R. G. Vanden Veer

Th: Jefferson

AUTHOR OF THE DECLARATION OF INDEPENDENCE

THE

LIFE AND TIMES

OF

THOMAS JEFFERSON.

BY

SAMUEL M. SCHMUCKER, LL.D.,

AUTHOR OF "THE EMPEROR NICHOLAS I.," "CATHERINE II. OF RUSSIA," "LIFE AND TIMES OF ALEXANDER HAMILTON," "ARCTIC EXPLORATIONS AND DISCOVERIES," ETC.

PHILADELPHIA:
JOHN E. POTTER AND COMPANY,
No. 617 SANSOM STREET.

PREFACE.

THOMAS JEFFERSON was one of the great representative heroes of the age in which he lived. He will always remain a very prominent and remarkable character in American history. Several biographies of him have already appeared; but they have not satisfied the wants of the reading public on the subject. They have all been partisan works, filled either with indiscriminate praise, or with wholesale censure. Thus the largest and most valuable of these productions, that written by Professor Tucker, is a glowing eulogy from beginning to end. Books of this description fail to present a correct and faithful historical picture of the subjects of which they treat.

I have endeavored in the following pages to throw as much light as possible upon the career and character of Mr. Jefferson; and to aid in accomplishing this end, have quoted largely from his own writings, from his Anas, his Memoirs, and his Correspondence. It is true that these are represented by his opponents as containing many partial and discolored statements; but this objection will not apply to any of the quotations made in the present work.

This book is neither a eulogy nor a tirade of censure. It has been the aim of the writer to present both the merits and the defects of Mr. Jefferson in their true light. The chief fault of this illustrious man was a pusillanimous and morbid terror of popular censure, and an insatiable thirsting after popular praise. He indeed saw very clearly, what every man of intelligence and observation must perceive, that a large proportion of mankind are in reality knaves and hypocrites; that vanity, selfishness, and perfidy, in various forms and under innumerable disguises, have always been the predominating qualities of human nature in every land and age; that even the divine principles and institutions of religion have been so perverted and distorted by human passions as to have become, in many instances, only the convenient tools for the aggrandizement of a more sanctimonious and aspiring form of selfishness; that were it not for a desire to preserve the "dignity of vice," resulting from the innate pride of human nature, even the empty boast of seeming virtue would rarely be heard, and the reality of it would scarcely ever be seen, on the face of the earth; in a word, that while the intellectual attributes of mankind assimilate them in many instances with angels, their propensities and their passions, in the majority of cases, leave an almost imperceptible interval between themselves and the brute creation.

Mr. Jefferson clearly perceived all this, and in his confidential letters to his most intimate friends—one of which I have inserted in this work—he has given utterance to his convictions on the subject. And yet he has made himself justly liable to the charge of insincerity and inconsistency by publicly proclaiming, during his whole lifetime, different and opposite sentiments; by upholding the dignity, grandeur, and majesty of human nature; by asserting the immaculate virtue of the multitude; by defending the infallibility of their judgments and the perfection of their decrees; and by making

1*

himself the great apostle and champion of those popular prerogatives which, in his inmost soul, he held in unutterable contempt.

After having set forth this defect in the character of Mr. Jefferson, together with the related weaknesses which naturally flowed from it, the residue of the description of him should be commendation of no ordinary character; it should be that rare praise which belongs to great talents devoted to the accomplishment of momentous results, and that too in the midst of imminent perils; persisted in through many long, vexatious years; opposed by tremendous obstacles; yet crowned at last with complete and overwhelming success.

PHILADELPHIA, *June*, 1857.

CONTENTS.

CHAPTER X.

CHAPTER XI.

CHAPTER XII.

CHAPTER XIII.

APPENDIX.

THOMAS JEFFERSON.

CHAPTER I.

BIRTH OF THOMAS JEFFERSON—HIS ANCESTORS—PETER JEFFERSON—THOMAS JEFFERSON BECOMES A PUPIL OF MAURY—HE ENTERS WILLIAM AND MARY COLLEGE—HIS HABITS AND PECULIARITIES—DR. WILLIAM SMALL—JEFFERSON'S ATTACHMENT TO MISS BURWELL—HIS LETTERS—GOVERNOR FAUQUIER—ELOQUENCE OF PATRICK HENRY—JEFFERSON'S JOURNEY TO PHILADELPHIA AND NEW YORK—HIS ADMISSION TO THE BAR—HIS QUALITIES AS A LAWYER—IS ELECTED TO THE VIRGINIA HOUSE OF BURGESSES—HIS ACTIVITY AND INFLUENCE IN THAT BODY.

VIRGINIA possesses the high distinction of being the mother both of great empires and of great men. From her bosom have gone forth, in successive generations, the sturdy and enterprising myriads who have peopled the vast domains which lie to the south and west of her own borders; and which now constitute so large and so important a portion of this confederacy. She has also given birth to many distinguished men, who, in different eras of the past, have shed lustre on their native land by their genius, their patriotism, and the splendor of their achievements. Foremost among all these is Washington, the most illustrious sage and hero of modern times. It had been sufficient glory for any country to have produced him alone. But very near that stately and sublime personage, there stands in the great pantheon of immortal fame another figure of impressive and solemn presence, to whom Virginia also gave existence,—and he is the subject of our present history.

THOMAS JEFFERSON was born at Shadwell, in Albemarle county, on the 2d of April, 1743. His ancestors, on his father's side, were of Welsh descent; and his immediate predecessors had been among the earliest inhabitants of the colony of Virginia. They enjoyed the reputation of having been intelligent, prosperous, and highly respectable citizens; and were the possessors of considerable wealth. The grandfather of Thomas Jefferson had three sons. One of these died at an early age. Another removed to the southern extremity of the State, and there passed an unobtrusive and an obscure existence. The third, who was named Peter, had removed from Chesterfield county where he had been reared, to Shadwell, where Thomas, his eldest child, was born. His wife was Jane Randolph, who was connected with one of the oldest and most reputable families in the colony. She was a woman of superior intelligence and amiability, and became the wife of Peter Jefferson in 1739, at the age of nineteen.

Peter Jefferson, the father of Thomas, had never enjoyed many facilities for mental cultivation; yet his natural talents were of a superior grade, and his industry in the pursuit of knowledge had been so persevering, while his judgment was regarded as so correct, that he was selected to perform the task of ascertaining and settling the boundary line between the territories of Virginia and North Carolina. His associate in this responsible task was Joshua Fry, the professor of mathematics in William and Mary College.

When five years old, Thomas Jefferson commenced his youthful studies at an English school. At nine he began the acquisition of the Latin, Greek, and French languages under the direction of a Scotch clergyman named Douglass. Peter Jefferson died in 1757, leaving two sons and six daughters. But they were not destitute; for to each of them their deceased parent had devised an estate. The plantation called Shadwell, where he first saw the light, was the portion which fell to the lot of the subject of this memoir—it also embraced the farm of Monticello.

After his father's death Thomas became the pupil of Mr. Maury, an eminent classical scholar of that day; and under his careful tuition he remained during two years. At this period he was already remarkable for his great industry, and for the rapid progress which he made in his studies. He seemed to possess an intuitive fondness for intellectual pursuits; yet he frequently took great delight in the exercise and diversion of hunting, for which the neighboring mountains, which traverse a portion of Albemarle county, furnished the most favorable opportunities.

In 1760, when seventeen years of age, Jefferson passed from the tuition of Mr. Maury to the higher studies and advantages of William and Mary College. He had been well prepared for the labors of this new sphere by the thorough instruction imparted to him by his former preceptors. He remained two years in connection with this institution, which was situated then as now at the city of Williamsburg; which place Jefferson, in his earlier letters to his most intimate friends, designated by the somewhat satirical epithet of "Devilsburg."

Respecting his pursuits and studies while at this institution Jefferson himself has furnished the most satisfactory account in his "Memoir." Says he: "It was my great good fortune, and what probably fixed the destinies of my life, that Dr. William Small of Scotland was the professor of mathematics, a man profound in most of the useful branches of science, with a happy talent of communication, correct and gentlemanly manners, and an enlarged and liberal mind. He, most happily for me, became soon attached to me, and made me his daily companion when not engaged in the school; and from his conversation I got my first views of the expansion of science, and of the system of things in which we are placed. Fortunately, the philosophical chair became vacant soon after my arrival at college, and he was appointed to fill it, *per interim;* and he was the first who ever gave, in that college, regular lectures in ethics, rhetoric, and belles lettres. He returned to Europe in 1762, having previously filled up the measure of his goodness to me, by procuring for me, from his most intimate friend, George Wythe, a reception as a student at law, under his direction, and introduced me to the acquaintance and familiar table of Governor Fauquier, the ablest man who had ever filled that office. With him, and at his table, Dr. Small and Mr. Wythe, his *amici omnium horarum*, and myself, formed a *partie guarre*, and to the habitual conversations on these occasions I owed much instruction. Mr. Wythe continued to be my faithful and beloved Mentor in youth, and my most affectionate friend through life. In 1767, he led me into the practice of the law at the bar of the general court, at which I continued until the Revolution shut up the courts of justice."

During the period of his residence at William and Mary College Jefferson was remarkable for the same habits of application, and for the same proficiency in his studies which he had previously displayed. His chief amusement was playing on the violin, in which agreeable art he acquired considerable skill. His letters of this date also furnish satisfactory proof that the future victor over British despotism was himself vanquished by the potent power of Cupid; and that he became even desperately in love. The object of his adoration was Miss Rebecca Burwell, a young lady of good family, and of considerable intelligence and beauty. For a time his ardent suit seemed to prosper. The lady bestowed upon her admirer a watch-paper containing her portrait. But this treasure, which Jefferson highly prized, was destined to be as evanescent as her love, for it was destroyed by the rain.

We will here introduce the only specimens of the early epistolary writings of the future statesman of Virginia, which are now in existence. They are valuable both as being illustrative of his style of thought and expression at this youthful period, and as containing details of his life and experiences which throw considerable light on his feelings, character and pursuits. They were addressed to John Page, afterward Governor Page, of Virginia; and were furnished by his son to one of the biographers of Mr. Jefferson.

"FAIRFIELD, December 25, 1762.

"DEAR PAGE:

"This very day, to others the day of greatest mirth and jolity, sees me overwhelmed with more and greater misfortunes than have befallen a descendant of Adam for these thousand years past I am sure; and perhaps, after excepting Job, since the creation of the world. I think his misfortunes were somewhat greater than mine: for although we may be pretty nearly on a level in other respects, yet, I thank my God, I have the advantage of brother Job in this, that Satan has not as yet put forth his hand to load me with bodily afflictions. You must know, dear Page, that I am now in a house surrounded with enemies who take counsel together against my soul; and when I lay me down to rest, they say among themselves, 'Come, let us destroy him.' I am sure if there is such a thing as a Devil in this world, he must have been here last night and have had some hand in contriving what happened to me. Do you think the cursed rats (at his instigation, I suppose) did not eat up my pocket-book, which was in my pocket, within a foot of my head? And not contented with plenty for the present, they carried away my jemmy-worked silk garters, and half a dozen new minuets I had just got, to serve, I suppose, as provision for the winter. But of this I should not have accused the Devil, (because, you know rats will be rats, and hunger, without the addition of his instigations, might have urged them to do this,) if something worse, and from a different quarter, had not happened. You know it rained last night, or if you do not know it, I am sure I do. When I went to bed, I laid my watch in the usual place, and going to take her up, after I arose this morning, I found her in the same place, it's true, but! *Quantum mutatus ab illo!* all afloat in water, let in at a leak in the roof of the house, and as silent and still as the rats that had eat my pocket-book. Now, you know, if chance had had any thing to do in this matter, there were a thousand other spots where it might have chanced to leak as well as at this one, which was perpendicularly over my watch. But I'll tell you; it's my opinion that the Devil came and bored the hole over it on purpose. Well, as I was saying, my poor watch had lost her speech. I should not have cared much for this, but something worse attended it; the subtle particles of the water with which the case was filled, had, by their penetration, so overcome the cohesion of the particles of the paper, of which my dear picture and watch-paper were composed, that, in attempting to take them out to dry them, good God! *Mens horret referre!* my cursed fingers gave them such a rent as, I fear, I shall never get over. This, cried I, was the last stroke Satan had in reserve for me; he knew I cared not for any thing else he could do to me, and was determind to try this last most fatal expedient. '*Multis fortunæ vulneribus, percussus, huic uni me imparem sensi, et penitus succubui!*' I would have cried bitterly, but I thought it beneath the dignity of a man, and a man too who had read των οντων, τα μεν εφ'ἡμιν, τα δ'ȣκ εφ'ἡμιν. However, whatever misfortunes may attend the picture or lover, my hearty prayers shall be, that all the health and happiness which Heaven can send may be the portion of the original, and that so much goodness may ever meet with what may be most agreeable in this world, as I am sure it must be in the next. And now, although the picture be defaced, there is so lively an image of her imprinted in my mind, that I shall think of her too often, I fear, for my peace of mind; and too often, I am sure, to get through old Coke this winter; for God knows I have not seen him since I packed him up in my trunk in Williamsburg. Well, Page, I do wish the Devil had old Coke, for I am sure I never was so tired of an old dull scoundrel in my life. What! are there so few inquietudes tacked to this momentary life of ours, that we must need be loading ourselves with a thousand more? Or, as brother Job says, (who, by-the-by, I think, began to whine a little under his afflictions,) 'Are not my days few? Cease, then, that I may take comfort a little before I go whence I shall not return, even to the land of darkness and the shadow of death." But the old fellows say we must read to gain knowledge, and gain knowledge to make us happy and be admired. *Mere jargon!* Is there any such thing as happiness in this world? No. And as for admiration, I am sure the man who powders most, perfumes most, embroiders most, and talks most nonsense, is most admired. Though to be candid, there are some who have too much good sense to esteem such monkey-like animals as these, in whose formation, as the saying is, the tailors and barbers go halves with God Almighty; and since these are the only persons whose esteem is worth a wish, I do not know but that, upon the whole, the advice of these old fellows may be worth following.

"You cannot conceive the satisfaction it would give me to have a letter from you. Write me very circumstantially every thing which happened at the wedding. Was she there? because, if she was, I ought to have been at the Devil for not being there too. If there is any news stirring in town or country, such as deaths, courtships, or marriages, in the circle of my acquaintance, let me know it. Remember me affectionately to all the young ladies of my acquaintance, particularly the Miss Burwells and Miss Potters, and tell them that though that heavy earthly part of me, my body, be absent, the better half of me, my soul, is ever with them; and that my best wishes shall ever attend them. Tell Miss Alice Corbin that I verily believe the rats knew I was to win a pair of garters from her, or they never would have been so cruel as to carry mine away. This very consideration makes me so sure of the bet, that I shall ask every body I see from that part of the world what pretty gentleman is making his addresses to her. I would fain ask the favor of Miss Becca Burwell to give me another watch paper of her own cutting, which I should esteem much more, though it were a plain round one, than the nicest in the world cut by other hands—however, I am afraid she would think this presumption, after my suffering the other to get spoiled. If you think you can excuse me to her for this, I should be glad if you would ask her. Tell Miss Sukey Potter that I heard, just before I came out of town, that she was offended with me about something, what it is I do not know; but this I know, that I never was guilty of the least disrespect to her in my life, either in word or deed; as far from it as it has been possible for one to be. I suppose when we meet next, she will be *endeavoring* to repay an imaginary affront with a real one; but she may save herself the trouble, for nothing that she can say or do to me shall ever lessen her in my esteem; and I am determined always to look upon her as the same honest-hearted, good-humored, agreeable lady I ever did. Tell—tell—in short, tell them all ten thousand things more than either you or I can now or ever shall think of as long as we live.

"My mind has been so taken up with thinking of my acquaintances, that, till this moment, I almost imagined myself in Williamsburg, talking to you in our old unreserved way; and never observed, till I turned over the leaf, to what an immoderate size I had swelled my letter—however, that I may not tire your patience by further additions, I will make but this one more, that I am sincerely and affectionately,

Dear Page, your friend and servant.

"P. S. I am now within an easy day's ride of Shadwell, whither I shall proceed in two or three days."

"SHADWELL, Jan. 20th, 1763.

"DEAR PAGE:

"To tell you the plain truth, I have not a syllable to write to you about. For I do not conceive that any thing can happen in my world which you would give a curse to know, or I either. All things here appear to me to trudge on in one and the same round: we rise in the morning that we may eat breakfast, dinner and supper, and go to bed again that we may get up the next morning and do the same: so that you never saw two peas more alike than our yesterday and to-day. Under these circumstances, what would you have me say? Would you that I should write nothing but truth? I tell you I know nothing that is true. Or would you rather that I should write you a pack of lies? Why, unless they were more ingenious than I am able to invent, they would furnish you with little amusement. What can I do then? nothing, but ask you the news in your world. How have you done since I saw you? How did Nancy look at you when you danced with her at Southall's? Have you any glimmering of hope? How does R. B. do? Had I better stay here and do nothing, or go down and do less? or, in other words, had I better stay here while I am here, or go down that I may have the pleasure of sailing up the river again in a full-rigged flat? Inclination tells me to go, receive my sentence, and be no longer in suspense: but reason says, if you go, and your attempt proves unsuccessful, you will be ten times more wretched than ever. In my last to you, dated Fairfield, Dec. 25, I wrote to you of the losses I had sustained; in the present I may mention one more, which is the loss of the whites of my eyes, in the room of which I have got reds, which gives me such exquisite pain that I have not attempted to read any thing since a few days after Jack Walker went down; and God knows when I shall be able to do it. I have some thoughts of going to Petersburg, if the actors go there in May. If I do, I do not know but I may keep on to Williamsburg, as the birth night will be near. I hear that Ben Harrison has been to Wilton: let me know his success. Have you an inclination to travel, Page? because if you have, I shall be glad of your company. For you must know that as soon as the Rebecca (the name I intend to give the vessel above mentioned) is completely finished, I intend to hoist sail and away. I shall visit particularly England, Holland, France, Spain, Italy, (where I would buy me a good fiddle,) and Egypt, and return through the British provinces to the Northward, home. This to be sure, would take us two or three years, and if we should not both be cured of love in that time, I think the Devil would be in it. After desiring you to remember me to acquaintances below, male and female, I subscribe myself,

Dear Page, your friend and servant."

"SHADWELL, July 15th, 1765.

"DEAR PAGE:

"Yours of May 30th came safe to hand. The rival you mentioned I know not whether to think formidable or not, as there has been so great an opening for him during my absence. I say *has been*, because I expect there is one no longer, since you have undertaken to act as my attorney. You advise me to go immediately and lay siege *in form*. You certainly did not think, at the time you wrote this, of that paragraph in my letter wherein I mentioned to you my resolution of going to Britain. And to begin an affair of that kind now, and carry it on so long a time in form, is by no means a proper plan. No, no, Page; whatever assurances I may give her in private of my esteem for her, or whatever assurances I may ask in return from her, depend on it—they must be kept in private. Necessity will oblige me to proceed in a method which is not generally thought fair; that of treating with a ward before obtaining the approbation of her guardian. I say necessity will oblige me to it, because I never can bear to remain in suspense so long a time. If I am to succeed, the sooner I know it, the less uneasiness I shall have to go through. If I am to meet with a disappointment, the sooner I know it, the more of life I shall have to wear it off: and if I do meet with one, I hope in God, and verily believe, it will be the last. I assure you, that I almost envy you your present freedom; and if Belinda will not accept of my service, it shall never be offered to another. That she may, I pray most sincerely; but that she will, she never gave me reason to hope. With regard to my not proceeding in form, I do not know how she may like it. I am afraid not much. That her guardians would not, if they should know of it, is very certain. But I should think that if they were consulted after I return, it would be sufficient. The greatest inconvenience would be my not having the liberty of visiting so freely. This is a subject worth your talking over with her; and I wish you would, and would transmit to me your whole confab at length. I should be scared to death at making her so unreasonable a proposal as that of waiting until I return from Britain, unless she could first be prepared for it. I am afraid it will make my chance of succeeding considerably worse. But the event at last must be this, that if she consents, I shall be happy; if she does not, I must *endeavor* to be as much so as possible. I have thought a good deal on your case; and as mine may perhaps be similar, I must endeavor to look on it in the same light in which I have often advised you to look on yours. Perfect happiness, I believe, was never intended by the Deity to be the lot of one of his creatures in this world; but that he has very much put in our power the nearness of our approaches to it, is what I have steadfastly believed.

"The most fortunate of us, in our journey through life, frequently meet with calamities and misfortunes which may greatly afflict us; and, to fortify our minds against the attacks of these calamities and misfortunes, should be one of the principal studies and endeavors of our lives. The only method of doing this is to assume a perfect resignation to the Divine will, to consider that whatever does happen, must happen; and that by our uneasiness, we cannot prevent the blow before it does fall, but we may add to its force after it has fallen. These considerations, and others such as these, may enable us in some measure to surmount the difficulties thrown in our way; to bear up with a tolerable degree of patience under this burthen of life; and to proceed with a pious and unshaken resignation, till we arrive at our journey's end, when we may deliver up our trust into the hands of Him who gave it, and receive such reward as to Him shall seemed proportioned to our merit. Such, dear Page, will be the language of the man who considers his situation in this life, and such should be the language of every man who would wish to render that situation as easy as the nature of it will admit. Few things will disturb him at all: nothing will disturb him much.

"If this letter was to fall into the hands of some of our gay acquaintance, your correspondent and his solemn notions would probably be the subjects of a great deal of mirth and raillery, but to you, I think, I can venture to send it. It is in effect a continuation of the many conversations we have had on subjects of this kind; and I heartily wish we could now continue these conversations face to face. The time will not be very long now before we may do it, as I expect to be in Williamsburg by the first of October, if not sooner. I do not know that I shall have occasion to return, if I can rent rooms in town to lodge in; and to prevent the inconvenience of moving my lodgings for the future, I think to build: no castle though, I assure you: only a small house, which shall contain a room for myself and another for you, and no more, unless

Belinda should think proper to favor us with her company, in which case, I will enlarge the plan as much as she pleases. Make my compliments to her particularly, as also to Sukey Potter, Judy Burwell, and such others of my acquaintance as inquire after me. I am,

Dear Page, your sincere friend," &c.

"WILLIAMSBURG, October 7, 1763.

"DEAR PAGE:

"In the most melancholy fit that ever any poor soul was, I sit down to write to you. Last night, as merry as agreeable company and dancing with Belinda in the Apollo could make me, I never could have thought the succeeding sun would have seen me so wretched as I now am! I was prepared to say a great deal: I had dressed up in my own mind, such thoughts as occurred to me, in as moving language as I knew how, and expected to have performed in a tolerably creditable manner. But, good God! When I had an opportunity of venting them, a few broken sentences, uttered in great disorder, and interrupted with pauses of uncommon length, were the too visible marks of my strange confusion! The whole confab I will tell you, word for word, if I can, when I see you, which God send may be soon. Affairs at W. and M. are in the greatest confusion. Walker, M'Clurg and Wat Jones are expelled *pro tempore*, or, as Horrox softens it, rusticated for a month. Lewis Burwell, Warner Lewis, and one Thompson have fled to escape flagellation. I should have excepted Warner Lewis, who came off of his own accord. Jack Walker leaves town on Monday. The court is now at hand, which I must attend constantly, so that unless you come to town, there is little probability of my meeting with you any where else. For God's sake come.

I am, dear Page,

Your sincere friend," &c.

Jefferson is described at this period as having been very tall, thin and raw-boned. His hair was red, his features were sharp and pointed, and his face was freckled. Yet, to counterbalance these disadvantages, his countenance was very intelligent and expressive, his conversation was lively and entertaining, and not a few indications were constantly given, both by his language and by his actions, of the possession of a superior and a powerful intellect.

During the college terms of Jefferson, he was an acquaintance and favorite of Mr. Farquier, at that time the British governor of the colony. This gentleman was remarkable for his superior talents, his literary acquirements, and his polished manners. From these qualities of his friend Jefferson derived much benefit; for being thrown into frequent and kindly intercourse with the governor, he was enabled to improve himself by imitating so excellent a model. But Governor Farquier had other peculiarities which were not so commendable. These were his approval of infidel sentiments, both in philosophy and in religion, and an excessive fondness for gambling. It is not improbable that the frequent conversations which occurred between Jefferson and his accomplished friend may have resulted in a similarity of opinions to some extent, and may have laid the foundation for that boldness of speculation which characterized Jefferson throughout his whole life. It does not appear, however, that he imitated the governor in his devotion to the vice of gaming.

Mr. Jefferson was still a student of William and Mary College when the memorable dispute began between Great Britain and the Colonies. A young man of his superior intelligence would very naturally take a deep interest in such a controversy. Accordingly he embraced every opportunity to attend the sittings of the Virginia House of Burgesses, and listened to the debates which there took place in reference to the encroachments and prerogatives of the British monarch. It was in May, 1765, that he first heard the unrivalled and thrilling eloquence of Patrick Henry, the Mirabeau of the American Revolution. Jefferson always contended that, during his whole subsequent life he had never listened to so powerful and so consummate an oration as Henry delivered on that occasion. Whether this estimate of the oratorical abilities of this celebrated man was just; or whether much allowance should be made for the profound impression which such an unusual display would make upon a young and susceptible person who was then unfamiliar with the triumphs of that great art, it is difficult now to determine. At any rate, the whole soul of Jefferson was then already enlisted in behalf of the independence and the rights of the colonies, and his ardor in the cause continued from that period without abatement.

At length having completed his studies at William and Mary College, Jefferson returned to Shadwell. He employed his first leisure in making a journey to Philadelphia and New York, the object of which was to obtain inoculation for the small-pox, and to enlarge his acquaintance with the colonies and their chief cities. He traveled three hundred miles in a one-horse chaise; and the inconveniences which attended locomotion at that period may be inferred from the fact that, in a single journey, he was frequently drenched with rain, and was several times in danger of being drowned when fording the streams which had been swollen by the rains.

Immediately on his return from this excursion, Jefferson was elected a justice of the peace of Albemarle county, having subsequently completed his legal studies under Mr. Wythe, and having been admitted to practice as an attorney in 1767. As already stated in the extract quoted from his "Memoir," Jefferson established himself at Williamsburg. Seven years were passed by him in the quiet performance of his professional labors. He exhibited the same qualities as a lawyer which marked him previously as a student, and which adorned him subsequently as a statesman. He was not brilliant or showy in his forensic efforts; but he was laborious, thorough and learned. His manuscript notes gave abundant evidence that he prepared his cases with the most patient research. He was gradually advancing to a prominent position among the ablest lawyers of Virginia, at the period when the revolutionary struggle called him away to a higher and more important sphere.* As a speaker, Jefferson

* The language of William Wirt on this subject is explicit: says he—"Permit me to correct an error which seems to have prevailed. It has been thought that Mr. Jefferson made no figure at the Bar;

could never have been eminent. His voice had neither compass, flexibility, or power. But as a writer and thinker his great superiority was clearly manifest on every occasion, and it was not without sufficient reason that he was subsequently selected from among the large body of able and distinguished men who composed the Continental Congress, to compose the immortal *magna charta* of a nation's freedom.

When twenty-six years of age, in 1769, Jefferson was elected a member of the Virginia House of Burgesses for the county of Albemarle. From the moment that he entered this important body he became remarkable for his industry, his prominence, and the decisive stand which he took either in the proposal or in the support of patriotic measures. Only a short time previous to this period, the British parliament had passed resolutions which severely condemned the stand which the Legislature of Massachusetts had taken against the growing encroachments of British tyranny. The Legislature of Virginia, on the receipt of this information, adopted a series of resolutions in which they

but the case was far otherwise. There are still extant, in his own fair and neat hand, in the manner of his master, a number of arguments which were delivered by him at the Bar upon some of the most intricate questions of the law; which, if they shall ever see the light, will vindicate his claims to the first honors of the profession."

boldly declared that the right to levy taxes in Virginia belonged exclusively to themselves; that they possessed, and that they should always exercise, the privilege of petitioning the king for a redress of grievances; and they further declared, that the transportation to England of persons accused of treason in the colonies, in order there to be tried, was illegal, unconstitutional, and unjust. In the discussion and the passage of these resolutions, Mr. Jefferson took a decided and prominent part.

No sooner were the resolutions passed than the governor, Lord Bottetourt, dissolved the Assembly. A crisis had at length arrived, and it now became the duty of the friends of liberty to take a resolute and determined course. Indecisive measures were no longer available. The next day a large number of the members of the dissolved legislature met at the Raleigh Tavern in Williamsburg, and formed an association for the purpose of carrying forward and completing the movement which had already been begun. These persons pledged their honors not to import or purchase certain specified articles of British merchandise, as long as the act of parliament authorizing the taxation of the colonies remained unrepealed. Eighty-eight members of the legislature signed this compact, and among the number were George Washington, Patrick Henry,

Richard Henry Lee, and Thomas Jefferson. Thus was the first decisive stand taken in Virginia against British despotism by an an association of patriots, all the most prominent of whom were young men, whose names and abilities were as yet almost wholly unknown to the country.

It was also during this first term of his service in the legislature, that Mr. Jefferson proposed the adoption of measures having reference to the subject of negro slavery. He did not urge the general manumission of the slaves, as has sometimes been asserted; but he suggested that the restrictions which then existed, and which prevented owners from conferring freedom on their slaves when they even desired so to do, should be removed. Yet his efforts were fruitless; and it was only in 1782 that even this cautious and limited policy was allowed to prevail.

CHAPTER II.

BURNING OF JEFFERSON'S RESIDENCE—HIS MARRIAGE—EVENTS OF 1773—PROCEEDINGS IN RHODE ISLAND—MEASURES OF THE VIRGINIA HOUSE OF BURGESSES—COMMITTEES OF CORRESPONDENCE—BRITISH AGGRESSIONS—STEPS OF RESISTANCE TAKEN IN VIRGINIA—ACTIVITY OF MR. JEFFERSON—THE CONVENTION—RESOLUTIONS ADOPTED BY THAT BODY—THE "SUMMARY VIEW OF THE RIGHTS OF BRITISH AMERICA"—DELEGATES TO THE FIRST CONTINENTAL CONGRESS—JEFFERSON'S RESOLUTIONS IN THE VIRGINIA LEGISLATURE—HIS ANSWER TO LORD NORTH'S PROPOSITION.

THE year 1770 opened with the occurrence of a personal calamity of no small moment to Mr. Jefferson. His residence at Shadwell, where he had spent his youth, and which was then the abode of his widowed mother, was burnt to the ground. This misfortune occurred during his absence, and his loss was not confined simply to the destruction of the edifice. His library, for which he had paid about a thousand dollars, and all his manuscripts, notes, and papers fell a prey to the flames. Not a solitary piece of writing remained. The loss of his law books was particularly severe, inasmuch as they could not be easily replaced, and that loss greatly exceeded their nominal value.

The following letter was written by young Jefferson in reference to this calamity, to his intimate friend Page; and throws much light upon the nature of hismisfortune, and the feelings with which he endured it.

"CHARLOTTESVILLE, Feb. 21, 1770.

"DEAR PAGE:

"I am to acquaint Mrs. Page of the loss of my favorite pullet; the consequence of which will readily occur to her. I promised also to give her some Virginia silk which I had expected, and I begin to wish my expectation may not prove vain. I fear she will think me but an ungainly acquaintance. My late loss may perhaps have reached you by this time; I mean the loss of my mother's house by fire, and in it of every paper I had in the world, and almost every book. On a reasonable estimate I calculate the *cost* of the books burned to have been £200 sterling. Would to God it had been the money, *then* had it never cost me a sigh! To make the loss more sensible, it fell principally on my books of Common Law, of which I have but one left, at that time lent out. Of papers too of every kind I am utterly destitute. All of these, whether public or private, of business or of amusement, have perished in the flames. I had made some progress in preparing for the succeeding General Court; and having, as was my custom, thrown my thoughts into the form of notes, I troubled my head no more with them. These are gone, and like the baseless fabric of a vision, leave not a trace behind. The records also, and other papers which furnished me with states of the several cases, having shared the same fate, I have no foundation whereon to set out anew. I have in vain attempted to recollect some of them; the defect sometimes of one, sometimes of more circumstances, rendering them so imperfect, that I can make nothing of them. What am I to do then in April? The resolution which the court has declared of admitting no continuances of causes seemed to be unalterable; yet it might surely be urged, that my case is too singular to admit of their being often troubled with the like excuse. Should it be asked, what are the misfortunes of an individual to a court? The answer of a court, as well as of an individual, if left to me, should be in the words of Terence, "*homo sum; humani nil a me alienum puto*"—but a truce with this disagreeable subject.

"Am I never more to have a letter from you? Why the devil don't you write? But I suppose you are always in the moon, or some of the planetary regions. I mean you are there in idea; and unless you mend, you shall have my consent to be there *de facto;* at least, during the vacations of the

Court of Assembly. If your spirit is too elevated to advert to sublunary subjects, depute my friend Mrs. Page to support your correspondences. Methinks I should, with wonderful pleasure, open and peruse a letter written by so fair, and (what is better) so friendly hands. If thinking much of you would entitle me to the civility of a letter, I assure you I merit a very long one. If this conflagration, by which I am burned out of a home, had come before I had advanced so far in preparing another, I do not know but I might have cherished some treasonable thoughts of leaving these my native hills; indeed I should be much happier were I nearer to Rosewell and Severn hills—however, the gods, I fancy, were apprehensive that if we were placed together, we should pull down the moon, or play some such devilish prank with their works. I reflect often with pleasure on the philosophical evenings I passed at Rosewell in my last visits there. I was always fond of philosophy, even in its drier forms; but from a ruby lip, it comes with charms irresistible. Such a feast of sentiment must exhilarate and lengthen life, at least as much as the feast of the sensualist shortens it—in a word, I prize it so highly, that, if you will at any time collect the same *Belle Assemblée*, on giving me three days previous notice, I shall certainly repair t‹ ‹‹v place as a member of it. Should it not happen before I come down, I will carry Sally Nicholas in the green chair to Newquarter, where your periagua (how the —— should I spell that word?) will meet us, automaton-like, of its own accord. You know I had a wagon which moved itself—cannot we construct a boat then which shall row itself? *Amicus noster, Fons, quo modo agit, et quid agit?* You may be all dead for any thing we can tell here. I expect he will follow the good old rule of driving one passion out by letting another in. *Clavum clavo pangere* was your advice to me on a similar occasion. I hope you will watch his immersion as narrowly as if he were one of Jupiter's satellites; and give me immediate notice, that I may prepare a dish of advice. I do not mean, Madam, to advise him against it. On the contrary, I am become an advocate for the passion; for I too am *cœla tactus, Currus bene se habet.* He speaks, thinks, and dreams of nothing but his young son. This friend of ours, Page, in a very small house, with a table, half a dozen chairs, and one or two servants, is the happiest man in the universe. Every incident in life he so takes as to render it a source of pleasure. With as much benevolence as the heart of a man will hold, but with an utter neglect of the costly apparatus of life, he exhibits to the world a new phenomenon in philosophy—the Samian sage in the tub of the cynic. Name me sometimes *homunculo tuo*, not forgetting little *dic mendacium.* I am determined not to enter on the next page, lest I should extend this nonsense to the bottom of that also. *A dieu je vous commis*, not doubting his care of you both."

Nevertheless, he immediately set to work to remedy the misfortune as rapidly as possible. Several years then passed away in the performance of his professional duties. On the 1st of January, 1772, he was married to Mrs. Martha Skelton, the widow of Bathurst Skelton. She was the daughter of John Wayles, a prominent member of the Virginia Bar. This gentleman died in 1773, and left a large estate, one-third of which fell to the lot of Mr. Jefferson. This union proved to be a peculiarly happy one, and during many subsequent years became the source of the utmost domestic enjoyment to both parties.

During 1772 the political storms which had previously begun to agitate the country to some extent subsided, in consequence of the partial repeal of the obnoxious duties formerly imposed by the British parliament. New causes of discontent arose in Rhode Island, in 1773. A Court of Inquiry was held in that province, vested with power to send persons accused of treason to England for trial. It had already become the determined purpose of Jefferson, and a few congenial spirits in Virginia, to take advantage of every occasion to keep alive the spirit of resistance to British tyranny in the colonies, as being preparatory to the final great act of entire and absolute separation. Accordingly, as soon as information of the proceedings of Rhode Island had reached Virginia, a few prominent members of the legislature, then in session at Williamsburg, determined to bring this matter before that body. Previous to taking this step, however, they met privately at the Raleigh Tavern, on the 11th of March, 1773, to deliberate on the measures which it behooved them to adopt. The leaders of this movement were Jefferson, Patrick Henry, R. H. Lee, F. L. Lee, and Dabney Carr. These patriots adopted the plan of appointing Committees of Correspondence between the legislatures of the different colonies. The ultimate aim of these committees was to propose the meeting of deputies from all the colonies in a general Congress. Mr. Jefferson was appointed to draft a series of resolutions recommending to the legislature the appointment of such committees; and also another resolution requesting an inquiry to be made in reference to the obnoxious and tyrannical proceedings which had but recently occurred in Rhode Island. Mr. Dabney Carr was selected, in consequence of his superior oratorical abilities, to offer the resolutions in the legislature, and to support them by his eloquence.

Accordingly, on the next morning, the resolutions were proposed by Mr. Carr in the House of Burgesses, and were supported by him with extraordinary pathos and fervor. They were adopted unanimously on the same day. The support given to these resolutions by Mr. Carr at once raised him to a high eminence among his distinguished associates; and a very brilliant future was naturally predicted for him. But his name never once occurs again in the stirring history of those times. He died suddenly and unexpectedly only two months after the passage of the resolutions.

But though Mr. Carr himself vanished so quickly from the scene, the influence and the rich results of his activity remained. The legislature was immediately dissolved by the governor in consequence of these events; yet his measures were utterly impotent to stop the mighty tide of popular feeling which had already begun to flow. The committee of correspondence was immediately appointed. They organized themselves without delay, and commenced operations. They prepared a circular, copies of which they addressed to the chairmen of the legislatures of the various colonies, and these they dispatched, without delay, to their respective destinations by expresses. The consequence of these measures was, that similar committees of correspondence were appointed by all the different colonies; a channel of direct communication was thus opened between them; an interchange of sentiment and of purpose took place; energetic plans were discussed; unity of purpose was introduced; and the grand result followed that, in the ensuing year, the general Congress assembled to deliberate upon the great questions of political life and death, which then agitated the whole continent.

It is true that the first *idea* of appointing a committee of correspondence between the colonies was due, not to the patriots of Virginia, but to those of Massachusetts. In 1765, immediately after the passage of the Stamp Act, the legislature of that State proposed a meeting of deputies from the several colonies to consult together on their common difficulties. And subsequently, in 1770, a similar resolution was adopted by the same body. But it is also true, that these resolutions were in neither case practically carried out. They remained in substance a dead letter. But Virginia possesses the credit not only of following this excellent example, but also of being the first to execute the resolutions thus adopted. To Massachusetts belongs the honor of first suggesting this admirable plan of furthering the aims of freedom; to Virginia that of giving that plan practical fulfillment and efficacy.

Other difficulties soon arose between England and her incensed colonies. In consequence of the diminution of trade between the two countries, a vast amount of tea had accumulated in the warehouses of the East India Company. This immense monopoly was a favorite of the British government; and it obtained permission to transport their tea to the American ports free of duty, on the unjust condition that, on its arrival at its destination, a duty of three-pence per pound should be paid. This unfair arrangement at once threw the inhabitants of Massachusetts into a state of intense indignation. The first cargo was totally destroyed in December, 1773. As a measure of retaliation, the British government passed the Boston Port Bill, by which that town was to be deprived of all its foreign trade from and after June, 1774. The Legislature of Virginia was in session when these events transpired. Mr. Jefferson was still a member. At his instance the small body of patriots who had convened on a previous occasion, were again summoned in order to determine upon the proper measures to be taken.

He himself describes the events which took place at this crisis in the following language:

"The lead in the House, on these subjects, being no longer left to the old members, Mr. Henry, R. H. Lee, Fr. L. Lee, three or four other members, whom I do not recollect, and myself, agreeing that we must boldly take an unequivocal stand in the line of Massachusetts, determined to meet and consult on the proper measures, in the council chamber, for the benefit of the library in that room. We were under conviction of the necessity of rousing our people from the lethargy into which they had fallen, as to passing events; and thought that the appointment of a day of general fasting and prayer, would be most likely to call up and alarm their attention. No example of such a solemnity had existed since the days of our distresses in the war of '55, since which a new generation had grown up. With the help, therefore, of Rushworth, whom we rummaged over for the revolutionary precedents and forms of the Puritans of that day, preserved by him, *we cooked up a resolution*, somewhat moderating their phrases, for appointing the 1st day of June, on which the Port Bill was to commence, for a day of *fasting, humiliation, and prayer;* to implore Heaven to avert from us the evils of civil war, to inspire us with firmness in the support of our rights, and to turn the hearts of the king and parliament to moderation and justice."

This important instrument was duly presented to the legislature, and it was passed without opposition on the 24th of May.* But the patriots did not stop with this decisive step. They passed a resolution to recommend to the counties of the State to elect delegates who should meet in the ensuing August, who should select representatives for the State in the Continental Congress. In pursuance of this resolution, delegates were chosen to meet in convention. Mr. Jefferson was one of these. He prepared a draft of instructions to be given to the congressional representatives who would be chosen, which he termed "A Summary View of the Rights of British America." This paper was addressed to the king, and contained a clear and powerful exposition of the political relations which existed, and ought to exist between the colonies and the mother country. It was in consequence of the composition of

* Immediately after this event, the British governor, Lord Dunsmore, entered the House, and spoke as follows:—"Mr. Speaker and Gentlemen of the House of Burgesses—I have in my hand a paper published by order of your House, conceived in such terms as reflect highly upon his Majesty and the Parliament of Great Britain, which makes it necessary to dissolve you—and you are dissolved accordingly." As usual, the whole assembly repaired immediately to the Apollo Hall in the Raleigh Tavern, and resumed their deliberations.

this pamphlet, that Mr. Jefferson was threatened by Lord Dunsmore with a prosecution for treason, and his name was included in a list of proscriptions by the British ministry, intended for future prosecution and punishment.

Mr. Jefferson was prevented by a sudden attack of illness from attending the convention which assembled in Williamsburg in August, 1774. This was the first popular or republican legislative assembly which ever met in Virginia, without the authority of government, and at the call of the popular will. Though absent from its sessions, Mr. Jefferson sent his Instructions to Patrick Henry and Peyton Randolph, for the purpose of having them submitted to the convention. A copy was laid on the table for the inspection of the members, and it was read with much interest. But the measures of retaliation and resistance which it proposed were thought to be, at that stage of the conflict, too extreme and excessive. They were therefore not adopted; but they were printed by an order of the convention, and were subsequently widely diffused. In this production Mr. Jefferson took the ground that the relation between the colonies and Great Britain was the same as the relation between that country and Scotland after the accession of James, or between England and Hanover after the accession of the reigning house of the latter country to the British throne; that they had the same executive chief, but no other necessary political connections; and that the emigration of English subjects to America, gave the British monarch no more right over them, than the emigration of the Danes and Saxons to England gave to the Danish and Saxon monarchs over Englishmen. In substance, therefore, Mr. Jefferson first announced, in this able document, the great republican doctrine that there should be no taxation without representation—a doctrine afterward more clearly and ably stated by him in the Declaration of Independence.*

The labors of this convention consisted chiefly in passing resolutions to the following effect:—Not to import any British merchandise after the 1st of November ensuing; to import no slaves; to use no more tea; to purchase no East India goods; to export no more tobacco, but to encourage its home manufacture; to improve the breed of sheep; to contribute to the relief of the people of Boston; and that the speaker of the convention be empowered to convene the members again at such time and place as he might think proper. The convention then elected delegates to represent the State of Virgnia

* *Vide* Girardin's History of Virginia—Appendix, No. 12.

in the Continental Congress. These men were chosen with the care and deliberation which the importance of the occasion required. Peyton Randolph was selected in consequence of his superior acquaintance with the rules of parliamentary proceedings. George Washington was recommended by his military talents and experience. Richard Henry Lee was chosen for his great eloquence; Patrick Henry for the same reason; Edward Pendleton for his profound learning as a lawyer; Benjamin Harrison because he represented the wealthy planters; and Richard Bland in consequence of his ability as a writer.

Mr. Jefferson was not elected as a delegate to the first Continental Congress; but during the year 1775 he was not inactive in the legislature of his native State. At the request of Peyton Randolph, who had been chosen President of Congress, he drew up the answer of the General Assembly of Virginia to the conciliatory proposals which had been made by Lord North, and which finally passed the House, with some softening amendments. Mr. Jefferson was subsequently appointed by the house to convey to the congress assembled at Philadelphia, the result of their action and deliberations, which duty he performed on the 21st of June, 1775.

Thus far the mental activity and the patriotism

of Mr. Jefferson had been confined in their operation to the comparatively limited sphere of his native province. He was still a young man of thirty-two years; yet he had taken an honorable place, by virtue of his great talents and acquirements, among the leading men of the Old Dominion. In truth, he had been the most radical and resolute of the reformers in that State, the fiercest foe to British tyranny, the most extreme and uncompromising of all the patriots. It was he who had declared in the Convention of Virginia, which assembled for the second time on the 20th of March, 1775, that "by the God that made him, he would cease to exist before he yielded to such a connection with England, and on such terms as the British Parliament propose." It was he who had proclaimed that "his creed had been formed on unsheathing the sword at Lexington." It was he who supported a resolution which was proposed in this convention by Patrick Henry, that the colony should immediately be put in a state of defense, and that a committee be appointed to prepare a plan to arm and discipline a body of effective troops. This was the daring and desperate resolution which was earnestly opposed by Pendleton, Harrison, Nicholas, and Wythe—patriots of the purest virtue—because they thought it too ultra and decisive. But in spite of their opposition this resolution was carried by means of the powerful influence of Jefferson and Patrick Henry, and was ultimately executed. But in all these noble achievements, the talents and patriotism of Jefferson had been confined to a comparatively limited sphere. A man of such enlightened views, of such bold determination, of such fierce hostility to despotism, of such devotion to popular freedom, only needed a more enlarged and elevated sphere of activity to give him a distinguished place in the history of his time and of his country. Such an opportunity was soon afforded him; and it may with truth be said that, among all the distinguished men of the Revolution, he who was the bitterest and most uncompromising foe to British tyranny and prerogative, and he who was most determined, impetuous and resolved in accomplishing their overthrow in these colonies, was none other than Thomas Jefferson.

This fact was especially evinced in his answer to the "Conciliatory Propositions" of the British minister, Lord North. This document, addressed to the colonies, was specious, insidious, and crafty in the extreme. But Jefferson, who was appointed on the Committee of the House of Burgesses to answer it, could not be imposed upon by its artful declamation. He penetrated its real character, stript its infamous propositions of their false and fallacious coverings, exposed its cruelty and injustice, and gave it a blow from which it never recovered. This was the last service which Jefferson performed for the cause of freedom in his native State. On the 24th of June, 1775, the House adjourned; and it was the last Assembly which ever convened under the authority of the British monarch in the colony of Virginia. The governor, fearing an outburst of popular indignation, fled from his palace on board a British man-of-war, and his authority was never again recognized by the inhabitants of the colony. This was the loss of the first province, which was followed subsequently by the defection of the whole continent, and by their hostile and triumphant attitude against the supremacy of the mother country.

CHAPTER III.

MR. JEFFERSON ELECTED A MEMBER OF CONGRESS—HIS APPOINTMENT ON IMPORTANT COMMITTEES—HIS REPORTS—MR. DICKINSON OF PENNSYLVANIA—MR. JEFFERSON PREPARES A CONSTITUTION AND DECLARATION OF RIGHTS FOR VIRGINIA—THE LEGISLATURE OF VIRGINIA RECOMMENDS A DECLARATION OF INDEPENDENCE—MR. JEFFERSON'S INFLUENCE IN CONGRESS—RESOLUTION OF RICHARD HENRY LEE—MR. JEFFERSON DRAFTS THE ORIGINAL DECLARATION OF INDEPENDENCE—STATE OF PARTIES IN CONGRESS—ADOPTION AND PROMULGATION OF THE DECLARATION—EXCITEMENT THROUGHOUT THE COLONIES ON THE SUBJECT—LITERARY MERITS OF THE DECLARATION—ITS HISTORIC INFLUENCE AND IMPORTANCE—MR. JEFFERSON'S OPINION RESPECTING IT—ITS FUTURE INFLUENCE.

BEFORE the adjournment of the second session of the popular convention of Virginia, it became necessary for them to elect a delegate to the Continental Congress in place of Peyton Randolph, who, as speaker of the Virginia House of Burgesses, would soon be required to return to his native State. Accordingly in May, 1775, Mr. Jefferson was elected to fill the place of Mr. Randolph; and on the 21st of June he took his seat in the Continental Congress. He was then thirty-two years of age; and he brought to this high sphere in which he was destined afterward to act so eminent and distinguished a part, very considerable reputation for abilities, industry, and devotion to the cause of freedom and progress.

This reputation procured him an appointment on the committee instructed to prepare a report on the "Cause of taking up Arms against England," five days after his entrance into Congress. The portion of the report of this committee which Mr. Jefferson was requested to prepare, has been frequently quoted and admired for its beauty of style, and for the clearness and boldness with which it treats the subject.* On the 22d of July he was again honored with an appointment on a committee with Dr. Franklin, Mr. Adams, and R. H. Lee, to prepare an answer to Lord North's resolutions. Mr. Jefferson penned this important document. It sets forth in powerful language the fundamental doctrine that the colonies alone have the privilege of granting or

* Mr. Dickinson of Pennsylvania was a member of this committee, and he seems to have been the croaking owl of the Continental Congress. He opposed all expressions of vigorous resistance, or of open denunciation, in the reports of the committees; and it was he who, alone of all the members of Congress, subsequently refused to sign the Declaration of Independence. When the committee on the "Cause of taking up Arms against England" reported, their report had been softened down so completely by the trembling appeals of Mr. Dickinson, as scarcely to amount to any thing. On its passage he remarked, that there was only one word in it of which he yet disapproved, and that word was "Congress." Mr. Harrison instantly rose and said, that there was but one word in the document of which he did approve, and that was "Congress."

withholding their own money; and that this also involves the right of inquiry into its application, of determining its amount, and of applying it to proper uses; and it condemns the propositions of Lord North, because they do not propose the repeal of the oppressive statutes which had been passed. The tone and spirit of this report differ very essentially from those of the report of the committee to which Mr. Dickinson belonged. They were bold, resolute and defiant, and marked clearly an important step in advance among that immortal band of patriots who were destined to achieve the freedom of the nation. It was the passage of this report, written by Mr. Jefferson, then the youngest member of Congress save one, which cut off forever all hope of conciliation and union between the colonies and Great Britain. From that moment a desperate conflict was inevitable.

Mr. Jefferson had been elected to Congress by the Legislature of Virginia in August, 1775, and subsequently was re-elected in June, 1776. During his absence from his native State, he was not forgetful of her interests. The regal authority had been already dissolved in that colony. A popular government had been quietly substituted. But no settled form for the administration of the government had been adopted. This then was the first task which demanded the attention of her patriots. A conven tion accordingly assembled at Williamsburg, on the 6th of May, 1776, for the purpose of adopting a declaration of rights and a constitution. On the 15th of May, after previous deliberations, a committee was appointed to report on the subject. Mr. George Mason was the leading member of that committee. On the 29th of June the constitution which they reported, after ample discussion, was adopted. But during this interval Mr. Jefferson had not been idle. He himself had prepared a form of constitution for the consideration of the house, together with a preamble, declaration of rights, and an entire plan of government. These important documents he sent to Mr. Wythe, but they arrived too late for the consideration of the house. They had already discussed and adopted a complete form of government, and had agreed upon a declaration of rights. Nevertheless some use was made of the valuable labors of Mr. Jefferson. Two or three parts of his plan were added to that already passed, and the entire preamble which accompanied his own form of government was adopted and added to that which had already received the legislative sanction. George Mason was the author of the declaration of rights. This constitution and declaration were unanimously adopted on the 29th of June, 1776, and thus was established the first institution of free government, by a written compact, which existed in the new world. Virginia "was the first of the nations of the earth," says Mr. Jefferson, speaking of this event, "which assembled its wise men peaceably together to form a fundamental constitution, to commit it to writing, and place it among their archives, where every one should be free to appeal to its text."

But this session of the convention in Virginia is rendered remarkable by another act, which possesses a national and not a local interest. They passed a resolution "that the delegates appointed to represent Virginia in General Congress be instructed to propose to that respectable body *to declare the United Colonies free and independent States*, absolved from all allegiance to or dependence on the crown or parliament of Great Britain; and that they give the assent of this colony to such declaration, and to whatever measures may be thought proper and necessary by the Congress for forming foreign alliances, and a *confederation of the colonies*, at such time and in the manner as to them shall seem best: provided that the power of forming governments for, and the regulation of, the internal concerns of each colony, be left to the respective colonial legislatures."

Thus rapidly and steadily were the representatives of the nation approaching the decisive moment and the irretrievable deed, which were to decide the fate of so many millions of human beings. And it must be conceded that, in this perilous and immortal race, Mr. Jefferson holds no secondary place. He, though one of the youngest members of Congress, though he had much at stake, though he could not be unmindful of the many and great dangers which clustered around his path, yet he did not hesitate. He was unquestionably the boldest, most determined, and most radical member of the national representation. Others pulled back, hesitated, and deprecated haste and rashness. He constantly urged forward, endeavored to inflame the minds of his associates with extreme hostility to England, and with unconquerable resolution to overthrow her supremacy in the colonies. Accordingly, on the 28th of May, 1776, he moved in Congress that "an animated address be published to impress the minds of the people with the necessity of now stepping forward to save their country, their freedom, and their property." He was appointed chairman of this committee; and he prepared an address whose temper and spirit were in accordance with this resolution, and which was admirably adapted to prepare the way for the grand and decisive step which was about to follow.

As soon as the delegates from Virginia received the instructions of the legislature of that State, in reference to making a declaration of national freedom, they prepared to execute them. Richard Henry Lee was the oldest and the most eloquent member of the Virginia delegation. Accordingly it fell to his lot to perform this responsible and honorable duty; and on the 7th of June, 1776, he rose in Congress, then sitting in the State House in the city of Philadelphia, and moved that "Congress should declare that these United States are, and of right ought to be, free and independent states; that they are absolved from all allegiance to the British crown; that all political connection between them and the state of Great Britain is and ought to be totally dissolved; that measures should be immediately taken for procuring the assistance of foreign powers, and that a confederation be formed to bind the colonies more closely together.

The consideration of this resolution was postponed until the next day. It was then taken up and debated for several successive days. Messrs. Adams, R. H. Lee, Wythe, Jefferson, and others, were in favor of the resolution. Messrs. Wilson, Robert Livingston, Rutledge and Dickinson opposed it. All the arguments of the latter gentlemen, however, except as a matter of course those of Mr. Dickinson, applied only to the most suitable *period* of passing such a resolution, and not to the abstract propriety or necessity of the act.

As unanimity of sentiment on the subject did not seem then to prevail, it was deemed advisable to postpone a final vote on the resolution until the 1st of July, but a committee was appointed in the meantime to prepare a document which might be appropriate to the purpose contemplated. At this crisis Mr. Lee received information of the dangerous illness of a member of his family. He was compelled immediately to leave Congress, and could not serve upon the committee which was about to be appointed, nor act as its chairman, as he would have been entitled to do as the mover of the resolution. A committee was then selected by the house, which chose the following persons: John Adams, Dr. Franklin, Roger Sherman, Robert Livingston, and Thomas Jefferson. As Mr. Jefferson had received the highest number of votes, he was appointed president of the committee, and thus was the preparation of the most illustrious and important state paper of all ages entrusted to his hands. After its preparation it was submitted privately to the examination of Dr. Franklin and Mr. Adams. They made a few minor alterations, and then it was examined before the whole committee. It received their unanimous approval, and on Friday, the 28th of June, Mr. Jefferson reported it to Congress. It was read, and then ordered to lie on the table.

On the 1st of July the house resolved itself into a committee of the whole, and resumed the discussion of the preliminary question, whether a declaration of independence should be made. After a long debate this question was carried in the affirmative. All the States represented in Congress voted in its favor, except Pennsylvania and South Carolina. Delaware was represented by only two members, and as they were divided in sentiment, her vote was indecisive. The delegates from New York requested permission to withdraw, in consequence of the fact that they had received no instructions from their constituents on the subject. The final vote on the resolution was taken on the 2d of July. On this ballot South Carolina voted affirmatively; an additional delegate had arrived from Delaware, which gave the voice of that State in the same way; the representatives of New York had received instructions to give their influence in favor of the measure and Pennsylvania had happily changed some of her representatives during the interval. A unanimous vote was therefore obtained at last in favor of the original motion, to declare the colonies independent of British rule.

Much more difficulty was experienced when the discussion of the Declaration itself which the committee had prepared, came before the house. Great violence and intense excitement prevailed. Every clause and every expression were rigidly criticised. Every sentiment uttered and every principle announced were fiercely combatted and assailed. Inch by inch was the great battle fought, on the issue of which depended such vital and inestimable interests. The clause condemning the slave trade was struck out in accordance with the peremptory demands of South Carolina and Georgia. The whole amount which was eventually erased, equalled one-third of the original composition. The battle raged for three days, during which the most intense excitement prevailed. John Adams especially distinguished himself by his eloquent support of the document in its unaltered state. Mr. Jefferson, thirty-seven years afterward described Mr. Adams as having been a colossus on the floor of the house on this great occasion, and in debate powerful and convincing in the highest degree. It became evident that it would only be by a spirit of compromise that unanimity could finally be obtained. In effecting these compromises, several of the best passages of this remarkable production were erased.*

* In the Appendix the reader will find the Declaration in its original form, with the changes and emendations which were introduced into it, before its final adoption. A difference of opinion may well exist as to whether much or even any advantage was derived from the expurgating process through which it passed.

The Declaration as thus amended in committee of the whole was reported to the house on the 4th of July. On this day it was adopted, and signed by every member then present, excepting one. The recusant was the pusillanimous member from Pennsylvania, Mr. Dickinson. Other representatives, who happened on that day to be absent, appended their signatures at subsequent periods. On the 20th of July Pennsylvania elected five new representatives, omitting Mr. Dickinson from the number, and all of these subsequently signed. The ignominious eminence of being the only person in the whole Continental Congress who shrank from the glory and the danger of giving his influence in favor of this immortal declaration, belongs to the discarded representative from Pennsylvania. On the 19th of July it was ordered to be engrossed; and on the 2d of August, after having been carefully compared and verified by the original, the parchment was again signed with all those whose names were appended to the manuscript copy.

Thus was consummated the most memorable event of modern times; an event, the influence of which on the destinies of the world in all climes, has exceeded in importance that of any other event, and which through all coming ages will be the subject of congratulation to countless millions of freemen.

It would be difficult to find among the most renowned and felicitous productions of the human intellect, one which has higher claims to admiration than this Declaration. Its chief merit consists in its admirable adaptation to the purpose for which it was intended. It is indeed remarkable for the polish and beauty of its language, for its clearness and force of expression. But its directness, its comprehensiveness, and its condensation of thought are higher merits still. Within the narrow compass to which it is necessarily confined, it utters volumes of ponderous and unanswerable truth. It is a singular and admirable combination of argument, of pathos, of vindication, and of invective. It is pathetic enough to enlist the warmest sympathies of the reader, and it is argumentative enough to convince his reason. It is not more pathetic than is necessary, lest its authors might seem to have been defective in argument; and it is not too argumentative, lest a suspicion might be excited that its authors were conscious that the weakness of their cause required an elaborate defense. Its style is declamatory, but not sufficiently so as to render it vulgar or undignified; while at the same time its manly dignity does not degenerate into haughtiness. Had it been more condensed, it might have become either obscure or flippant. Had it been more expanded, it might have lost in vigor and directness. The very best evidence which can be adduced in favor of its claims to admiration and approval, is the universal judgment which the civilized world has passed upon its merits. The highest encomium which can be bestowed upon it, is to assert that it is a production worthy of the memorable occasion with which it was connected, and whose matchless glories it aided so effectually to increase and to perpetuate. Had Jefferson accomplished nothing more during his long life of eighty-three years than elaborate this immortal document, he would have deserved to be held in honorable remembrance for ages to come; and having accomplished this noble task, it is venturing nothing to say that his name will be forever rescued from the common oblivion, and will be numbered among the bright catalogue of the world's greatest heroes until the latest period of recorded time.

On the 8th of July the Declaration of Independence was publicly promulgated in Philadelphia, and rapidly the glorious news of its adoption spread through the whole country. It was received with transports of joy by many millions, and throughout the whole length and breadth of the continent a universal frenzy of delight prevailed. The declaration was published in New York on the 11th, in presence of the American army there assembled; and was greeted with the utmost pomp and splendor of military pageantry. When the news arrived in Boston, the public excitement became unparalleled. All the civil authorities, the military, and a vast multitude assembled in front of the Capitol, where the document was read, and was received with the most enthusiastic plaudits. An immense banquet was afterward given, at which innumerable toasts were drank in praise of liberty, and in denunciation of tyrants. During the ensuing night every ensign of royalty, and every badge of kingly power which existed in Boston, was defaced and removed.

Similar scenes occurred throughout all the colonies. In Virginia the name of the king was erased by an act of the legislature from the liturgy of the established religion. All the emblems of the fallen monarchy were at once obliterated; and a new coat of arms was ordered for the rising commonwealth, just then emerging from chaos into a vigorous and splendid existence. This commendable example was followed in all the remaining States. The declaration seemed to have inspired new life into the hearts of patriots, and to have steeped the spirits of the minions of despotism in despair.

Mr. Jefferson was himself fully conscious of the importance of the event which had just taken place, and of the high dignity of the drama in which he had acted so prominent a part. He regarded the proclamation of the declaration of American independence as the great starting point in the race for freedom in modern times; as the initial step in the emancipation of all civilized nations from the supremacy and the outrages of despots. It was in his judgment the first chapter in a glorious history. It was the summons which spoke in thunder-tones to the cringing millions who were yet slumbering in the dark night and gloom of tyranny, inviting them to arouse, to shake off their shackles, to assert their long plundered rights, and their dignity as men, and to achieve their liberties. Nor were these anticipations disappointed. The noble example thus set before the world was not lost. The leaven soon began to work vigorously in the mighty mass of humanity. France was the first nation to follow this example; but she followed it after a fashion of her own, and her endeavors were marked by the peculiarities of the national character. To the declaration of American independence may justly be attributed, as their ultimate and original cause, all the revolutionary movements which have since occurred, with such various successes and with such conflicting and dissimilar incidents, in Poland, in Italy, in Hungary, in Spain, in Germany, and in Central and Southern America.

And it is scarce.y hazarding too much to say, that the potent influence of the example given and of the principles inculcated by this declaration, will continue to operate until republican freedom and republican governments will replace all the rotten thrones and despotic institutions which now afflict and disgrace the world. Such is the inherent and unconquerable power of truth!

CHAPTER IV.

MR. JEFFERSON DECLINES A RE-ELECTION TO CONGRESS—RESULTS OF HIS LABORS IN CONGRESS—APPOINTED COMMISSIONER TO FRANCE—HE DECLINES—HE TAKES HIS SEAT IN THE LEGISLATURE OF VIRGINIA—HE PROPOSES A LAW FOR THE REORGANIZATION OF THE COURTS OF JUSTICE—HE PROPOSES A LAW FOR THE ABOLITION OF ENTAILS—HE PROPOSES A BILL TO OVERTHROW THE ESTABLISHED CHURCH IN VIRGINIA—FIERCE CONFLICTS WHICH ENSUED—THE FINAL RESULT—JEFFERSON'S ULTIMATE TRIUMPH—ESTABLISHMENT OF ABSOLUTE RELIGIOUS FREEDOM IN VIRGINIA—MR. JEFFERSON OBTAINS THE PASSAGE OF A LAW ABOLISHING THE FOREIGN SLAVE TRADE IN VIRGINIA—HISTORY OF THAT REFORM IN FOREIGN COUNTRIES.

MR. JEFFERSON's term of service in the Continental Congress expired on the 11th of August, 1776. Before the arrival of that period he had notified the convention of Virginia that he declined a re-election. Nevertheless that body chose to act contrary to his wishes, and he was again unanimously re-elected. This result did not alter his own purpose, and he again wrote to the chairman of the convention, resigning positively the proffered honor. Two causes induced him at this period to withdraw from the national councils. One of these was the necessity which existed that he should attend to his private affairs at home. But the chief reason was a desire to participate in the formation of the new constitution and government which were about to be formed and adopted in Virginia. Says he: "The new government in Virginia was now organized, a meeting of the legislature was to be held in October, and I had been elected a member by my county. I knew that our legislation, under the royal government, had many very vicious points which urgently required reformation; and I thought I could be of more use in forwarding that work. I therefore retired from my seat in Congress." On the 2d of September, 1776, Mr. Harrison, his successor, arrived at Philadelphia, and Jefferson immediately returned to Virginia. The period of his actual presence in the national councils had been only nine months; and yet at the early age of thirty-three he had taken the first rank among the leading patriots of the colonies; he had led their opinions and moulded their measures; and he had impressed the stamp of his genius and of his principles upon the great title deeds and symbols of the nation's rights and liberties.

On the 30th of September he received another evidence of the confidence with which he had inspired the members of the Continental Congress. They appointed him a joint-commissioner to France, with Dr. Franklin and Silas Dean, to negotiate treaties of alliance and commerce with that government. This was a trust of the greatest importance to the interests of the nation; and yet so earnest was the desire of Mr. Jefferson to superintend and assist in the establishment of the new government and constitution of his native State, that he again declined an honorable appointment which would have interfered with the realization of his wishes on that subject.

We have now reached that period in the life and labors of Mr. Jefferson when he ceases to be an exponent and representative of national measures, and assumes the attitude of the founder of a new and distinct school of politics; and when he began the proposal and defense of doctrines which have not unjustly won for him the epithet of the "*Father of American Democracy.*" This course, it will be seen, he consistently pursued throughout the many years of high official position which marked his subsequent life.

Mr. Jefferson took his seat in the Legislature of Virginia on the 7th of October, 1776. Five days afterward he moved for leave to introduce a bill for the reorganization and establishment of the courts of justice. He was appointed chairman of the committee to whom the matter was referred; and he drew up an ordinance, which he submitted to the committee. They approved of all its provisions.

It was then reported to the house, by whom, after a thorough and careful examination, and the introduction of a few unimportant changes, it was unanimously adopted.

The provisions of the law prepared by Mr. Jefferson possess the qualities of simplicity, symmetry, and the spirit and form of republicanism. But in addition to these it could also claim the merit of great originality; for although a similar arrangement exists in the judicial institutions of other States at the present time, that proposed by Mr. Jefferson was the model after which they have all been drawn and executed. He divided the State into counties, and devised three courts of ascending grades, called the County, the Superior, and the Supreme Courts. The jurisdictions of these courts, and their relative number, were found admirably adapted to meet all the wants of the community. He gave new prominence and importance to the trial by jury, as the great bulwark of the rights of the people. He ordained that in all questions of law and of fact combined, as well as in all pure questions of fact, the reference to a jury was made imperative and unavoidable in the courts of law; and he would have carried this principle also into the Courts of Chancery, had he not, in this movement, been opposed and defeated by the efforts of

Edmund Pendleton, the ablest lawyer in the State, who was opposed to the extreme measures of popular reform introduced by Mr. Jefferson. The chief features of the law on this subject, as proposed by Mr. Jefferson, remain in force in Virginia till the present day.

On the 12th October Mr. Jefferson continued his labors by introducing a bill for the abolition of the law of entails in Virginia. This was a measure of much greater importance than the preceding one. It was a desperate and destructive blow struck directly at the aristocratic order in that State. Nowhere else on the continent had the lines of demarcation between the higher and the lower ranks, between the gentle and the vulgar, between the exclusive and the popular, been drawn with so much distinctness as in the Old Dominion. And that distinction was based not simply on differences of education, birth, and breeding; but also on the more unpopular one of the possession of wealth. The State having been settled at an early period by a body of men who had embraced the privileges granted them of taking vast tracts of the free domain of nature—these estates had become immensely valuable with the progress of time; and in accordance with the English law of entail, they had been devised from generation to generation in fee-tail to the eldest son of the family. This aristocratic transmission of estates had gradually created a body of men who formed a patrician order in the State, whose wealth, luxury, and expensive and ostentatious establishments were little in harmony with the simplicity of republican manners. Together with the possession of the land, this class of men gradually absorbed all the political power, which only increased the evil, and rendered the state of things more obnoxious to the friends of liberty and reform.

If this aristocratic class of the community were useless to the State, the other existing orders of society in Virginia were such, that some of them invited, and others of them demanded, a reformation on this subject. Next below the great landowners, in the social and political scale, were the class known as "half-breeds." These were the descendants of the younger sons and daughters of the aristocrats, who inherited the pride without the wealth or the influence of their ancestors. Below these again were the upstarts, or pretenders, who were usually men of talent, and having obtained wealth by means of their superior enterprise and abilities, were desirous of separating themselves from the class in which they were born and to which they originally belonged, and of imitating the manners and habits of the aristocracy, and if possible to obtain admission to their society. Below these again were the plain, substantial yeomen, who were industrious, simple, frugal, who knew nothing and cared less about aristocratic splendor, rank, or wealth, and whose whole attention was confined to the cultivation of the small farms which they possessed, or to their mechanical trades. Below all these again, and the vilest of the race, were the class of persons termed "overseers," who tyrannized over the slaves, who were the most cringing of human beings to their superiors, and most the tyrannical to their subordinates and victims.

By abolishing the law of entails in Virginia, Mr. Jefferson destroyed the entire fabric of this social structure; for the whole of it gradually grew up around, and in consequence of that institution. His purpose was also to open the way for an aristocracy of intellect and talent, as being more in accordance with the spirit of a republic. And although this measure was resisted with the utmost violence by the representatives of the aristocratic order in the legislature, led on by men of the highest ability—such as Edmund Pendleton and John Robinson, the measure was finally adopted. Entails were abolished, and a law passed by which real estate, as well as personal property was distributed, on the death of the possessor in equitable proportions among the whole of his children. Mr. Jefferson also subsequently introduced another bill, which rendered this reform complete, which destroyed the preference given to the male over the female sex, and to the eldest child over the younger children.*

After accomplishing this great republican movement, which gave a new appearance and form to the secular and material interests of the State, Mr. Jef-

* Mr. Jefferson describes his labors in reference to this event in the following language:

"On the 12th, I obtained leave to bring in a bill declaring tenants in tail to hold their lands in fee simple. In the earlier times of the colony, when lands were to be obtained for little or nothing, some provident individuals procured large grants; and desirous of *founding great families for themselves*, settled them on their descendants in fee tail. The transmission of this property from generation to generation, in the same name, raised up a distinct set of families, who being privileged *by law in the perpetuation of their wealth*, were thus formed into a *patrician order*, distinguished by the splendor and luxury of their establishments. From this order, too, the king habitually selected his counselors of state; the hope of which distinction devoted the whole corps to the interests and will of the crown. To annul this privilege, and instead of an *aristocracy of wealth*, of more harm and danger than benefit to society, to make an opening for the *aristocracy* of *virtue* and *talent*, which nature has wisely provided for the direction of the interests of society, and scattered with equal hand through all its conditions, was deemed essential to a well-ordered republic. To effect it, no violence was necessary, no deprivation of natural right, but rather an enlargement of it, by a repeal of the law. For this would authorize the present holder to divide the property among his children equally, as his affections were divided; and would place them, by natural generation, on the level of their fellow-citizens."

ferson directed his attention to the religious relations and interests of the community. He introduced a bill to abolish the church establishment in Virginia, and to place all religious sects on an equal footing.

The establishment of the Church of England in Virginia had taken place at the period of the first immigration thither. The charter granted to Sir Walter Raleigh contained an express clause, which provided that the laws of the new colony to be founded by him, should in no respect militate against the true Christian faith as then professed by the Church of England, and established by law in the realm. At an early day the colony had been divided into parishes, and in each parish a minister had been settled, a church built, a glebe and parsonage assigned, and a support provided for the incumbent from the proceeds of a specified amount of tobacco. Schismatics were severely punished. It was a penal offense in parents to prevent their children from being baptized by the minister of the established church. The assembling of Quakers was forbidden by law; and they had been ordered to leave the State, with the penalty of death if they returned. In 1705, a law had been passed to the effect that he who denied the truth of the Christian religion, or the existence of the trinity, or the inspiration of the Scriptures, should be incapable of holding any office, civil, military, or ecclesiastical, and should further suffer three years' imprisonment. Even the Declaration of Rights, passed in 1776, had not abolished and obliterated these infamous enactments; although the legislature, in that year, had been overflowed with the most urgent petitions from thousands of respectable and influential citizens asking their repeal. In the progress of the several centuries which preceded this date, the morals of the established clergy had become a by-word and a disgrace to the Christian name. They were, in the majority of instances drunken, idle and debauched. Numerous dissenters of intelligence, piety, and wealth had gradually immigrated into the State; and at the period of Mr. Jefferson's activity in the legislature, they formed an important portion of the community. The Presbyterians especially had attained a high position in point of importance, wealth and social influence, in many portions of the commonwealth.

With this large class of citizens the labors of Mr. Jefferson met with much favor. They supported him with numerous petitions to the legislature. The opposing faction, long secure in its prerogatives, and undisturbed in its domination, awoke from its lethargy, fiercely fought against the project of change, and presented numerous memorials against the proposed reforms. Many arguments were urged by the supporters of the established religion, the most cogent of which was that the Episcopal clergy had entered on their livings with the understanding, on the part of the government, that they should hold them for life; and that, though the form of government had been changed, yet the tenure of these rights was as sacred as that by which the citizens held their private property.

The conflict between the advocates of conservatism and progress in the legislature was violent in the extreme. Mr. Jefferson describes them as having been the most furious in which he had ever engaged. Nor were the efforts of his opponents without effect; for so vigorous was their resistance that they compelled him to change his position from the absolute to the partial abolition of the establishment. He eventually succeeded in obtaining the passage of a law, which removed the penalty which had formerly been inflicted for maintaining irreligious opinions, for refusing to attend church, and for the exercise of any other than the established mode of religious worship. He also obtained the exemption of dissenters from contributing to the support of the established church. But Mr. Jefferson was not a man to yield in the full accomplishment of his purposes, to any degree of opposition. He accordingly persisted in his endeavors for three successive years, until at last, by unwearied exertions, he succeeded in attaining his end in the final passage of a law which enacted that no general assessment should be established by law, on any one, either for the support of the Church of England, or for that of other sects; but that every one should be permitted to exercise his own free will in reference to the maintenance of any form of religious service. The passage of this law not only overthrew the power of the Church of England in Virginia, but it established religious liberty on the fullest and largest basis. It is true that he was at that time not a member of the legislature, but the governor of the State; yet it was well understood that the final triumph of the measure was secured through his influence, by his assistance, and in accordance with his wishes.

The next measure of reform proposed by Mr. Jefferson had reference to the slave-trade. His opinions on this important subject were that the emancipation of the slaves, accompanied with their colonization, was practicable. But his efforts at this period were not directed to the attainment of this result; for he undoubtedly perceived that the period for the accomplishment of so radical a measure had not yet arrived. But he proposed a law abolishing the foreign slave-trade; and in the attainment of this result he was eminently useful and successful; a law making the foreign slave-trade piracy having finally passed the legislature in 1778.

The honor of having *led the van* in this great reform, among all the nations of the earth, belongs to Virginia; and the honor of having proposed and accomplished this result in Virginia belongs to Mr. Jefferson. The praise of priority in this matter has long been claimed for Mr. Wilberforce, and for Great Britain; but the claim is unjust. It was in 1791 that Mr. Wilberforce introduced his bill to abolish the Foreign Slave Trade into the English parliament. He failed in carrying his motion through both branches of the legislature, during fourteen successive years; until he triumphed at last on the 25th of March, 1807. In March, 1792, Denmark passed a similar law, interdicting the slave-trade on the part of Danish subjects after January, 1803. Sweden passed a similar law in 1813; Netherland in 1814. Bonaparte forbade the traffic in 1815. Spain followed with a prohibitory decree in 1816, to take effect in 1820; and Portugal did the same in 1828. Thus it appears that the credit of leading the way in this great and beneficent revolution belongs to Virginia, acting under the promptings and guidance of Thomas Jefferson; inasmuch as her statute on the subject was passed, and went into full and permanent operation in 1778, and consequently long prior to any of the rest.

CHAPTER V.

PROPOSITION TO CODIFY THE LAWS OF VIRGINIA—A COMMITTEE APPOINTED FOR THE PURPOSE—MR. JEFFERSON'S PORTION OF THE TASK—CHANGES IN THE LAW OF DESCENTS—CHANGES IN THE CRIMINAL LAW—MEETING OF THE COMMITTEE—THEIR REPORT TO THE LEGISLATURE—LEADING REFORMS INTRODUCED BY MR. JEFFERSON INTO THE CODE—RELIGIOUS FREEDOM—ABOLITION OF SLAVERY—GENERAL SYSTEM OF EDUCATION—THE CAPTIVE ARMY OF BURGOYNE QUARTERED AT CHARLOTTESVILLE—POPULAR EXCITEMENT—USEFUL AND BENEVOLENT ACTIVITY OF JEFFERSON IN REFERENCE TO THE CAPTIVES.

Mr. Jefferson deserves to occupy the first place among the eminent men who have labored to republicanize the institutions of America, both those of the Federal government and those of the States. Having succeeded in introducing those important reforms into Virginia which have been described in the foregoing chapter, he proceeded on the 24th of October, 1776, to introduce a bill providing for the appointment of a committee of five persons, who should prepare a new code of laws for the government of the State, by revising, altering, amending, and repealing what already existed, or by adding new enactments thereto. This measure was in substance providing for the erection of an entirely new system of laws in the State, and the total destruction of the civil, political, and religious institutions of the past.

The committee appointed by the joint ballot of both houses of the legislature to perform this important task, were Mr. Jefferson as chairman, Edmund Pendleton, George Wythe, George Mason, and Thomas Ludwell Lee. So important were the duties entrusted to this committee supposed to be, that the legislature excused Mr. Wythe from his attendance in Congress, in order to enable him to perform the more responsible labors which devolved upon him as a member of this committee. The committee appointed their first meeting at Fredericksburg on the ensuing 13th of January, for the purpose of making a distribution of the respective portions of their onerous work.

When the committee met, the arrangement which was adopted threw the most difficult and laborious portion of the work on the shoulders of Mr. Jefferson. To him was committed the codification of the Common Law and of the British statutes down to the period of James I., when a separate legislature was first introduced into Virginia. The same statutes from the reign of James I. to the then existing period were committed to Mr. Wythe. The statutes of Virginia already in existence were consigned to Mr. Pendleton. The two remaining members of the committee resigned without taking any share in the work, on the ground that they were not lawyers, and therefore not competent to the duties which would have devolved upon them. No substitutes were ever appointed in their place; and the whole of this immense labor was performed, in about two years, by the three remaining members of the committee.

The department of criminal law and the law of descents both fell within the range of Mr. Jefferson's task; and he embraced the opportunity thus afforded to impress upon both, the peculiar sentiments which he entertained on those subjects. In speaking of his labors in a letter to Mr. Wythe, in November, 1778, he said: "In style I have aimed at accuracy, brevity and simplicity, preserving however the very words of the established law, whether their meaning had been sanctioned by judicial decisions or rendered technical by usage. The same matter, if couched in modern statutory language, with all its tautologies, redundancies, and circumlocutions, would have spread itself over many pages, and been unintelligible to those whom it concerns." When re-enacting English statutes he took care not to change their ancient diction, lest he should give rise to new disputes by introducing new phraseology;

at the same time avoiding all useless amplification of language.

In regard to the criminal law, Mr. Jefferson adopted the fundamental rule to recommend penalties not repugnant to benevolence, to abolish the barbarous remains of ancient usages and punishments, and to inflict death only for the crimes of murder and treason. At that period the penal code of England affixed the penalty of death to two hundred different offenses. The humanity therefore which Mr. Jefferson recommended was at that time the more remarkable, as it was so far in advance of the age in which he lived.

The changes which he introduced into the law of descents were radical and extreme. He proposed to abolish the law of primogeniture, and to make real estate heritable in equal partition by the next of kin, as personal property already was by the statute of distribution. This project, which harmonized with the acts of the legislature already adopted on the subject, was violently opposed by Mr. Pendleton, who was also one of the committee; but Mr. Jefferson persisted in his purpose, and introduced this reform fully and prominently into the new code.

After the continued labors of two years the committee assembled in February, 1779, at Williamsburg, to review, approve, and consolidate their respective labors into one general and complete report. Day after day the several parts were read, examined, criticised, altered, amended and confirmed according to the decision of the majority of the committee. They had embodied in their labors all the Common Law, all the British statutes, and all the existing laws of Virginia; and had condensed this vast mass of jurisprudence into a single printed folio volume of ninety pages only, comprising one hundred and twenty-six bills.

On the 18th of June, 1779, the committee of revision reported the results of their labors to the general assembly. These were not adopted in a mass, but single portions were taken up from time to time, discussed and approved. It was not till 1785, after the conclusion of the Revolutionary war, that the whole code had received the sanction of law. The peculiar and most remarkable principles which Mr. Jefferson elaborated, and incorporated into this code, were important in the highest degree, and indicate the great originality and boldness of his views. In addition to the repeal of the law of entails which he introduced into the code, and the abrogation of the law of primogeniture, together with the equal division of inheritances among children, he asserted the right of expatriation, or a republican definition of the terms on which aliens may become citizens, and citizens may make themselves aliens. He also proposed the establishment of religious equality and liberty upon the broadest foundation. He advised the emancipation of all the slaves born in Virginia after the passage of the act, and their colonization or deportation at a proper age. This measure was entirely stricken out by the legislature. He recommended the abolition of capital punishment in all cases except treason and murder; and the graduation of all other punishments upon the principle of humanity and reason. He devised the establishment of a systematic plan of general education, reaching to all classes of the citizens, and adapted to every grade of capacity. This portion of his labors was not carried into effect by the legislature.

The act providing for the establishment of religious freedom is the most remarkable and praiseworthy of all Mr. Jefferson's productions, except the Declaration of Independence; and it exhibits the largeness and liberality of his views in the most impressive manner. It was the work which stood second in the author's own estimation of all his labors; and he proudly ordered that a reference to it should be inscribed upon his tombstone. And yet it was with very considerable difficulty that he succeeded in obtaining its passage by the legislature.

That portion however of Mr. Jefferson's labors as a codifier in which he took the greatest interest, which met with the fiercest opposition, and in the establishment of which he was totally defeated, had reference to the domestic slave-trade. He himself declared that on that subject he could scarcely write or speak temperately. His proposed law provided that after a certain period all negroes born in the State should be free, and afterward at an adult age be transported to some foreign colony. As his opinions on this subject are of great interest and importance, the following extract from his own writings are quoted. It was penned at the age of seventy-seven, and shows that the progress of many years had made no change in his sentiments. Says he: "The principles of the amendment, however, were agreed on in the committee, that is to say, the freedom of all born after a certain day, and deportation at a proper age. But it was found that the public mind would not yet bear the proposition, nor will it bear it even at this day, (1821.) Yet the day is not distant when it must bear and adopt it, or worse will follow. *Nothing is more certainly written in the book of fate than that these people are to be free; nor is it less certain, that the two races, equally free, cannot live in the same government.* Nature, habit and opinion, have drawn indelible lines of distinction between them. It is still in our power to direct the process of emancipation and deportation, peaceably, and in such slow degree, as that the evil will wear off insensibly, and their place be, *pari passu*, filled up by free white laborers. If, on the contrary, it is left to force itself on, human nature must shudder at the prospect held up. We should in vain look for an example in the Spanish deportation or deletion of the Moors. This precedent would fall far short of our case."

The bill providing for the introduction of a general system of education contains three prominent and remarkable divisions. It proposed the establishment of elementary schools throughout the State, for all children generally, without distinction of rich or poor. It recommended the erection of colleges, or more properly speaking, of academies in each district, to impart a middle range of instruction. It advised the creation and endowment of a general university, wherein the highest and ultimate grade of instruction should be given. An addition which he added to this bill called for the establishment of a public library, and a gallery for the exhibition of paintings and sculptures. The first portion only of the bill, providing for the establishment of elementary schools, received the approbation of the legislature.

Having concluded his labors as a codifier, and having obtained the authority of law for a large portion of his bills, Mr. Jefferson's agency as a legislator for the present ceased. Nor should it be forgotten that these elaborate researches were carried on, and these legislative reforms were effected, at a period when the whole country, and Virginia particularly, was convulsed by the vicissitudes of a desperate, protracted and uncertain conflict. The storms of the revolutionary war were then raging, and many dark and gloomy hours harassed the spirit of this faithful and devoted servant of the popular interests and supremacy. But none of these things diverted his attention from the important task which he had assumed. To this day the laws, legislation and jurisprudence of Virginia bear upon their front the deep and ineffaceable impress of the master mind and the indefatigable industry of Thomas Jefferson.

In January, 1779, an incident occurred of a more personal nature, which serves to illustrate clearly the qualities of Mr. Jefferson's disposition, and which proves that his views of reform and amelioration were not theories merely, but were substantial and practical realities. After the capture of Burgoyne by General Gates, four thousand British troops became prisoners of war. At first they were quartered at Boston. After twelve months they were removed to Charlottesville in Virginia, six miles from Monticello. This arrival in their midst threw the inhabitants of that district into the utmost terror. The scarcity of provisions and other causes induced them to imagine that the presence of this large force would lead to a famine.

Mr. Jefferson immediately exerted himself to quell the popular excitement. He assisted in the erection of capacious barracks, in establishing suitable accommodations for the officers, and in providing rations for the troops. Soon the residence of the prisoners became the abode of comfort and contentment. He frequently entertained the officers at Monticello. His large and valuable library was at their disposal. Gradually the presence of these captive troops was found to be a great advantage and profit to the surrounding planters, and universal contentment reigned. At this period Patrick Henry, then Governor of the State, formed the resolution to order the removal of these troops from Charlottesville to another location. This step would have been exceedingly impolitic and unwise. The whole community revolted against it, loud complaints were made both by the people and by the troops, and a riot was apprehended.

At this crisis Mr. Jefferson addressed an energetic

appeal to Governor Henry, urging the relinquishment of the proposed change, at great length. The governor and his council carefully deliberated on the arguments of Mr. Jefferson, and finally concluded to acquiesce in his views. His agency in this matter won for him the enthusiastic applause of the whole people in the neighborhood of Monticello, and especially were the officers of the British troops, who had derived so many advantages from the proximity of Mr. Jefferson, intensely grateful. Some of these were Hessians, and many years afterward, when Mr. Jefferson was traveling in Germany, he had the pleasure of meeting some of these officers again, and of receiving their demonstrations of gratitude and esteem. When the foreign officers eventually left Charlottesville, they addressed letters of acknowledgment to their benefactor, which indicated how greatly they considered themselves under obligations to him.

The communication addressed by Mr. Jefferson on this occasion to Governor Henry, is so peculiar in its style and spirit, that we will here introduce a portion of it. It is as follows:

"It is for the benefit of mankind to mitigate the horrors of war as much as possible. The practice, therefore, of modern nations of treating captive enemies with politeness and generosity, is not only delightful in contemplation, but really interesting to all the world, friends, foes, and neutrals. Let us apply this: the officers, after considerable hardships, have all procured quarters, comfortable and satisfactory to them. In order to do this, they were obliged, in many instances, to hire houses for a year, certain, and at such exorbitant rents, as were sufficient to tempt independent owners to go out of them, and shift as they could. These houses, in most cases, were much out of repair. They have repaired them at a considerable expense. One of the general officers has taken a place for two years, advanced the rent for the whole time, and been obliged, moreover, to erect additional buildings, for the accommodation of a part of his family, for which there was not room in the house rented. Independent of the brickwork, for the carpentry of these additional buildings I know he is to pay fifteen hundred dollars. The same gentleman, to my knowledge, has paid to one person three thousand six hundred and seventy dollars, for different articles, to fix himself commodiously. They have, generally, laid in their stocks of grain, and other provisions; for it is well known that officers do not live on their rations. They have purchased cows, sheep, &c.; set into farming; prepared their gardens, and have a prospect of quiet and comfort before them. To turn to the soldiers—the environs of the barracks are delightful, the ground cleared, laid off in hundreds of gardens, each inclosed in its separate paling; these well prepared, and exhibiting a fine appearance. General Reidésel alone laid out upward of two hundred pounds in garden seeds for the German troops only. Judge what an extent of ground these seeds would cover. There is little doubt, that their own gardens will furnish them with a great abundance of vegetables through the year. Their poultry, pigeons, and other preparations of that kind, present to the mind the idea of a company of farmers, rather than a camp of soldiers. In addition to the barracks built for them by the public, and now very comfortable, they have built great numbers for themselves, in such messes as fancied each other; and the whole corps, both officers and men, seem now happy and satisfied with their situation. Having thus found the art of rendering captivity itself comfortable, and carried it into execution, at their own great expense and labor, their spirits sustained by the prospect of gratifications rising before their eyes, does not every sentiment of humanity revolt against the proposition of stripping them of all this, and removing them into new situations, where, from the advanced season of the year, no preparations can be made for carrying themselves comfortably through the heats of summer; and when it is known that the necessary advances for the conveniences already provided, have exhausted their funds, and left them unable to make the like exertions anew?"

CHAPTER VI.

MR. JEFFERSON ELECTED GOVERNOR OF VIRGINIA—HIS MEASURES OF RETALIATION UPON THE BRITISH—ARREST OF HENRY HAMILTON—WASHINGTON APPROVES OF JEFFERSON'S MEASURES—TARLTON'S INVASION OF VIRGINIA—JEFFERSON'S ACTIVITY—HIS LETTER TO WASHINGTON—ATTACK OF THE BRITISH ON RICHMOND—SCHEMES TO CAPTURE ARNOLD—THEIR FAILURE—ATTEMPT OF THE BRITISH TO TAKE JEFFERSON AT MONTICELLO—HIS ESCAPE—EFFORTS MADE TO IMPEACH JEFFERSON IN THE LEGISLATURE—THEIR DEFEAT—JEFFERSON'S DEFENSE OF HIS OFFICIAL ACTS.

ON withdrawing from the legislature of Virginia, Mr. Jefferson was complimented with the highest trust within their gift. He was elected governor of the State. This event took place on the 1st of June, 1779.

One of the first steps which the new governor took was of a retributory nature toward the fierce and implacable foes who were then ravaging the land, laboring to crush the liberties of the people, and striving to destroy their military defenders. The generous example of their conduct toward the captive army of Burgoyne, was now totally lost upon them. The American officers and soldiers who had been taken prisoners were loaded with chains. They were confined in crowded and filthy dungeons and prison ships. Their food was pernicious and detestable. Many had been transported, tried, convicted, and punished in England. Mr. Jefferson determined at this crisis to try the effect of a just severity upon those prisoners then in his power, in order to soften the measures pursued by the foe. The cruel and rapacious governor of Detroit, Henry Hamilton, was then in the hands of the Americans, together with Philip Dejean, a justice of the peace of Detroit, and William Lamotte, a captain, all of whom had been taken prisoners by Col. Clarke at Fort Vincennes, and brought under guard to Williamsburg. These men had been notorious for their great barbarity toward the Americans. Hamilton especially had been unequalled for his crimes of blood. He had spurred on the Indians to acts of the utmost cruelty to the settlers; and to increase the number of murders he had given a high reward for scalps, and had refused all rewards for prisoners. All of these men had rendered themselves notorious for the scalping parties which they had organized and led over the frontier settlements, in which excursions they had butchered, with indiscriminate ferocity, men, women, and children.*

To punish these villains, and to strike a wholesome terror into their former associates, Mr. Jefferson ordered that they should be put in irons, con

* Vide Jefferson's Works. Vol. I. Appendix, note A.

fined in a dungeon in the public prison, deprived of all use of pen, ink and paper, and be forbidden to hold communication with any one except their keepers.

These decisive steps received the unqualified approbation of General Washington. He thought it highly desirable that at least one solemn proof should be given, that the patriots of the Revolution could be just as well as generous. That proof could again be repeated, should a repetition be deemed advisable. The first effect which these measures produced upon the British was to retaliate. They published a declaration that no officer of the Virginia line should be exchanged as long as Hamilton and his friends remained in captivity. As soon as Jefferson received information of this resolution, he ordered all exchange of British prisoners to be stopped. He intended to retain them as pledges for the security of the captive patriots. A prison ship was fitted up for their especial accommodation. Special means were used to ascertain the kind of treatment the Americans received at the hands of their captors. The final result of this retaliative process on both sides was precisely such as Mr. Jefferson had anticipated. The appeals of the British prisoners to their own countrymen became so urgent and so pertinacious, that the latter were at last compelled to yield, to treat the American captives with the humanity required by the laws of civilized warfare, and by so doing to secure the comfort of those minions of the British despot who had fallen into the hands of the patriots.

The period of the memorable invasion of Virginia by the notorious Tarlton now arrived. His pathway through the young commonwealth was marked by blood and rapine. Terror spread rapidly throughout the whole community; but the prevalence of terror did not prevent those who were in imminent danger from arousing themselves to energetic deeds of fortitude and self-defense. At this crisis very great responsibility lay upon Mr. Jefferson as the chief magistrate of the State. He employed all his influence and abilities to provide proper means of protection against the common foe. He called upon the legislature to act with promptness and decision. That body immediately clothed the governor with extraordinary powers. The summer of 1779 passed away in repeated alarms, and in hurried preparations for resistance. On the 11th of June Mr. Jefferson addressed the following letter to General Washington, advising him of the critical state of affairs in the State, and the surrounding colonies:

"Our intelligence from the southward is most

lamentably defective. Though Charleston has now been in the hands of the enemy nearly a month, we hear nothing of their movements which can be relied upon. Rumors say they are penetrating northward. To remedy this defect, I shall immediately establish a line of expresses from hence to a neighborhood of their army, and send thither a sensible, judicious person, to give us information of their movements. This intelligence will, I hope, be conveyed at the rate of one hundred and twenty miles in the twenty-four hours. They set out to their stations to-morrow. I wish it were possible that a like speedy line of communication could be formed from hence to your excellency's head-quarters. Perfect and speedy information of what is passing in the south, might put it in your power perhaps to frame your measures by theirs. There is really nothing to oppose the enemy northward, but the cautious principle of the military art. North Carolina is without arms. They do not abound with us. Those we have are freely imparted to them; but such is the state of their resources that they have not been able to move a single musket from this State to theirs. All the wagons we can collect here have been furnished to the Baron de Kalb, and are assembled for the march of 2500 men under General Stevens, of Culpepper, who will move on the 19th inst. I have written to

Congress to hasten supplies of arms and military stores for the southern States, and particularly to aid us with cartridge paper and boxes, the want of which articles, small as they are, renders our stores useless. The want of money cramps every effort. This will be supplied by the most unpalatable of all substitutes, force. Your excellency will readily conceive that, after the loss of one army, our eyes are turned toward the other, and that we comfort ourselves with the hope that, if any aids can be furnished by you, without defeating the operations more beneficial to the Union, they will be furnished. At the same time, I am happy to find that the wishes of the people go no further, as far as I have an opportunity of hearing their sentiments. Could arms be furnished, I think this State and North Carolina would embody from ten to fifteen thousand militia immediately, and more if necessary. I hope ere long to be able to give you a more certain statement of the enemy's as well as our own situation."

On the 30th of December Mr. Jefferson received information that twenty-seven British ships had entered the capes of Virginia on the preceding day. He immediately sent General Nelson to the lower counties of the State, for the purpose of calling out the militia. The fleet proceeded up James river. On the 3d of January, 1780, it anchored at Jamestown. At Westover one thousand men were landed under the command of the traitor Arnold, and they proceeded at once toward Richmond. This was a complete surprise; for no attack at that point had been expected, and all the militia had been marched to Williamsburg. The legislature immediately dispersed. When the British were at Four Mile Creek, twelve miles from Richmond, Mr. Jefferson also deserted the capital at seven o'clock at night. He proceeded to join his family at Tuckahoe, eight miles from Richmond. There he remained until the approach of the enemy compelled him to retreat to Manchester. While halting at this place he was visited by some of the citizens of Richmond, who conveyed an offer from Arnold not to burn the town, provided the tobacco there deposited was delivered up to the possession of the foe. This offer was instantly rejected. As soon as Arnold reached Richmond, he destroyed the cannon foundry, and a large quantity of tobacco as well as many public and private buildings were burned. He then returned to his ships after an excursion of forty-eight hours; and committing deeds which will involve his name in eternal infamy, as the foe and assailant of his native land. Immediately after the departure of Arnold from Richmond, Mr. Jefferson devised a scheme for the capture of the traitor. He addressed the following letter to General Muhlenberg on the subject:

"Sir: Acquainted as you are with the treasons of Arnold, I need say nothing for your information, or to give you a proper sentiment of them. You will readily suppose that it is above all things desirable to drag him from those under whose wing he is now sheltered. On his march to and from this place, I am certain it might have been done with facility, by men of enterprise and firmness. I think it may still be done, though perhaps not quite so easily. Having peculiar confidence in the men from the western side of the mountains, I meant, as soon as they should come down, to get the enterprise proposed to a chosen number of them, such whose courage and whose fidelity would be above all doubt. Your perfect knowledge of these men personally, and my confidence in your discretion, induce me to ask you to seek from among them proper characters, in such numbers as you think best; to reveal to them our desire; and engage them to undertake to seize and bring off this greatest of all traitors. Whether this may be best effected by their going in as friends, and awaiting their opportunity, or otherwise, is left to themselves. The smaller the number the better, so that they may be sufficient to manage him. Every necessary caution must be used on their part, to prevent a discovery of their design by the enemy. I will undertake, if they are successful in bringing him off alive, that they shall receive five thousand guineas reward among them; and to men formed for such an enterprise, it must be a great incitement to know that their names will be recorded with glory in history, with those of Vanwert, Paulding, and Williams."

The guilty fears of Arnold rendered him doubly cautious, and the plan of his capture was not successful. Nevertheless Jefferson was not disheartened, but devised a second trap, in which he was to receive the assistance of General Washington and the French fleet. That plan was to block up the river by means of the land and naval forces of the patriots as to completely hem in the foe, and eventually to secure his capture. But the arrival of a British squadron of superior size drove the French fleet from the Chesapeake, and again defeated the plan of Jefferson for the capture of the arch-traitor.

Arnold having retreated from Virginia, Lord Cornwallis immediately afterward entered the State from the south. The legislature convened at Charlottesville on the 28th of May, and soon began to discuss and adopt measures of vigorous resistance. The very day the legislature assembled, Mr. Jefferson addressed the following letter to General Washington:

"I have just been advised, he says, that the British have evacuated Petersburg, been joined by a considerable reinforcement from New York, and crossed James River at Westover. They were, on the 26th instant, three miles advanced toward Richmond, at which place Major-General the Marquis Fayette lay with three thousand men, regulars and militia, that being the whole number we could arm, until the arrival of the 1100 stand of arms from Rhode Island, which are about this time at the place where our public stores are deposited. The whole force of the enemy within this State, from the best intelligence I have been able to get, is, I think, about 7000 men, including the garrison left at Portsmouth. A number of privateers, which are constantly ravaging the shores of our rivers, prevent us from receiving any aid from the counties lying on navigable waters; and powerful operations meditated against our western frontier, by a joint force of British and Indian savages, have, as your excellency before knew, obliged us to embody between two and three thousand men in that quarter. Your excellency will judge from this state of things, and from what you know of your own country, what it may probably suffer during the present campaign. Should the enemy be able to obtain no opportunity of annihilating the marquis's army, a small proportion of their force may yet restrain his movements effectually, while the greater part is employed in detachments to waste an unarmed country, and lead the minds of the people to acquiesce under those events which they see no human power prepared to ward off. We are too far removed from the other scenes of war, to say whether the main force of the enemy be within this State; but I suppose they cannot any where spare so great an army for the operations of the field. Were it possible for this circumstance to justify, in your excellency, a determination to lend us your personal aid, it is evident from the *universal voice, that the presence* of their beloved countryman, whose talents have so long been successfully employed in establishing the freedom of *kindred States*, to whose person they have still flattered themselves they retained some right, and have ever looked upon as their *dernier resort* in distress; that your appearance, among them, I say, *would restore full* confidence of salvation, and would *render them equal* to whatever is not impossible. I cannot undertake to foresee and obviate the difficulties which lie in the way of such a resolution. The whole subject is before you, of which I see only detached parts. Should the danger of the State, and its consequences to the Union, be such as to render it best for the whole that you should repair to its assistance, the difficulty would then be how to keep men out of the field. I have undertaken to hint this matter to your excellency, not only on my own sense of its importance to us, but at the solicitation of many members of weight in our legislature, which has not yet assembled to speak its own desires. A few days will bring to me that relief, which the Constitution has prepared for those oppressed with the labors of my office; and a long declared resolution of relinquishing it to abler hands, has prepared my way for retirement to a private station; still, as an individual, I should feel the comfortable effects of your presence, and have (what I thought could not have been) an additional motive for that gratitude, esteem and respect, which I have long felt for your excellency."

It was at this period that Tarlton made his famous attempt to surprise and capture Mr. Jefferson at Monticello. Having approached within ten miles of that place with his whole force, he sent a detachment of horse rapidly in advance, under the command of Captain McLeod, to accomplish that purpose. But several of Mr. Jefferson's friends had apprized him of his peril, and he was able to make his escape, about ten minutes before the arrival of the foe. He rode rapidly on horseback through the adjacent forests to the house of Edward Carter, six miles distant, and thus eluded the British.

The following extract from the defense which was made by Mr. Jefferson against the charges which had been preferred against him, at once both vindicates him from the accusations of his foes, and exhibits the peculiar spirit with which he repelled their malignant attacks upon his honor and his fame.

"M. de La Fayette, about this time, arrived at Richmond with some continental troops, with which, and the militia collected in the neighborhood, he continued to occupy that place, and the north bank of the river, while Phillips and Arnold held Manchester and the south bank. But Lord Cornwallis, about the middle of May, joining them with the main southern army, M. de La Fayette was obliged to retire. The enemy crossed the river and advanced up into the country, about fifty miles, and within thirty miles of Charlottesville, at which place the legislature being to meet in June, the governor proceeded to his seat at Monticello, two or three miles from it. His office was now near expiring—the country under invasion by a powerful army—no services but military of any avail—unprepared by his line of life and education for the command of armies, he believed it right not to stand in the way of talents better fitted than his own to the circumstances under which the country was placed. He, therefore, himself proposed to his friends in the legislature, that General Nelson, who commanded the militia of the state, should be appointed governor, as he was sensible that the union of the civil and military power in the same hands, at this time, would greatly facilitate military measures. This appointment accordingly took place on the 12th of June, 1781."

After narrating the particulars of Tarlton's attempt to surprise him at Monticello, he thus comments on the charge which his enemies had founded on that enterprise:

"This is the famous adventure of Carter's Mountain, which has been so often resounded through the slanderous chronicles of federalism. But they have taken care never to detail the facts, lest these should show that this favorite charge amounted to nothing more than that he did not remain in his house, and there singly fight a whole troop of horse, or suffer himself to be taken prisoner. Having accompanied his family one day's journey, he returned to Monticello. Tarlton had retired after eighteen hours' stay in Charlottesville. Mr. Jefferson then rejoined his family, and proceeded with them to an estate he had in Bedford, about eighty miles south-west, where, riding on his farm, some time after, he was thrown from his horse, and disabled from riding on horseback for a considerable time. But Mr. Turner finds it more convenient to give him this fall, in his retreat before Tarlton, which had happened some weeks before, as a proof that he withdrew from a troop of horse with a precipitancy which Don Quixotte would not have practiced.

"The facts here stated most particularly, with date of time and place, are taken from the notes made by the writer hereof, for his own satisfaction at the time—the others are from memory, but so well recollected, that he is satisfied there is no material fact misstated. Should any person undertake to contradict any particular, on evidence which may at all merit the public respect, the writer will take the trouble (though not at all in the best situation for it) to produce the proofs in support of it. He finds, indeed, that of the persons whom he recollects to have been present on the occasion, few have survived the intermediate lapse of four and twenty years. Yet he trusts that some, as well as himself, are yet among the living; and he is positively certain that no man can falsify any material fact here stated. He well remembers, indeed, that there were then, as there are at all times, some who blamed every thing done contrary to their own opinion, although their opinions were formed on a very partial knowledge of facts. The censures which have been hazarded by such men as Mr. Turner, are nothing but revivals of these half-informed opinions. Mr. George Nicholas, then a very young man, but always a very honest one, was prompted by these persons to bring specific charges against Mr. Jefferson. The heads of these, in writing, were communicated through a mutual friend to Mr. Jefferson, who committed to writing also the heads of justification on each of them. I well remember this paper, and believe the original of it still exists; and though framed when every real fact was fresh in the knowledge of every one, this fabricated flight from Richmond was not among the charges stated in this paper, nor any charge against Mr. Jefferson for not fighting, singly, the troop of horse. Mr. Nicholas candidly relinquished further proceeding. The House of Representatives of Virginia pronounced an honorable sentence of entire approbation of Mr. Jefferson's conduct, and so much the more honorable, as themselves had been witnesses to it. And Mr. George Nicholas took a conspicuous occasion afterward, of his own free will, and when the matter was entirely at rest, to retract publicly the erroneous opinions he had been led into on that occasion, and to make just reparation by a candid acknowledgment of them."

While Mr. Jefferson was confined at Poplar Forest, his estate in Bedford, in consequence of the fall from his horse, and was thereby incapable of any active employment, public or private. He occupied himself with answering the queries which Mons. de Marbois, then secretary of the French Legation to the United States, had submitted to him respecting the physical and political condition of Virginia; which answers were afterward published by him, under the title of "Notes on Virginia." When we consider how difficult it is, even in the present day, to get an accurate knowledge of such details of our country, and how much greater the difficulty must have then been, we are surprised at the extent of the information which a single individual had been able to acquire, as to the physical features of the State—the course, length and depth of its rivers, its zoological and botanical productions, its Indian tribes, its statistics and its laws. After the lapse of more than half a century, by much the larger part of this work still gives us the fullest and most accurate information which we possess in reference to the subjects of which it treats.

CHAPTER VII.

MR. JEFFERSON CHOSEN A PLENIPOTENTIARY TO ENGLAND—DEATH OF MRS. JEFFERSON—MISSION TO ENGLAND ABANDONED—MR. JEFFERSON ELECTED A DELEGATE TO CONGRESS—IMPROVEMENTS IN THE CURRENCY—WASHINGTON RESIGNS HIS COMMISSION TO CONGRESS AT ANNAPOLIS—THE DEFINITIVE TREATY WITH ENGLAND—ANTI-SLAVERY ORDINANCES PROPOSED BY MR. JEFFERSON IN CONGRESS IN 1784—HE IS APPOINTED PLENIPOTENTIARY TO FRANCE—CONFERENCES WITH THE FRENCH MINISTRY—ATTEMPT TO NEGOTIATE A COMMERCIAL TREATY WITH GREAT BRITAIN.

On the 15th of June, 1781, Mr. Jefferson was chosen by Congress, in connection with Messrs. Adams, Franklin, Jay and Laurens, as minister-plenipotentiary, to negotiate a peace which was then contemplated with England, through the mediation of Russia. He however declined the appointment. The expected mediation of Russia never took place, and very soon the memorable capture of Cornwallis at Yorktown rendered it unnecessary. The cause of tyranny became thereafter hopeless in the United Colonies, and the enemy was compelled at once to treat. On this important occasion Mr. Jefferson was again chosen to represent the interests of this country. This appointment he accepted, and among the motives which influenced him so to do, was one of a domestic and painful nature.

In September, 1782, Mrs. Jefferson died, and this bereavement produced a deep effect upon her husband's mind. He had three daughters who survived their mother, and to every member of his family he was tenderly attached. He supposed that a change of scene might produce a beneficial effect upon his spirits. Mrs. Randolph, his favorite daughter, thus speaks of the effect which the death of Mrs. Jefferson produced upon the mind of the subject of this memoir:

"As a nurse, no female ever had more tenderness or anxiety. He nursed my poor mother, in turn, with aunt Carr and his own sisters; sitting up with her, and administering her medicines and drink to the last. For four months that she lingered, he was never out of calling. When not at her bed-side, he was writing in a small room that opened immediately at the head of her bed. A moment before the closing scene, he was led from the room almost in a state of insensibility by his sister, Mrs. Carr, who with difficulty got him into his library, where he fainted, and remained so long insensible, that they became apprehensive he never would revive. The scene that followed I did not witness; but the violence of his grief, (when, by stealth, I entered his room at night,) I dare not trust myself to describe. He kept his room three weeks, during which I was never a moment from his side. He walked almost incessantly, night and day, lying down only occasionally, when nature was completely exhausted, on a pallet, that had been brought in during his long fainting fit. My aunts remained constantly with him for some weeks; I do not remember how many. When at last he left his room, he rode out and from that time he was incessantly on horseback, rambling about the mountains, in the least frequented roads, and just as often through the woods."

Having accepted the mission offered him by Congress, Mr. Jefferson started on the 19th of December, 1782, for Philadelphia. There he arrived after a journey of eight days. He proposed to embark at that place; but the French minister, M. Lucerne, offering him a passage in a frigate then lying below Baltimore, he proceeded thither. The ice still impeded and suspended the navigation, and he was compelled to wait during several months. In the mean time, however, a provisional treaty of peace had been signed by the American commissioners on the 3d of September; and this event precluding the necessity of the further agency of the new commissioners, Mr. Jefferson returned on the 15th of May to Monticello.

On the 6th of June, the Legislature of Virginia appointed him a delegate to Congress. He left

Monticello on the 16th of October, and arrived at Trenton, where Congress then sat, on the 4th of November. On the 25th of that month Congress adjourned to meet at Annapolis, the capital of Maryland; but it was not until the 13th of December that a quorum could be obtained.

The first subject which engaged his attention as a member of this Congress, was that of the currency. The colonies had always experienced the want of a sufficient supply of the precious metals; and although their currency was nominally the same as that of the mother country, it had greatly depreciated, not only abroad, but even among the States themselves. A hundred pounds of English money were then equivalent to a hundred and thirty-three and a third pounds in Virginia and through New England. In other States the disproportion was still greater. The attention of Congress had been first called to this subject by Robert Morris in 1782. That great financier made an elaborate report, showing the importance of a general standard value of money. At the session of Congress which then convened, the subject was referred to a committee, of which Mr. Jefferson was a member. He suggested a plan, in favor of which the committee eventually reported. This plan of arranging the currency was adopted by Congress during the following year. He suggested the introduction of the dollar as our unit of account and payment; and its division and subdivision in the decimal ratio, into dimes, cents, and mills. He proposed the same principle in the regulation of weights, measures, and distances. The plan has been found admirable in reference to the coin; but it has never been tried in regard to the other matters.

On the 19th December General Washington arrived at Annapolis for the purpose of resigning to Congress the high military command with which he had been intrusted, and which he had exercised with such success and glory.

A committee, of which Mr. Jefferson was chairman, was appointed to make arrangements for the occasion. The ceremony took place in the State House Hall, at 12 o'clock, on the 23d of December, in the presence of all the officers of the federal and state governments and of numerous spectators. The moral grandeur of the scene, and the patriotic exultation it was likely to call forth, could not suppress a feeling of tender melancholy on beholding that connection dissolved which had been the source of so much national pride and glory; and many of the spectators, yielding to this emotion, melted into tears. The principal actors themselves, General Washington and the president of Congress, General

Mifflin, were almost overpowered by their feelings. This closing act of the great drama made a deep impression on the whole American people, and forms one of the interesting subjects with which Trumbull's gifted pencil has adorned the Capitol at Washington. The addresses of the general, and of the president of Congress in reply to him, exhibit the same beautiful simplicity, both as to thought and diction, which was suited to the occasion. That of the president, ascribed to the pen of Mr. Jefferson, is quoted as a specimen of his happiest manner.

Sir: The United States, in Congress assembled, receive with emotions too affecting for utterance, the solemn resignation of the authorities under which you have led their troops with success through a perilous and doubtful war. Called upon by your country to defend its invaded rights, you accepted the sacred charge, before it had formed alliances, and whilst it was without funds, or a government to support you. You have conducted the great military contest with wisdom and fortitude, invariably regarding the rights of the civil power through all disasters and changes. You have, by the love and confidence of your fellow-citizens, enabled them to display their martial genius, and transmit their fame to posterity. You have persevered, till these United

States, aided by a magnanimous king and nation, have been enabled, under a just Providence, to close the war in freedom, safety and independence; on which happy event we sincerely join you in congratulations.

"Having defended the standard of liberty in this new world; having taught a lesson useful to those who inflict, and to those who feel oppression, you retire from the great theatre of action, with the blessings of your fellow-citizens—but the glory of your virtues will not terminate with your military command, it will continue to animate remotest ages.

"We feel with you our obligations to the army in general, and will particularly charge ourselves with the interests of those confidential officers, who have attended your person to this affecting moment.

"We join you in commending the interests of our dearest country to the protection of Almighty God, beseeching him to dispose the hearts and minds of its citizens to improve the opportunity afforded them of becoming a happy and respectable nation. And for you we address to him our earnest prayers, that a life so beloved may be fostered with all his care; that your days may be happy as they have been illustrious; and that he will finally give you that reward which this world cannot give."

Immediately after this event the definitive treaty with England arrived at Annapolis, and its provisions became the subject of protracted arguments and discussions. In reference to this occasion Mr Jefferson has said: "Our body was little numerous but very contentious. Day after day was wasted on the most unimportant questions. A member, one of those afflicted with the morbid rage of debate, of an ardent mind, prompt imagination, and copious flow of words, who heard with impatience any logic which was not his own, sitting near me, on some occasion of a trifling but wordy debate, asked me how I could sit in silence, hearing so much false reasoning, which a word should refute? I observed to him, that to refute indeed was easy, but to silence impossible; that in measures brought forward by myself I took the laboring oar, as was incumbent on me; but that in general I was willing to listen; that if every sound argument or objection was used by some one or other of the numerous debaters, it was enough; if not, I thought it sufficient to suggest the omission, without going into a repetition of what had been already said by others: that this was a waste and abuse of the time and patience of the house, which could not be justified. And I believe, that if the members of deliberative bodies were to observe this course generally, they would do in a day what takes them a week; and it is really more questionable than may at first be thought, whether Bonaparte's dumb legislature, which said nothing and did much, may not be preferable to one which talks much and does nothing. I served with General Washington in the Legislature of Virginia, before the Revolution, and during it with Dr. Franklin in Congress; I never heard either of them speak ten minutes at a time, nor to any but the main point which was to decide the question. They laid their shoulders to the great points, knowing that the little ones would follow of themselves. If the present Congress errs in too much talking, how can it be otherwise in a body to which the people send one hundred and fifty lawyers, whose trade it is to question every thing, yield nothing, and talk by the hour? That one hundred and fifty lawyers should do business together ought not to be expected."

At length, on the 14th of January, the delegates from nine States having arrived, the treaty was ratified without a dissenting voice.

Subsequent to the conclusion of this important matter, on the 1st of March, 1784, a committee consisting of Messrs. Jefferson, Chase of Maryland, and Howell of Rhode Island, reported to Congress the following celebrated ordinance for the government of all the national territory lying beyond the limits of the thirteen States, and not merely the North-Western Territory, *and for the exclusion of slavery therefrom.*

"*Resolved*, That the territory ceded or to be ceded by individual States to the United States, whensoever the same shall have been purchased of the Indian inhabitants and offered for sale by the United States, shall be formed into additional States, bounded in the following manner, as nearly as such cessions will admit; that is to say, northwardly and southwardly by parallels of latitude, so that each State shall comprehend from south to north two degrees of latitude, beginning to count from the completion of thirty-one degrees north of the equator; but any territory northwardly of the forty-seventh degree shall make part of the State next below. And eastwardly and westwardly they shall be bounded, those on the Mississippi, by that river on one side and the meridian of the lowest point of the rapids of the Ohio on the other; and those adjoining on the east, by the same meridian on their western side, and on their eastern by the meridian of the western cape of the mouth of the great Kanawha. And the territory eastward of this last meridian, between the Ohio, Lake Erie, and Pennsylvania, shall be one State.

"That the settlers within the territory so to be purchased and offered for sale shall, either on their own petition or on the order of Congress, receive authority from them, with appointments of time and place, for their free males of full age to meet together for the purpose of establishing a temporary government, to adopt the constitution and laws of any one of these States, so that such laws nevertheless shall be subject to alteration by their ordinary Legislature, and to erect, subject to a like alteration, counties or townships for the election of members for their legislature.

"That such temporary government shall only continue in force in any State until it shall have acquired twenty thousand free inhabitants, when, giving the due proof thereof to Congress, they shall receive from them authority, with appointments of time and place, to call a convention of representatives to establish a permanent constitution and government for themselves; provided, that both the temporary and permanent governments be established on these principles as their basis:

"1. That they shall forever remain a part of the United States of America.

"2. That in their persons, property, and territory, they shall be subject to the Government of the United States in Congress assembled, and to the Articles of Confederation in all those cases in which the original States shall be so subject.

"3. That they shall be subject to pay a part of the Federal debts, contracted or to be contracted, to be apportioned on them by Congress according to the same common rule and measure by which apportionments thereof shall be made on the other States.

"4. That their respective governments shall be in republican forms, and shall admit no person to be a citizen who holds any hereditary title.

"5. That after the year 1800 of the Christian era, there shall be neither *slavery nor involuntary servitude* in any of the said States, otherwise than in punishment of crimes, whereof the party shall have been duly convicted to have been personally guilty.

"That whenever any of the said States shall have, of free inhabitants, as many as shall then be in any one of the least numerous of the thirteen original States, such State shall be admitted, by its delegates, into the Congress of the United States, on an equal footing with the said original States; after which the assent of two-thirds of the United States, in Congress assembled, shall be requisite in all those cases wherein, by the confederation, the assent of nine States is now required, provided the consent of nine States to such admission may be obtained according to the eleventh of the Articles of Confederation. Until such admission by their delegates into Congress, any of the said States, after the establishment of their temporary government, shall have authority to keep a sitting member in Congress, with a right of debating, but not of voting.

"That the territory northward of the forty-fifth degree, that is to say, of the completion of forty-five degrees from the equator, and extending to the Lake of the Woods, shall be called *Sylvania;* that of the territory under the forty-fifth and forty-fourth degrees, that which lies westward of Lake Michigan, shall be called *Michigania;* and that which is eastward thereof, within the peninsula formed by the lakes and waters of Michigan, Huron, St. Clair, and Erie, shall be called *Chersonesus*, and shall include any part of the peninsula which may extend above the forty-fifth degree. Of the territory under the forty-third and forty-second degrees, that to the westward, through which the Assenisipi or Rock River runs, shall be called *Assenisipia;* and that to the eastward, in which are the fountains of the Muskingum, the two Miamies of the Ohio, the Wabash, the Illinois, the Miami of the Lake, and the Sandusky rivers, shall be called *Metropotamia.* Of the territory which lies under the forty-first and fortieth degrees, the western, through which the river Illinois runs, shall be called *Illinoia;* the next adjoining to the eastward, *Saratoga;* and that between this last and Pennsylvania, and extending from the Ohio to Lake Erie, shall be called *Washington.* Of the terrritory which lies under the thirty-ninth and thirty-eighth degrees, to which shall be added so much of the point of land within the fork of the Ohio and Mississippi as lies under the thirty-seventh degree; that to the westward, within and adjacent to which are the confluences of the rivers Wabash, Shawanee, Tanisee, Ohio, Illinois, Mississippi, and Missouri, shall be called *Polypotamia;* and that to the eastward, further up the Ohio, otherwise called the Pelisipi, shall be called *Pelisipia.*

"That all the preceding articles shall be formed into a charter of compact, shall be duly executed by the President of the United States in Congress assembled, under his hand and the seal of the United States, shall be promulgated, and shall stand as fundamental conditions between the thirteen original States and those newly described, unalterable but by the joint consent of the United States, in Congress assembled, and of the particular State within which such alteration is proposed to be made."

On a test vote on adopting the anti-slavery provision above, sixteen voted aye, and seven no; but the requisite number of States failing to vote in the affirmative, it was lost. And three years later the Ordinance of 1787, for the North-western Territory alone, was adopted.

Congress having resolved to send another minister to Europe for the purpose of negotiating treaties of commerce there, in addition to Messrs. Franklin and Adams, Mr. Jefferson was appointed for that post. He accepted the proffered honor, which allured him by the highest inducements, both of usefulness, fame and pleasure, so to do. He thus describes his voyage: "I left Annapolis on the 11th, took with me my eldest daughter, then at Philadelphia (the two others being too young for the voyage,) and proceeded to Boston in quest of a passage. While passing through the different States, I made a point of informing myself of the state of the commerce of each; went on to New Hampshire with the same view, and returned to Boston. Thence I sailed on the 5th of July, in the *Ceres*, a merchant ship of Mr. Nathaniel Tracy, bound to Cowes. He was himself a passenger, and after a pleasant voyage of nineteen days, we arrived at Cowes on the 26th. I was detained there a few days by the indisposition of my daughter. On the 30th we embarked for Havre, arrived there on the 31st, left it on the 3d of August, and arrived at Paris on the 6th. I called immediately on Dr. Franklin, at Passy, communicated to him our charge, and we wrote to Mr. Adams, then at the Hague, to join us at Paris."

In Europe, the services of Mr. Jefferson were highly beneficial to his country; for independent of his diplomatic talent, the moral force of his character as a statesman, a man of science, a philosopher and a sage, elevated the reputation of his country, and extorted that respect which civilized mankind always pay as the tribue of reason to the power of intellect. Having negotiated several treaties of commerce, Dr. Franklin returned home; and Mr. Adams having been appointed ambassador at St. James', Mr. Jefferson was left as minister at the court of Versailles.

A treaty with Prussia and Morocco was the only fruit of the labors of the three ambassadors.

At the request of Mr. Adams, Jefferson now went over to London to attempt a treaty with that power; but returned to Paris covered with disappointment, mortification and chagrin at the cold reception which the overture had received.

From Paris, Mr. Jefferson found leisure to travel into Italy, and to explore Holland; and his powers of observation fully enabled him to amass a fund of information as useful to his country as it proved beneficial to himself.

In France, a long residence and a perfect mastery

of the language could not fail to imbue him deeply with European politics. His prepossessions in favor of the French were warm and evident; he did not conceal his attachment to the French character, and to French modes of thinking, acting and feeling; and he therefore naturally became a favorite with their philosophers and men of letters; nor was it a slight honor to call D'Alembert his friend, to embrace Condorcet as a companion, and to acknowledge the Abbe Morrellet as his literary godfather, who from love to the author translated his Notes on Virginia.

Although at a foreign court, the thoughts of Jefferson were too much directed homeward to allow him to overlook what was going on, in the formation of the new constitution, to which he looked with an anxiety and solicitude proportioned to the magnitude and importance of the subject. As it will forever remain an interesting subject of rational curiosity, as well as of political importance, to know in what light he viewed the constitution at the time of its adoption, we will quote from his memoirs and correspondence all that appears to bear directly upon this great point. He says, page 63: "Our first essay in America, to establish a federative government, had fallen, on trial, very short of its object. During the War of Independence, while the pressure of an external enemy hooped us together, and their enterprises kept us necessarily on the alert, the spirit of the people, excited by danger, was a supplement to the confederation, and urged them to zealous exertions, whether claimed by that instrument or not; but when peace and safety were restored, and every man became engaged in useful and profitable occupation, less attention was paid to the calls of Congress. The fundamental defect of the confederation was, that Congress was not authorized to act immediately on the people, and by its own officers. Their power was only requisitory, and those requisitions were addressed to the several legislatures, to be by them carried into execution, without other coercion than the moral principle of duty. This allowed, in fact, a negative to every legislature on every measure proposed by Congress; a negative so frequently exercised in practice, as to benumb the action of the federal government, and to render it inefficient in its general objects, and more especially in pecuniary and foreign concerns. The want, too, of a separation of the legislative, executive and judiciary functions worked disadvantageously in practice. Yet this state of things afforded a happy augury of the future march of our confederacy, when it was seen that the good sense and good dispositions of the people, as soon as they perceived the incompetence of their first compact, instead of leaving its correction to insurrection and civil war, agreed with one voice to elect deputies to a general convention."

Immediately on his arrival in Paris, Mr. Jefferson rented a house in the *Cul de Sac Têtebout*, near the Boulevards, and furnished it in an elegant and expensive manner. His household consisted of Colonel Humphreys, the secretary of legation, Mr. Short, his private secretary, and his daughter, who was afterward placed in a convent for her education. One of the first projects which occupied his attention was the printing of his Notes on Virginia. He had refrained from publishing the work in America in consequence of the expense. He found that the cost in Europe would be only about one-fourth of the price in his own country. Two hundred copies only were printed at first. One of these fell into the hands of a Parisian publisher, who procured a French translation to be made, but so imperfectly was it done as to deface and deform the work. Mr. Jefferson then negotiated with a London bookseller to have the volume properly given to the world, and thus introduce it to general diffusion.

The Legislature of Virginia had authorized him and his colleagues to employ a competent artist to execute a statue of General Washington. In the performance of this duty, Mr. Jefferson selected a distinguished French artist named *Houdon* for the task. This person visited the United States, in the execution of the work, and the result of his labors now adorn the Capitol of the State of Virginia. Mr. Jefferson also recommended Houdon as a suitable person to execute the equestrian statue of Washington which Congress had resolved upon. But difficulties postponed and subsequently entirely defeated the realization of this enterprise.

On the 15th of August, 1785, Mr. Jefferson opened his negotiations with the French minister, Count de Vergennes, in reference to the establishment of a commercial treaty between France and the United States. Mr. Adams had previously left Paris for London, Dr. Franklin had returned home, and Mr. Jefferson was left alone to conduct this important and difficult negotiation. He desired to place the trade in tobacco on a footing profitable to both countries. The policy of the French government in reference to this great staple had been exclusive and selfish, "contrary to the spirit of trade and to the dispositions of merchants to carry a commodity to any market where but one person is allowed to buy it, and where of course that person fixes its price, which the seller must receive or re-export his commodity at the loss of his voyage thither. Experience accordingly shows that they carry it to other markets, and that they take in exchange the merchandise of the place where they deliver it."

The deliberations were long, intricate and tedious. Mr. Jefferson was called on to answer many objections to his proposed arrangement. One of these was that the treaty would encourage smuggling. The answer to this argument was, that "the temptation to smuggling would be less, when what costs fourteen *sous* may now be sold for sixty, but will then sell for but forty." He desired to remove all restrictions on commerce, and he thus asserted fully and boldly the great democratic principle on that subject.

In a letter to Mr. Adams in July, 1785, he thus speaks of the policy of subjecting aliens to higher duties than are paid by citizens: "As far as my inquiries enable me to judge, France and Holland make no distinction of duties between aliens and natives. I also rather believe that the other states of Europe make none, England excepted, to whom this policy, as that of her navigation act, seems peculiar. The question then is, should we disarm ourselves of the power to make this distinction against all nations, in order to purchase an exemption from the alien duties in England only? for if we put her importatious on the footing of native, all other nations with whom we treat will have a right to claim the same. I think we should, because against other nations who make no distinctions in their ports between us and their own subjects, we ought not to make a distinction in ours. And if the English will agree in like manner to make none, we should with equal reason abandon the right as against them. I think all the world would gain by setting commerce at perfect liberty. I remember that when we were digesting the general form of our treaty, this proposition to put foreigners and natives on the same footing was considered; and we were all three, Dr. Franklin, as well as you and myself, in favor of it."

In a letter received from Mr. Jay, he had been asked "Whether it would be useful to us to carry all our own productions, or none?" and he evidently shows a preference for the Chinese policy. This opinion may seem inconsistent with a clear perception of the benefits of free trade; but on this occasion he postpones pecuniary gain to what he deemed the higher considerations of national policy.

"We have now," he says, "lands enough to employ an infinite number of people in their cultivation. Cultivators of the earth are the most valuable citizens. They are the most vigorous, the most independent, the most virtuous, and they are tied to their country, and wedded to its liberty and interests by the most lasting bonds. As long, therefore, as they can find employment in this line, I would not convert them into mariners, artisans, or any thing else. But our citizens will find employment in this line, till their numbers, and of course their productions, become too great for the demand, both internal and foreign. This is not the case as yet, and probably will not be for a considerable time. As soon as it is, the surplus of hands must be turned to something else. I should then, perhaps, wish to turn them to the sea, in preference to manufactures; because, comparing the characters of the two classes, I find the former the most valuable citizens. I consider the class of artificers as the panders of vice, and the instruments by which the liberties of a country are generally overturned. However, we are not free to decide this question on principles of theory only. Our people are decided in the opinion that it is necessary for us to take a share in the occupation of the ocean, and their established habits induce them to require that the sea be kept open for them, and that that line of policy be pursued which will render the use of that element to them as great as possible. I think it a duty in those entrusted with the administration of their affairs, to conform themselves to the decided choice of their constituents: and that, therefore, we should in every instance preserve an equality of right to them, in the transportation of commodities, in the right of fishing, and in the other uses of the sea."

But he thinks that wars will be the inevitable consequence: "That their property will be violated on the sea, and in foreign ports their persons will be insulted, imprisoned, &c., which outrages we must resent. That the only way to deter injustice will be to put ourselves, by means of a naval force, in a situation to punish it. I think it," he says, "to our interest to punish the first insult; because an insult unpunished is the parent of many others." In case of a war with England, he thought we should abandon the carrying trade, because we could not protect it. "Foreign nations must in that case be invited to bring us what we want, and take our productions in their own bottoms. This alone could prevent the loss of those productions to us, and the acquisition of them to our enemy. Our seamen might be employed in depredations on their trade." He afterward adds: "Our vicinity to their West India possessions and to the fisheries, is a bridle which a small naval force on our part would hold in the mouths of the most powerful of these countries. I hope our Land Office will rid us of our debts, and that our first attention then will be to the beginning of a naval force of some sort. This alone can countenance our people as carriers on the water, and I suppose them to be determined to continue such."

In March, 1787, Mr. Jefferson proceeded to London to assist Mr. Adams in perfecting the treaties which were then in progress of negotiation with Tripoli, Tunis and Portugal, together with that then pending with England. Mr. Jefferson at this time uttered the conviction to one of his correspondents, that notwithstanding the treaty which had already been ratified with England and the United States, the former was the enemy of the latter; that her hatred was deeply rooted and cordial; and that nothing was wanting with her but the power to crush her rebellious colonies from the face of the earth. And this opinion seemed founded in truth, and was supported by ample evidence furnished by the press, the parliament and the court of England at that moment. The ulcerations of the king's mind seemed to be so great as to hold out no hope of reconciliation whatever. On the presentation of Messrs. Jefferson and Adams, their reception "by their majesties" was most ungracious. Before leav ing England, Mr. Jefferson wrote as follows to Mr Jay, then Secretary of Foreign Affairs:

"With this country nothing is done; and that nothing is intended to be done on their part, admits not the smallest doubt. The nation is against any change of measures; the ministers are against it; some from principle, others from subserviency; and the king, more than all men, is against it. If we take a retrospect to the beginning of the present reign, we observe that amidst all the changes of ministry, no change of measures with respect to America ever took place, excepting only at the moment of the peace, and the minister of that movement was immediately removed. Judging of the future by the past, I do not expect a change of disposition during the present reign, which bids fair to be a long one, as the king is healthy and temperate. That he is persevering we know. If he ever changes his plan, it will be in consequence of events which at present neither himself nor his ministers place among those which are probable. Even the opposition dare not open their lips in favor of a connection with us, so unpopular would be the topic. It is not that they think our commerce unimportant to them. I find that the merchants have set sufficient value on it. But they are sure of keeping it on their own terms. No better proof can be shown of the security in which the ministers think themselves on this head, than that they have not thought it worth while to give us a conference on the subject, though on my arrival we exhibited to them our commission, observed to them that it would expire on the 12th of next month, and that I had come over on purpose to see if any arrangements could be made before that time. Of two months which then remained, six weeks have elapsed without one scrip of a pen, or one word from a minister, except a vague proposition at an accidental meeting. We availed ourselves even of that to make another essay, to extort some sort of a declaration from the court; but their silence is invincible."

CHAPTER VIII.

THE CONVENTION AT ANNAPOLIS—SUMMONING OF THE FEDERAL CONVENTION —ADOPTION OF THE NEW CONSTITUTION—ORIGIN AND STATE OF POLITICAL PARTIES IN THE UNITED STATES—JEFFERSON'S OPINIONS IN REFERENCE TO THE FEDERAL CONSTITUTION—HIS LETTERS ON THE SUBJECT—OPPOSING OPINIONS OF WASHINGTON—VOX POPULI, VOX DEI—JEFFERSON'S TRAVELS IN EUROPE—HIS DIPLOMATIC LABORS—EVENTS OF THE FRENCH REVOLUTION—JEFFERSON'S OPINIONS IN REFERENCE TO THOSE EVENTS.

IN January, 1786, the General Assembly of Vir ginia resolved to appoint eight commissioners to meet those of other States to digest a system of uni form commercial regulations. The convention was appointed to meet at Annapolis in the ensuing September. When that time arrived five States only sent their representatives to the Convention. These were New York, New Jersey, Pennsylvania, Maryland and Virginia. Mr. Dickerson was appointed president, and the members proceeded to deliberate. They found their powers too limited, and their numbers too few to secure any benefit or authority from their labors. They accordingly adjourned, but before doing so agreed upon a report to be submitted to the different States, in which they set forth the expediency of revising and extending the federal system, and recommended the appointment of deputies by the various State legislatures to meet at Philadelphia on the 2d of May, 1787. On the 21st of February, 1787, Congress passed a resolution declaring such a Convention expedient. On the 25th of May deputies from nine States assembled in Philadelphia. Washington was elected president. Rhode Island subsequently sent her representatives, and the whole number composing the Convention was fifty-five. After long and careful deliberations a Federal Constitution was agreed upon. Alexander Hamilton drew the first draft, which was afterward adopted with some modifications. The instrument was sent to Congress on the 28th of September, 1787, and by them submitted to the several States for their ratification. It was approved by Delaware, Pennsylvania and New Jersey in 1787; by Georgia, Connecticut, Massachusetts, Maryland, South Carolina, New Hampshire, Virginia and New York in 1788; North Carolina ratified it in November, 1789, and Rhode Island in May, 1790.

It was mainly on the ground of "State sovereignty" that the Constitution reported by this convention was opposed on the part of some of the States; and that parties arrayed against federal power entered warmly into the discussion of its merits, in the interim between its promulgation by the Convention and its final ratification by the States. To elucidate its merits, and enforce and illustrate its virtues, three of the most distinguished friends of Washington, noted for their political acumen, profound knowledge of jurisprudence, power of argument, and force of style, united their labors in a series of papers under the title of *The Federalist;* the joint production of Alexander Hamilton, John Jay and James Madison. On the side of State sovereignty, popular rights and limited government, were arrayed the powerful pens of the great champions of democracy; each party straining every nerve to prevent or secure its ratification by the States.

Here again the weight and influence of Washington's character secured a result which without the authority of his name, and the magic power of his virtues, could not have been produced; for there is conclusive reason to believe, that had the State conventions been left purely to the naked merits of the Constitution, the ratification by the number of States required to give it effect could not have been obtained. Even Marshall is constrained to admit that in some of the adopting States a majority of the people were in opposition to it, and were only brought to acquiesce in its provisions from a just dread of the calamitous consequences of a dismemberment of the Union, rather than from an approbation of the instrument which had been submitted for their sanction; and from a deference to the character of Washington, which no other man could have inspired.

Although the Federal Constitution was adopted while Mr. Jefferson was residing in Paris, he did not view the subject with less interest than if he was personally engaged in the direct discussion of its provisions. He communicated his sentiments very freely to Mr. Madison; and his letters constantly express his great confidence in the capacity of the people for self-government, and his jealousy of their delegates. He was decidedly in favor of separating the executive, legislative, and judiciary powers. He was opposed to the negative proposed to be given on the legislative acts of the several States. He said:

"It fails in an essential character; the hole and the patch should be commensurate. But this proposes to mend a small hole by covering the whole garment. Not more than one out of a hundred State acts concern the confederacy. This proposition then, in order to give them one degree of power which they ought to have, gives them ninety-nine more which they ought not to have, upon a presumption that they will not exercise the ninety-nine. But upon every act there will be a preliminary question: Does this act concern the confederacy? And was there ever a proposition so plain as to pass Congress without debate? Their decisions are almost always wise; they are like pure metal; but you know of how much dross this is the result."

He suggested as a better method of accomplishing the object aimed at, by conferring such a check on the Federal government, that there should be an appeal from the State judicature to the Federal, where the Constitution controlled the question. In reference to the powers of coercion on the States which the Articles of Confederation conferred upon Congress, he thus writes to Mr. Carrington of Virginia, in August, 1787: "My general plan would be to make the States one as to every thing connected with foreign nations, and several as to every thing purely domestic. But with all the imperfections of our present government, it is without comparison the best existing, or that ever did exist. Its greatest defect is the imperfect manner in which matters of commerce have been provided for. It has been so often said as to be generally believed, that Congress have no power by the confederation to enforce any thing; for example, contributions of money. It was not necessary to give them that power expressly; they have it by the law of nature. When two parties make a compact, there results to each a power of compelling the other to execute it. Compulsion was never so easy as in our case, where a single frigate would soon levy on the commerce of any State the deficiency of its contributions; nor more safe than in the hands of Congress, which has always shown that it would wait, as it ought to do, to the last extremities before it would execute any of the powers that are disagreeable."

To his esteemed friend Mr. Wythe he thus speaks of the Federal Convention; "My own general idea was that States should generally preserve their sovereignty in whatever concerns themselves alone; and that whatever may concern another State, or any foreign nation, should be made a part of the Federal sovereignty. That the exercise of the Federal sovereignty should be divided among three several bodies—legislative, executive and judiciary, as the State sovereignties are; and that some peaceable means should be contrived for the Federal head to force compliance on the part of the States." Knowing his correspondent's classical predilections, in adverting to the recent rupture between the Turks and Russians, he adds, "Constantinople is the key of Asia—Who shall have it? is the question. I cannot help looking forward to the re-establishment of the Greeks as a people, and the language of Homer becoming again a living language, as among possible events. You have now with you Mr. Paradise, who can tell you how easily the modern may be improved into the ancient Greek."

In November, 1787, he thus writes to Mr. Adams more fully and explicitly: "How do you like our new Constitution? I confess there are things in it which stagger all my dispositions to subscribe to what such an assembly has proposed. The house of federal representatives will not be adequate to the management of affairs, either foreign or federal. Their president seems a bad edition of a Polish king. He may be elected from four years to four years for life. Reason and experience prove to us that a chief magistrate so continuable is an office for life. When one or two generations shall have proved that there is an office for life, it becomes on every succession worthy of intrigue, of bribery, force, and even of foreign interference. It will be of great consequence to France and England to have America governed by a Galloman or Angloman. Once in office, and possessing the military force of the Union without the aid or check of a council, he would not be easily dethroned, even if the people could be induced to withdraw their votes from him. I wish at the end of the four years they had made him for ever ineligible a second time."

To Colonel Smith he says of the Constitution:

"There are very good articles in it, and very bad. I do not know which preponderate. What we have lately read in the history of Holland, in the chapter on the stadtholder, would have sufficed to set me against a chief magistrate eligible for a long duration, if I have ever been disposed toward one: and what we had always read of the elections of Polish kings, would have forever excluded the idea of one continuable for life." Apprehending that arguments would be drawn for this enlargement of the powers of the Federal Government generally, and of its executive in particular, from the recent insurrection in Massachusetts, he speaks of it not only as an unimportant affair, but as scarcely to be deprecated. "God forbid," he exclaims, "we should ever be twenty years without such a rebellion. The people cannot be all, and always well informed. The part which is wrong will be discontented in proportion to the importance of the facts they misconceive. If they remain quiet under such misconceptions, it is a lethargy, the forerunner of death to the public liberty. We have had thirteen States independent for eleven years. What country before ever existed a century and a half without a rebellion? And what country can preserve its liberties if its rulers are not warned from time to time that this people preserve the spirit of resistance? Let them take arms. The remedy is to set them right as to facts, pardon and pacify them, What signify a few lives lost in a century or two? The tree of liberty must be refreshed from time to time with the blood of patriots and tyrants. It is its natural manure. Our Con vention has been too much impressed by the insurrection of Massachusetts; and on the spur of the moment, they are setting up a kite to keep the hen-yard in order."

But in a letter to Mr. Madison, in December, he discloses his opinions more at length. The features of the Constitution of which he approved were the self-acting power of the general government, by which it could peaceably go on without recurring to the State legislatures; the separation of the legislative, executive and judiciary powers; the powers of taxation given to the legislature; and the election of the House of Representatives by the people. He doubted however whether the members would be as well qualified for their duties when chosen by the people, as if they were chosen by the legislature. He was captivated by the compromise between the great and the small States—the latter having the equality they asserted in the Senate; the former the proportion of influence they regarded as their right in the House of Representatives. He preferred too the voting by persons instead of by States; and he approved the qualified negative given to the executive, though he would have liked it still better if the judiciary had been invested with a similar check.

Still futher light is thrown upon Mr. Jefferson's views in reference to the provisions and merits of the Federal Constitution, by his letter to Mr. Hopkinson in March, 1788, and by another written to Mr. Madison, in which he expresses an opinion hostile to the consolidation of the powers of the government. To Mr. Madison he says:

"I own I am not a friend to a very energetic government; it is always oppressive; it places the governors indeed more at their ease, but at the expence of the people. The late rebellion in Massachusetts has given more alarm than I think it should have done. Calculate that one rebellion in thirteen States in the course of eleven years, is but one for each State in a century and a half. No country should be so long without one, nor will any degree of power in the hands of government prevent insurrections. In England, where the hand of power is heavier than with us, there are seldom half a dozen years without an insurrection. In France, where it is still heavier but less despotic, as Montesquieu supposes, than in some other countries, and where there are always two or three hundred thousand men ready to crush insurrections, there have been three in the course of the three years I have been here, in every one of which greater numbers were engaged than in Massachusetts, and a great deal more blood was spilt. In Turkey, where the sole nod of the despot is death, insurrections are the events of every day. Compare again the ferocious depredations of their insurgents with the order, the moderation, and the almost self-extinguishment of ours, and say finally whether peace is best preserved by giving energy to the government or information to the people. This last is the most certain and the most legitimate engine of government. Educate and inform the whole mass of the people, enable them to see that it is their interest to preserve peace and order, and they will preserve it; and it requires no very high degree of education to convince them of this; they are the only sure reliance for the preservation of our liberty. After all, it is my principle that the will of the majority should prevail. If they approve the proposed Constitution in all its parts I shall concur in it cheerfully, in hopes they will mend it whenever they shall find it works wrong."

It may not be uninteresting to place here in opposition to these sentiments of Mr. Jefferson the opposing views of his illustrious friend Washington on the same subject, and in reference to the disputed virtues of the same Constitution. In a letter to Mr.

Jay, Washington thus expresses himself: "Your sentiments that our affairs are drawing rapidly to a crisis, accord with my own. What the event will be is also beyond the reach of my foresight. We have errors to correct; we have probably had too good an opinion of human nature in forming our confederation. Experience has taught us that men will not adopt and carry into execution measures the best calculated for their own good without the intervention of coercive power. I do not conceive we can exist long as a nation without lodging somewhere a power which will pervade the whole Union in as energetic a manner as the authority of the State governments extends over the several States. To be fearful of investing Congress, constituted as that body is, with ample authorities for national purposes, appears to me the very climax of popular absurdity and madness. Could Congress exert them for the detriment of the people, without injuring themselves in an equal or greater proportion? Are not their interests inseparably connected with those of their constituents? Many are of opinion that Congress have too frequently made use of the suppliant humble tone of requisition in applications to the States, when they had a right to assert their imperial dignity and command obedience. Be that as it may, requisitions are a perfect nullity, where thirteen sovereign, independent, disunited States are in the habit of discussing, and refusing or complying with them at their option. Requisitions are actually little better than a jest and a bye-word throughout the land. If you tell the legislatures they have violated the treaty of peace, and invaded the prerogatives of the confederacy, they will laugh in your face. What then is to be done? Things cannot go on in the same train forever. It is much to be feared, as you observe, that the better kind of people, being disgusted with these circumstances, will have their minds prepared for any revolution whatever. We are apt to run from one extreme into another. To anticipate and prevent disastrous contingencies, would be the part of wisdom and patriotism."

Such was the difference of opinion entertained by these distinguished men in reference to the vital principles of the government. Washington and his trusted associate Hamilton placed no extravagant confidence in the virtues of the masses; but thought that they needed to be governed and restrained by the force of law and the corrective influence of less popular and more exclusive elements. Jefferson on the contrary loudly proclaimed himself a democrat, an admirer of the masses of the people. He regarded the *Vox populi* as the *Vox Dei.** He pretended the most unbounded confidence in the wisdom, im partiality and justice of the multitude, and regarded with suspicion the encroachments of the more wealthy, intelligent and cultivated few upon the rights of the many. He feared that if the Federal government were invested with strong powers it would crush the freedom of the several States, infringe the rights of the State governments, and lead to tyranny under another form and name, but not less detestable in character, than that of Great Britain herself.

Whatever serious apprehensions Mr. Jefferson may have indulged in reference to the operation of the Federal Constitution, the steady lapse of time has now clearly proved their fallacy. The respective powers and prerogatives of the States and of the general government were so wisely balanced, so evenly proportioned, and so admirably adjusted by it, that no storms or convulsions however furious, have yet been able to weaken or injure it. It is not

* This adage, *Vox populi, vox Dei*, is true, if by the Deity referred to, is meant the gods of ancient Greece and Rome; for very frequently the "voice of the people" resembles that of Bacchus, roaring after more drink; or that of Plutus, craving after greater riches; or that of Venus, inviting to impurity and lust; while once in a long while you hear a gentle whisper which reminds you of Minerva, and urging you to the pursuit and attainment of wisdom!

improbable that had Mr. Jefferson been a member of the Federal Convention, he would have succeeded in introducing more popular features into the Constitution than now exist in it; but whether such a change would have operated more beneficially for the interests of the nation, and for the perpetuity of its power and unity, may well be doubted.

During the period of Mr. Jefferson's absence in Europe, he embraced the opportunity thus afforded him, to enjoy the pleasures and advantages of foreign travel. He desired to see the great canal of Languedoc in order to acquire a knowledge of inland navigation, which could afterward be made available in his own country. He desired also to visit the sea-ports of the Mediterranean, and examine there the practical effects of the recent commercial regulations which had been established with the United States. He left Paris in the beginning of March, 1787. He traveled through Champagne, Burgundy, Dauphine, Languedoc, and the north of Italy. He visited Marseilles, Nantes, Bordeaux, Nismes, Nice, and traveled through a portion of Germany and Holland. He returned to Paris on the 11th of June. Speaking of this journey to La Fayette he says, as illustrative of its great advantages and its pleasures: "It will be a great comfort for you to know, from your own inspection, the condition of all the provinces of your own country, and it will be interesting to them, at some future day, to be known to you. This is perhaps the only moment of your life in which you can acquire that knowledge. And to do it most effectually you must be absolutely incognito; you must ferret the people out of their hovels as I have done; look into their kettles; eat their bread; loll on their beds, under pretence of resting yourself, but in fact to find if they are soft. You will feel a sublime pleasure in the course of this investigation, and a sublimer one hereafter, when you shall be able to apply your knowledge to the softening of their beds, or the throwing a morsel of meat into their kettle of vegetables."

In July he resumed his negotiations with M. de Montmorin, French Minister of Foreign Affairs, in reference to the pending treaty between France and the United States. While thus engaged in the performance of the difficult duties of his post, he was not an idle observer of the important events which were then passing around him in France. The great Revolution had commenced, and its mighty surges were sweeping in furious eddies to and fro, and dashing to the earth the monuments and institutions of the past. He expresses himself in the following language in reference to those events, the principles involved, and the results which they produced:

"The deed which closed the mortal course of these sovereigns I shall neither approve nor condemn. I am not prepared to say that the first magistrate of a nation cannot commit treason against his country, or is unamenable to its punishment; nor yet that where there is no written law, no regulated tribunal, there is not a law in our hearts, and a power in our hands, given for righteous employment in maintaining right and redressing wrong. Of those who judged the king, many thought him willfully criminal; many that his existence would keep the nation in perpetual conflict with the horde of kings who would war against a regeneration which might come home to themselves, and that it were better that one should die than all. I should not have voted with this portion of the legislature. I should have shut up the queen in a convent, putting harm out of her power, and placed the king in his station, investing him with limited powers, which I verily believe he would have honestly exercised according to the measure of his understanding. In this way no void would have been created, courting the usurpation of a military adventurer, nor occasion given for those enormities which demoralized the nations of the world, and destroyed, and is yet to destroy millions and millions of inhabitants. There are three epochs in history signalized by the total extinction of national morality. The first was of the successors of Alexander, not omitting himself; the next the successors of the first Cæsar; the third our own age. This was begun by the partition of Poland, followed by that of the treaty of Pilnitz; next the conflagration of Copenhagen; then the enormities of Bonaparte, partitioning the earth at his will, and devastating it with fire and sword."

He thus describes the state of France and of the French people in the midst of that great struggle. We quote from a letter to Col. Humphreys, dated 18th March, 1789: "The change in this country since you left it, is such as you can form no idea of. The frivolities of conversation have given way entirely to politics. Men, women and children talk nothing else; and all you know talk a great deal. The press groans with daily productions which in point of boldness makes an Englishman stare, who hitherto has thought himself the boldest of men. A complete revolution in this government has within the space of two years (for it began with the Notables of 1787,) been effected merely by the force of public opinion, aided indeed by the want of money, which the dissipations of the court had brought on. And this revolution has not cost a single life, unless we charge it to a little riot lately in Bretagne, which began about the price of bread, became afterward political, and ended in the loss of four or five lives."

It may readily be supposed that Mr. Jefferson changed his opinion materially of the merits of this revolution, of its actors and of its results, before their career was concluded. Like many more, he regarded it at its comencement as a "spirit of grace," but before its termination, he detested it as a "goblin damned!"

CHAPTER IX.

THE CONVOCATION OF THE STATES-GENERAL OF FRANCE—JEFFERSON'S DESCRIPTION OF FRENCH PARTIES—JEFFERSON'S PLAN FOR THE SETTLEMENT OF THE KINGDOM—HIS RETURN TO THE UNITED STATES—HIS RECEPTION AT MONTICELLO—HE IS INVITED BY WASHINGTON TO BECOME SECRETARY OF STATE—HE ACCEPTS THE OFFER—HIS VIEWS ON THE QUESTION OF PUBLIC CREDIT—HIS REPORTS ON THE COINAGE, WEIGHTS AND MEASURES—HIS LETTER TO THE NATIONAL ASSEMBLY OF FRANCE ON THE DEATH OF FRANKLIN—HIS VIEWS ON THE UNITED STATES BANK.

As the thrilling events of the French Revolution progressed, Mr. Jefferson took a deeper interest in their effects and probable results. He was present on the 5th of May, 1789, at the memorable convocation of the States-General which had been summoned by the unfortunate Louis XVI., and which had not been convened before for several centuries. To that assembly the whole French nation looked with intense emotions of mingled hope and fear. The higher orders were justly apprehensive that its deliberations and its acts might lead to the destruction of their ancient privileges, and to the enfranchisement of the people. The latter anticipated that this convocation would become a new era in the history of the nation; that it would be the birthday of liberty; that the wrongs and despotism of the past would be overturned; that the great evils which centuries of kingly and princely pomp, extravagance, tyranny, corruption and pride had produced, would then be remedied and forever removed. Nor were they disappointed in the realization of many of their hopes.

On the opening of the States-General, when scenes of imposing religious solemnity and splendor adorned the vast cathedral of Notre-Dame in Paris, when the crumbling monarchy once more and for the last time displayed its ancient grandeur, and when the uprising people and their representatives for the first time assumed a portentous air of dignity and power—in that immense assemblage, when all the magnificence of the decrepit monarchy was combined with all the intellectual vigor and moral grandeur of the indignant nation, represented by the men whose names were destined very soon afterward to acquire a world-wide but a bloody and revolting celebrity—in that assemblage Jefferson mingled, and surveyed the proceedings with a scrutinizing eye. Robespierre and Danton were there, though then unknown to fame. Napoleon Bonaparte was also there, though still more insignificant and obscure. And he who had penned the great charter of a nation's freedom, which had already been bought and secured by a nation's blood, looked on, and congratulated himself there that his own land had already happily passed through the crisis which was then just commencing in the country of his sojourn.* His opinion of the state of parties in France may be inferred from the following letter, addressed to Mr. Jay: "1. The *aristocrats*, comprehending the higher members of the clergy, military, nobility, and the parliaments of the whole kingdom. This forms a head without a body. 2. The *moderate royalists*, who wish for a constitution nearly similar to that of England. 3. The *republicans*, who are willing to let their first magistracy be hereditary, but to make it very subordinate to the legislature, and to have that legislature consist of a single chamber. 4. The *faction of Orleans*. The second and third descriptions are composed of honest, well-meaning men, differing in opinion only, but both wishing the establishment of as great a degree of liberty as can be preserved. They are considered as constituting the patriotic part of the Assembly, and they are supported by the soldiery of the army, the soldiery of the clergy, that is to say, the curés and

* During Mr. Jefferson's absence in Paris, the University in Harvard conferred on him the honorary degree of Doctor of Laws. This title, like other literary and scientific titles, was worth something at that period of our country's history.

monks, the dissenters and part of the nobility which is small, and the substantial Bourgeoisie of the whole nation."

During the progress of events, Mr. Jefferson was requested by La Fayette to suggest a plan for the guidance of the revolutionists, and to give him his advice as to the best policy to be pursued. He suggested that the king in a *seance royale* should come forward with a charter in his hand, to be signed by himself and all the members of the three Orders; and that this charter should contain the five great points which the Resultat of December offered on the part of the king, the abolition of the pecuniary privileges of the higher orders, the assumption of the national debt, and a grant of the sums asked from the nation. The charter of rights which Jefferson drew up for La Fayette consisted of the following ten articles:

"1. The States-General shall assemble uncalled on the first day of November annually, and shall remain together so long as they shall see cause. They shall regulate their own elections and proceedings; and until they shall ordain otherwise, their elections shall be in the form observed in the present year, and shall be triennial.

"2. The States-General alone shall levy money on the nation, and shall appropriate.

"3. Laws shall be made by the States-General only, with the consent of the king.

"4. No person shall be restrained of his liberty but by regular process from a court of justice, authorized by a general law. (Except that a noble may be imprisoned by order of a court of justice, on the prayer of twelve of his nearest relations.) On complaint of an unlawful imprisonment to any judge whatever, he shall have the prisoner immediately brought before him, and shall discharge him if his imprisonment be unlawful. The officer in whose custody the prisoner is shall obey the orders of the judge, and both judge and officer shall be responsible, civilly and criminally, for a failure of duty herein.

"5. The military shall be subordinate to the civil authority.

"6. Printers shall be liable to legal prosecution for printing and publishing false facts, injurious to the party prosecuting; but they shall be under no other restraint.

"7. All pecuniary privileges and exemptions enjoyed by any description of persons are abolished.

"8. All debts already contracted by the king are hereby made the debts of the nation, and the faith thereof is pledged for their payment in due time.

"9. Eighty millions of livres are now granted to

the king, to be raised by loan, and reimbursed by the nation; and the taxes heretofore paid shall continue to be paid to the end of the present year and no longer.

"10. The States-General shall now separate, and meet again on the 1st day of November next."

Having concluded his diplomatic duties in the French capital, Mr. Jefferson left Paris on the 26th of September, 1789. He had resided in France more than five years. He had been addressed previous to his return, by Mr. Madison, who had inquired of him whether he would accept any appointment at home; but in reply he had stated that he desired retirement; that all his appointments to office had been contrary to his own wishes (a declaration which was not strictly true); and that his object in withdrawing from the French mission was to resume his agricultural pursuits, and the enjoyment of total seclusion and rest.

He left Havre on the 8th of October, accompanied by his two daughters. He journeyed to Cowes, where he had taken passage in a vessel for Virginia. He was delayed at the Isle of Wight by contrary weather until the 22d. In consequence of a special application to Mr. Pitt from Colonel Trumbull, his baggage was exempted from search by the officers of the customs. His return voyage was prosperous;

and on the thirtieth day after his embarcation he landed at Norfolk. The dangers of the voyage clustered around its termination. As the vessel approached the coast a heavy mist prevailed and hid the land from view. For three days they beat about, looking for a pilot in vain. At length the captain boldly ran the vessel within the capes, and thus avoided the fury of a storm which in a few hours afterward swept the coast. Subsequent to this the vessel took fire, but the flames were subdued without any damage to Mr. Jefferson's baggage and papers.

Having disembarked he journeyed toward Monticello. There being no public conveyance at that time in that region, he was indebted to his friends for the means of reaching home. At Effington, on the way, he received a letter from General Washington inviting him to accept the office of Secretary of State. At length, on the 23d of December, he arrived at Monticello. His daughter, Mrs. Randolph, thus describes the scene which ensued: "The negroes discovered the approach of the carriage as soon as it reached Shadwell, and such a scene I never witnessed in my life. They collected in crowds around it, and almost drew it up the mountain by hand. The shouting, &c., had been sufficiently obstreperous before, but the moment the carriage arrived on the top it reached the climax. When the door of the carriage was opened, they received him in their arms and bore him into the house, crowding around and kissing his hands and feet—some blubbering and crying—others laughing. It appeared impossible to satisfy their eyes, or their anxiety to touch and even kiss the very earth that bore him. These were the first ebullitions of joy for his return after a long absence, which they would of course feel, but it is perhaps not out of place to add here that they were at all times very devoted in their attachment to him. They believed him to be one of the greatest, and they knew him to be one of the best of men and kindest of masters. They spoke to him freely, and applied confidingly to him in all their difficulties and distresses; and he watched over them in sickness and in health; interested himself in all their concerns; advising them, and showing esteem and confidence in the good, and indulgence to all."

Immediately after his return home, Mr. Jefferson's eldest daughter Martha was married to Mr. Thomas M. Randolph, eldest son of the Tuckahoe branch of the Randolphs. This gentleman afterward became Governor of Virginia. He had first seen Miss Jefferson during a visit to Paris. At the same period Mr. Jefferson received a second letter from the

President urging his acceptance of the office of Secretary of State, leaving him at the same time at liberty to follow his own inclinations. After some deliberation he accepted the appointment. He left Monticello for New York, where the Federal Government was then located, on the 1st of March, 1790.

At Philadelphia he called on Dr. Franklin, who was then on his death-bed, and who conversed with him with the resignation of a philosopher, and the animation of an enthusiast for liberty. The doctor confided to him a manuscript memoir of his life, which Mr. Jefferson, under a mistaken idea of the trust reposed in him, afterward delivered into the hands of his grandson, William Temple Franklin. This memoir Mr. Jefferson represents as containing valuable details; among others he thus relates a very important one: "I remember," he says, speaking of secret negotiations of Franklin to accommodate matters between the Colonies and Great Britain, "that Lord North's answers were dry, unyielding, in the spirit of unconditional submission, and betrayed an absolute indifference to the occurrence of a rupture; and he said to the mediators distinctly, at last, that '*a rebellion was not to be deprecated on the part of Great Britain; that the confiscations it would produce would provide for many of their friends.*' This expression was reported by the mediators to Dr. Franklin. Here the negotiation stopped."

Mr. Jefferson reached New York on the 20th of March, while Congress was in session, and commenced his duties as the second officer in the government. He was associated with Alexander Hamilton as Secretary of the Treasury, General Knox as Secretary of War, Edmund Randolph as Attorney-General. The second session of Congress under the administration of Washington commenced on the 4th of January, 1790. Its first deliberations were in reference to the elaborate and able report of Mr. Hamilton on the subject of the public credit, which had been submitted to Congress. That report laid the foundation for a new division of parties, which continued to prevail during four successive administrations. This report contended that the debts of the individual States contracted during the Revolution should be assumed by the general government; that the United States were bound to pay the interest as well as the principal of these public debts; that no distinction should be made between original holders of the evidences of these debts and those who had purchased them at a discount; and to diminish the part due to domestic creditors, not by greater taxation, but by giving them a satisfactory equivalent. This report called forth the most spirited debates in Congress. Mr. Jefferson arrived at the seat of government in the midst of it. His views of the state of the controversy may be gathered from the following extract from his writings:

"Here certainly I found a state of things which of all I had ever contemplated, I the least expected. I had léft France in the first year of her revolution, in the fervor of natural rights and zeal for reformation. My conscientious devotion to these rights could not be heightened, but it had been aroused and excited by daily exercise. The President received me cordially, and my colleagues and the circle of principal citizens apparently with welcome The courtesies of dinner-parties given me, as a stranger newly arrived among them, placed me at once in their familiar society. But I cannot describe the wonder and mortification with which the table conversation filled me. Politics were the chief topic, and a preference of kingly over republican government was evidently the favorite sentiment. An apostate I could not be, nor yet a hypocrite; and I found myself for the most part the only advocate on the republican side of the question, unless among the guests there chanced to be some member of that party from the legislative houses. Hamilton's financial system had then passed. It had two objects; 1st. As a puzzle, to exclude popular understanding and inquiry; 2d. As a machine for the corruption of the legislature; for he avowed the opinion that man could be governed by one of two motives only, force or interest; force, he observed, in this country was out of the question, and the interest therefore of the members must be laid hold of, to keep the legislature in unison with the executive. And with grief and shame it must be acknowledged that his machine was not without effect; that even in this, the birth of our government, some members were found sordid enough to bend their duty to their interests, and to look after personal rather than public good."

Whatever may have been the mercenary motives of some members of Congress who supported the policy recommended in Mr. Hamilton's report, it is absurd to charge *him* with a design to corrupt the legislature, or to promote his personal interests. The whole history of this memorable era proves that one of the most disinterested men, possessing the sternest integrity and honesty of purpose, who ever moved amid its stirring scenes, was the Secretary of the Treasury.

A compromise was at length effected between the contending factions, in reference to which Mr. Jefferson speaks as follows:

"This game was over, and another was on the carpet at the moment of my arrival; and to this I was most ignorantly and innocently made to hold the candle. This fiscal manœuvre is well known by the name of the Assumption. Independently of the debts of Congress, the States had during the war contracted separate and heavy debts; and Massachusetts particularly, in an absurd attempt, absurdly conducted, on the British post of Penobscot; and the more debt Hamilton could rake up the more plunder for his mercenaries. This money, whether wisely or foolishly spent, was pretended to have been spent for general purposes, and ought therefore to be paid from the general purse. But it was objected that nobody knew what these debts were, what their amount, or what their proofs. No matter; we will guess them to be twenty millions. But of these twenty millions we do not know how much should be reimbursed to one State, or how much to another. No matter; we will guess. And so another scramble was set on foot among the several States, and some got much, some little, some nothing. But the main object was obtained, the phalanx of the treasury was reinforced by additional recruits.

"This measure produced the most bitter and angry contests ever known in Congress, before or since the union of the States. I arrived in the midst of it. But a stranger to the ground, a stranger to the actors on it, so long absent as to have lost all familiarity with the subject, and as yet unaware of its object, I took no concern in it. The great and trying question however was lost in the House of Representatives. So high were the feuds excited by this subject, that on its rejection, business was suspended. Congress met and adjourned from day to day without doing any thing; the parties being too much out of temper to do business together. The eastern members particularly, who with Smith from South Carolina were the principal gamblers in these scenes, threatened a secession and dissolution. Hamilton was in despair. As I was going to the president's one day, I met him in the street. He walked me backward and forward before the president's door for half an hour. He painted pathetically the temper into which the legislature had been wrought; the disgust of those who were called the creditor States; the danger of the secession of their members, and the separation of the States. He observed that the members of the administration ought to act in concert; that though this question was not of my department, yet a common duty should make it a common concern; that the president was the centre on which all administrative questions ultimately rested, and that all of us should rally around him and support with joint efforts measures approved by him; and that the question having been lost by a small majority only, it was probable that an appeal from me to the judgment and discretion of some of my friends might effect a change in the vote, and the machine of government, now suspended, might be again set in motion.

"I told him that I was really a stranger to the whole subject; that not having yet informed myself of the system of finance adopted, I knew not how far this was a necessary sequence; that undoubtedly if its rejection endangered a dissolution of our Union at this incipient stage, I should deem that the most unfortunate of all consequences, to avert which all partial and temporary evils should be yielded. I proposed to him, however, to dine with me the next day, and I would invite another friend or two, bring them into conference together, and I thought it impossible that reasonable men, consulting together coolly, could fail by some mutual sacrifices of opinion, to form a compromise which was to save the Union. The discussion took place. I could take no part in it but an exhortatory one, because I was a stranger to the circumstances which should govern it. But it was finally agreed that whatever importance had been attached to the rejection of this proposition, the preservation of the Union and of concord among the States was more important, and that therefore it would be better that the vote of rejection should be rescinded, to effect which some members should change their votes. But it was observed that this pill would be peculiarly bitter to the Southern States, and that some concomitant measure should be adopted to sweeten it a little to them. There had before been propositions to fix the seat of government either at Philadelphia or at Georgetown, on the Potomac; and it was thought that by giving it to Philadelphia for ten years, and to Georgetown permanently afterward, this might as an anodyne calm in some degree the ferment which might be excited by the other measure alone. So two of the Potomac members (White and Lee, but White with a revulsion of stomach almost convulsive) agreed to change their votes, and Hamilton undertook to carry the other point. In doing this, the influence he had established over the eastern members, with the agency of Robert Morris with those of the middle States, effected his side of the engagement; and so the assumption was passed, and twenty millions of stock divided among favored States, and thrown in as a pabulum to the stock-jobbing herd. This added to the number of votaries to the treasury, and made its chief the master of every vote in the legislature which might give to the government the direction suited to his political views."

During the progress of 1790 Mr. Jefferson made two reports to Congress on subjects referred by them to him. One of these was in reference to a proposition made by an individual in England to furnish the United States with a supply of copper coinage. On this subject he held the doctrine that coinage being an attribute of sovereignty, it should not be submitted to another sovereign; that to exercise it in a foreign country would be on many accounts inconvenient, and was without an example; and he therefore opposed the proposition and recommended that a Mint be established at home.

The other report had reference to the subject of weights and measures. It recommended the pendulum in the latitude of 45° north, as the standard of lineal and other measures, and rain water at a given temperature as the standard of weight. It further recommended a system of decimal divisions both for measures and weights. The report on the coinage was adopted. The other seems never to have received any action of the legislature, and the reform on that subject remains to this day one of the *desiderata* of federal legislation.

In March, 1791, Mr. Jefferson, by order of the President, addressed a letter to the President of the

National Assembly of France in answer to their decree of the 11th of June, paying a just tribute to the memory and the virtues of Dr. Franklin, then recently deceased. A portion of that letter is as follows:

"That the loss of such a citizen should be lamented by us, among whom he lived, whom he so long and eminently served, and who feel their country advanced and honored by his birth, life and labors, was to be expected. But it remained for the National Assembly of France to set the first example of the representatives of one nation doing homage, by a public act, to the private citizen of another, and by withdrawing arbitrary lines of separation, to reduce into one fraternity the good and the great, wherever they have lived or died.

"That these separations may disappear between us in all times and circumstances, and that the union of sentiment which mingles our sorrows on this occasion may continue long to cement the friendship and the interests of our two nations, is our constant prayer. With no one is it more sincere than with him who, in being charged with the honor of conveying a public sentiment, is permitted that of expressing the homage of profound respect, with which he is, sir, your most obedient and most humble servant."

Another question which was warmly discussed in the cabinet between the great opposing leaders of the federal and republican parties—Hamilton and Jefferson—was that of the incorporation of the United States Bank.

That measure having produced a deep excitement in both Houses of Congress, as involving fundamental principles of constitutional power, naturally awakened the patriotism of Washington, which induced him to pause and deliberate with his usual coolness and ability, before he decided upon its final adoption. For this purpose he requested a written investigation of the merits of the question from Mr. Jefferson, in common with the other members of his cabinet; in complying with which this statesman exhibited a power of reasoning not inferior in brilliancy to that solidity of principle upon which he rested as the foundation of his arguments. Simple, broad, and comprehensive in his premises, he went upon the axiom that a limited constitution, restricted by special grants of power, could not authorize a sovereign exercise of authority, which no part of that instrument allowed or granted in express terms; that the power to create a national bank was in its very nature one too vast and influential over the whole rights and interests of the people, to be either a necessary or an incidental power to others expressly granted; and that it were better for the harmony and success of the whole Union, to forego the exercise of a doubtful power than to breed endless dissensions and heart-burnings, by assuming an authority which could not be sustained by the letter of the Constitution, to observe which the government was bound in the exercise of substantive powers. In this elucidation of one of the most controverted features of the federal government, he was decidedly opposed by the eloquent and brilliant exposition of Alexander Hamilton, who reasoning on opposite principles, and leaning to a government of more comprehensive and energetic nature, naturally carried with him the already prepossessed judgment of the President. But neither the force of Hamilton's reasoning nor the hourly augmenting weight of the influence of Washington himself, have been able to settle this disputed question; while the edifice of free principles erected by the republican logic of Jefferson will forever remain a monument of that inflexible and uncompromising democracy which made him so emphatically the man ot the people; and which have consecrated his opinions upon this subject as a perpetual rallying point for the advocates of free principles, State rights, and the equality of privileges throughout every portion of this great confederacy.

CHAPTER X.

DISPUTES IN THE CABINET OF WASHINGTON—JEFFERSON'S STATEMENT OF HAMILTON'S VIEWS—HAMILTON'S SUPERIORITY—MR. JEFFERSON'S PURPOSE OF RETIRING—GILES' RESOLUTIONS—JEFFERSON'S VINDICATION OF HIMSELF—HIS PROFOUND AND ABLE OPINION IN REFERENCE TO THE WAR WITH FRANCE—CONDUCT OF GENET, THE FRENCH MINISTER—THE LITTLE DEMOCRAT—GENET'S RECALL—JEFFERSON'S DESCRIPTION OF HIS ASSOCIATES IN THE CABINET.

THE great difference of sentiment which existed between Jefferson and Hamilton rendered it impossible that much harmony should exist between them, either in the deliberations of the cabinet or in the active measures of the administration. These differences increased with the progress of time, and gradually took the form of personal antagonism and hostility. In April, 1791, Washington visited the Southern States; and during his absence it became necessary for the members of the cabinet to consult together without the presence and the restraining influence of the President. On one occasion Mr. Jefferson invited Mr. Adams, the Vice President, Mr. Hamilton, General Knox and Mr. Randolph to dinner; and Mr. Jefferson has left on record an account of the opinions uttered by Mr. Hamilton on that occasion, for the purpose of illustrating the difference of sentiment existing between them, and to show what Mr. Jefferson held to be the anti-republican doctrines entertained by his rival. Jefferson went so far as to charge Hamilton with being in favor of a union with England, and that he thought the death of Washington would prove the termination of the existence of the Federal Government. But of the truth of these charges there is not the slightest evidence. The following statement of the opinions expressed by Mr. Hamilton on the occasion above referred to, possesses great interest; and for the truth of the narrative, Mr. Jefferson solemnly says, "I attest the God who made me!"

"After the cloth was removed and our question argued and dismissed, conversation began on other matters, and by some circumstance was led to the British constitution, on which Mr. Adams observed, 'Purge that constitution of its corruption, and give to its popular branch equality of representation, and it would be the most perfect constitution ever devised by the wit of man.' Hamilton paused and said, 'Purge it of its corruption, and give to its popular branch equality of representation, and it would become an impracticable government; as it stands at present, with all its supposed defects, it is the most perfect government which ever existed.'

And this was assuredly the exact line which separated the political creeds of these two gentlemen. The one was for two hereditary branches and an honest elective one; the other for an hereditary king, with a house of lords and commons corrupted to his will, and standing between him and the people. Hamilton was indeed a singular character. Of acute understanding, disinterested, honest and honorable in all private transactions, amiable in society, and duly valuing virtue in private life, yet so bewitched and perverted by the British example, as to be under thorough conviction that corruption was essential to the government of a nation. Mr. Adams had originally been a republican. The glare of royalty and nobility, during his mission to England, had made him believe their fascination a necessary ingredient in government; and Shay's rebellion, not sufficiently understood where he then was, seemed to prove that the absence of want and oppression was not a sufficient guarantee of order. His book on the American Constitution having made known his political bias, he was taken up by the monarchial federalists in his absence, and on his return to the United States he was by them made to believe that the general disposition of our citizens was favorable to monarchy. He here wrote his 'Davila' as a supplement to the former work, and his election to the

Presidency confirmed him in his errors. Innumerable addresses too, artfully and industriously poured in upon him, deceived him into a confidence that he was on the pinnacle of popularity when the gulf was yawning at his feet which was to swallow up him and his deceivers. For when General Washington was withdrawn, these *energumeni* of royalism, kept in check hitherto by the dread of his honesty, his firmness, his patriotism, and the authority of his name, now mounted on the car of state, and free from control, like Phaeton on that of the sun, drove headlong and wild, looking neither to right nor left, nor regarding ery thing but the objects they were driving at, until displaying these fully, the eyes of the nation were opened, and a general disbandment of them from the public councils took place."

On another occasion Mr. Jefferson writes that Mr. Hamilton having condemned Mr. Adams' writings, and particularly "Davila," as being opposed to the true policy of Washington's administration, proceeded to say:

"'I own it is my opinion, though I do not publish it in Dan or Beersheba, that the present government is not that which will answer the ends of society, by giving stability and protection to its rights, and that it will probably be found expedient to go into the British form. However, since we have undertaken the experiment, I am for giving it a fair course, whatever my expectations may be. The success indeed, so far, is greater than I had expected, and therefore at present success seems more probable than it had done heretofore, and there are still other and other stages of improvement which, if the present does not succeed, may be tried, and ought to be tried before we give up the republican form altogether; for that mind must be really depraved which would not prefer the equality of political rights, which is the foundation of pure republicanism, if it can be obtained consistently with order. Therefore whoever by his writings disturbs the present order of things is really blamable, however pure his attentions may be, and he was sure Mr. Adams' were pure.' This is the substance of a declaration made in much more lengthy terms, and which seemed to be more formal than usual for a private conversation between two, and as if intended to qualify some less guarded expression which had been dropped on former occasions. Thomas Jefferson has committed it to writing in the moment of A. Hamilton's leaving the room."

Yet it is but justice to Mr. Jefferson to say that, notwithstanding his frequent collisions with Mr. Hamilton, and the personal and political rivalry which existed between them, he possessed magnanimity enough on some occasions to render a tribute of praise to his great talents. Thus at a subsequent period, in reference to the treaty with England negotiated by Mr. Jay, he says:

"Hamilton is really a Colossus to the anti-republican party; without numbers he is a host within himself. They have got themselves into a defile, where they might be finished; but too much security on the republican part will give time to his talents and indefatigableness to extricate them. In truth when he comes forward there is nobody but yourself who can meet him.

"The merchants were certainly (except those of them who are English) as open-mouthed at first against the treaty as any. But the general expression of indignation has alarmed them for the strength of the government. They have feared the shock would be too great, and have chosen to tack about and support both treaty and government, rather than risk the government." He thus concludes: "There appears a pause at present in the public sentiment which may be followed by a revulsion. This is the effect of the desertion of the merchants, of the president's chiding answer to Boston and Richmond, of the writings of Curtius and Camillus, and of the quietism into which people naturally fall after first sensations are over. For

God's sake take up your pen and give a fundamental reply to Curtius and Camillus."

In consequence of the dissensions in the cabinet Mr. Jefferson began to contemplate, as early as February, 1792, his retirement from the post which he held in it. He also perceived that notwithstanding his utmost efforts to undermine his influence, Hamilton really controlled the judgment and measures of the President. He thought the influence and patronage attached to the Treasury department absorbed that of all the other branches of the government, and overshadowed them. The truth was, that prodigious genius of Hamilton, his indefatigable energy, the versatility of his powers, his elaborate reports, his unrivalled eloquence, his facility in the disposal of business, and the confidence of the nation in his patriotism, rendered him the commanding spirit in the administration. Notwithstanding the profound though less shining abilities of Jefferson, the greater glory belonged to his rival.

Washington received the intimation of his proposed withdrawal from Mr. Jefferson with sincere regret. His presence in the cabinet gave stronger unity to the nation. He represented the vast republican or democratic body in its deliberations, and he was a pillar of strength to the administration. Washington endeavored to dissuade him from the execution of his purpose, and succeeded so far as to induce him to postpone it for a time. The differences, however, which divided the cabinet were not healed. On the 23d of January, 1792, Mr. Giles introduced resolutions into the House of Representatives, designed to inculpate Mr. Hamilton as Secretary of the Treasury. These resolutions were proposed at the instance and with the approbation of Mr. Jefferson. In reference to these resolutions, Mr. Jefferson thus writes in his diary, under date of March 2d:

"He, (Mr. Giles,) and one or two others, were sanguine enough to believe that the palpableness of these resolutions rendered it impossible the house could reject them. Those who knew the composition of the house: 1, of bank directors; 2, holders of bank-stock; 3, stock-jobbers; 4, blind devotees; 5, ignorant persons, who did not comprehend them; 6, lazy and good-humored persons, who comprehended and acknowledged them, yet were too lazy to examine, or unwilling to pronounce censure; the persons who knew these characters foresaw that the three first descriptions making one-third of the house, the three latter would make one-half of the residue; and of course that they would be rejected by a majority of two to one. But they thought that even this rejection would do good, by showing the public the desperate and abandoned dispositions with which their affairs were conducted. The resolutions were proposed, and nothing spared to present them in the fullness of demonstration. There were not more than three or four who voted otherwise than had been expected."

The result of this investigation was favorable to the integrity of the Secretary of the Treasury, and in favor of the wisdom and prudence of the measures which he had recommended. This result had not tended to increase the kindness of feeling between the heads of the two great parties. Hostilities and recriminations continued between them. Mr. Jefferson thus defends himself against some anonymous attacks in the newspaper, which he attributed, without any evidence to support the supposition, to the agency of Mr. Hamilton:

"He charges me—1. With having written letters from Europe to my friends to oppose the present Constitution, while depending. 2. With a desire of not paying the public debt. 3. With setting up a paper to decry and slander the government.

"The first charge is most false. I approved as much of the Constitution as most persons, and more of it was disapproved by my accuser than by me, and of its parts most vitally republican. My objection to the Constitution was the want of a bill of rights

—Colonel Hamilton's that it wanted a king and house of lords. The sense of America has approved my objection, and added the bill of rights, and not the king and lords. I wanted the presidential term longer and not renewable; 'my country thought otherwise and I have acquiesced.' As to the public debt, he emphatically denies the charge, says he wishes "the debt paid off to-morrow; Colonel Hamilton never; but always to remain in existence for him to manage and corrupt the legislature."

Notwithstanding his repeatedly expressed determination to retire from office, Mr. Jefferson accepted a renewal of his appointment as Secretary of State under Washington's second administration, which commenced on the 4th of March, 1793. War having been declared by France against England, the policy of the United States under these circumstances toward the belligerents became involved in much difficulty. Washington immediately submitted to each member of his cabinet a series of propositions in writing on the subject. These same propositions were afteward discussed in the cabinet. The main question was, whether the existing treaties with France were then binding on the United States? The paper drawn up by Mr. Jefferson on this occasion is remarkable for the originality of its views, the vigor of its reasoning, and its general ability.

At this crisis M. Genet was appointed French minister to the United States. In reference to this person, Mr. Jefferson says:

"Never, in my opinion, was so calamitous an appointment made as that of the present minister of France here. Hot-headed, all imagination, no judgment, passionate, disrespectful, and even indecent toward the President in his written as well as his verbal communications before Congress or the public, they will excite indignation. He renders my position immensely difficult. He does me justice personally; and giving him time to vent himself, and become more cool, I am on a footing to advise him freely, and he respects it; but he will break out again on the very first occasion, so that he is incapable of correcting himself. To complete our misfortune, we have no channel through which we can correct the irritating representations he may make."

Genet insisted that French cruisers should have the right to bring their prizes into American ports, under the treaty of 1778. He also asserted that French citizens possessed the right to arm and equip their ships of war in American ports. These positions Mr. Jefferson denied, and he held that the assertion of the right of sovereignty by a neutral nation in its own ports become a duty, whenever it was violated to the injury of a belligerent. The sale of vessels taken by French cruisers was stopped at Philadelphia by the government. Genet immediately and insolently demanded restitution, damages and interest. He also demanded the payment of the debt due by the United States to France, amounting to two million three hundred thousand dollars. Genet then proceeded to speculate privately on his own account. He bought, equipped and commissioned a prize, called the *Little Democrat*, and prepared to dispatch her on a cruise. The governor of Pennsylvania, Mr. Mifflin, requested Genet to delay the departure of his vessel. He refused. The *Little Democrat*, on the 11th of July fell down the Delaware to Chester, on her outward voyage. The cabinet was convened. They resolved to detain all vessels of any of the belligerents which had been armed in the United States, together with their prizes, until the questions thereon arising could be definitely settled. But in defiance of this order the *Little Democrat* put to sea, and cruised along the American coasts. The government then determined to demand the recall of Genet, as French minister, as the only expedient whereby the offended dignity of the United States could be satisfied without involving both countries in the horrors and calamities of a war. With unexpected magnanimity the French Directory recalled Genet, censured his conduct, and resolved to send four commissioners to the United States, to send Genet home a prisoner, and to augment the good feeling and unity which existed between the two nations. The sudden overthrow of the government at home defeated the execution of this purpose. Genet was deprived of his diplomatic powers, but remained permanently in the United States. Mr. Jefferson describes in the following sarcastic and scarcely excusable language, the deliberations of his associates in the cabinet, in reference to the movements of Genet. We extract from a letter to Mr. Madison, dated August 11, 1793.

"I believe it will be true wisdom in the republican party to approve unequivocally of a state of neutrality; to avoid little cavils about who should declare it; to abandon Genet entirely, with expressions of strong friendship and adherence to his nation, and confidence that he has acted against their sense. In this way we shall keep the people on our side, by keeping ourselves in the right. They made the establishment of the democratic society here the ground for sounding the alarm that this society, (which they considered as the antifederal and discontented faction,) was put into motion by M. Genet, and would by their corresponding societies, in all the States, draw the mass of the people by dint of misinformation into their vortex, and overset the government. The President was strongly impressed by this picture, drawn by Hamilton, in three speeches of three-quarters of an hour's length each. I opposed it totally; told the President plainly, in their presence, that the intention was to dismount him from being the head of the nation, and make him the head of a party; that this would be the effect of making him, in an appeal to the people, declare war against the republican party. Randolph, according to his half-way system between wrong and right, urged the putting off the appeal. The President came into his idea, or rather concluded that the question on it might be put off indefinitely, to be governed by events. If the demonstrations of popular adherence to him become as general and as warm as I believe they will, I think he will never again bring on the question; if there is an appearance of their supporting Genet, he will probably make the appeal. Knox is the poorest creature I ever saw, having no color of his own, and reflecting that nearest to him. When he is with me he is a whig, when with Hamilton he is a tory, when he is with the President he is what he thinks will please him. . . . . *The President always acquiesces in the majority!*

"You ask the sense of France with regard to the

defensive quality of the guarantee. I know it no otherwise than from Genet. His doctrine is, that without waiting to be called on—without waiting 'till the islands were attacked, the moment France was engaged in a war, it was our duty to fly to arms as a nation, and the duty of every one to do it as an individual."

CHAPTER XI.

MR. JEFFERSON'S RETIREMENT FROM THE CABINET OF WASHINGTON—HIS MOTIVES FOR SO DOING—HIS LETTERS TO MR. MADISON—HIS LAST REPORT TO CONGRESS—HIS LETTER OF RESIGNATION—CAUSES OF PREVIOUS DISSENSIONS IN THE CABINET—MR. JEFFERSON'S CHARGES AGAINST MR. HAMILTON—EVIDENCE OF THEIR FALSEHOOD—THE NATIONAL GAZETTE—FRENEAU—MR. JEFFERSON REFUSES TO SUPPRESS THE NATIONAL GAZETTE—HIS RETURN TO MONTICELLO—HIS CELEBRATED LETTER TO MAZZEI—JEFFERSON'S APOLOGY TO WASHINGTON FOR ITS STRICTURES ON HIM.

ON the 31st of December, 1793, Mr. Jefferson executed his long-threatened purpose of retiring from the office of Secretary of State. His motives for so doing have been frequently discussed, commended and censured. They seem in reality to have been of a complex nature, and quite varied and dissimilar in their character. It is doubtless true that he was fond of rural and agricultural life; that he desired greater leisure to cultivate his taste for literature and science; that he delighted in the society of his daughters and grand-children; and that he had already served the public through many years of laborious activity. But it seems to be also true, that the preponderating cause of his withdrawal at this time from the cares ot office was the fact that

Hamilton had secured the ascendency over Washington and his cabinet; that Jefferson's popularity at this period was on the wane; and that the prospects of the administration, of which he was an important member, were then gloomy and forbidding. At this period party dissensions began to rage with greater fury; and a revolution in popular sentiment threatened soon to leave the administration of Washington in a helpless minority. Jefferson being attached to the ultra doctrines of liberty was associated in the cabinet with men whose love of freedom was tempered by a regard for authority, a reverence for the past, and esteem for order and subordination. Among such men Mr. Jefferson was not at home; and though his great talents and reflective sagacity gave him importance and respectability, they could not secure him a predominating influence. He seized the most appropriate opportunity to escape from the falling wreck with safety, security, and honor. Jefferson thought he foresaw that the popularity of Washington was about to be destroyed by an outburst of popular indignation; and he did not wish to incur any portion of that obloquy which the baseness and ingratitude of a thankless nation were about to inflict, as he feared, upon the author of their liberties Jefferson also thought that the tide of democratic sentiment was rising rapidly throughout the nation; and the result eventually proved the sagacity of his calculations. How far he co-operated, after his retirement, in the attainment of this result, it is difficult to say; but it is unquestionable that he still cherished a dislike to Washington, a hatred of Hamilton, and a detestation of their party, as will appear from the following letters to Mr. Madison, dated April 3d, and December 28th, 1794

"DEAR SIR: Our post having ceased to ride ever since the inoculation began in Richmond till now, I received three days ago, and all together, your friendly favors of March 2, 9, 12, 14, and Colonel Monroe's of March 3 and 16. I have been particularly gratified by the receipt of the papers containing yours and Smith's discussion of your regulating propositions. These debates had not been seen here but in a very short and mutilated form. I am at no loss to ascribe Smith's speech to its true father. Every tittle of it is Hamilton's except the introduction. There is scarcely any thing there which I have not heard from him in our various private, though official discussions. The very turn of the arguments is the same and others will see as well as myself, that the style is Hamilton's. The sophistry is too fine, too ingenious, even to have been comprehended by Smith, much less devised by him. His reply shows that he did not understand his first speech; as its general inferiority proves its legitimacy, as evidently as it does the bastardy of the original. You know we had understood that Hamilton had prepared a counter report, and that some of his humble servants in the Senate were to move a reference to him in order to produce it. But I suppose they thought it would have a better effect if fired off in the House of Representatives. I find the report, however, so fully justified, that the anxieties with which I left it are perfectly quieted. In this quarter all espouse your propositions with ardor, and without a dissenting voice.

"The rumor of a declaration of war has given an opportunity of seeing that the people here, though attentive to the loss of value of their produce in such an event, yet find in it a gratification of some other passions, and particularly of their ancient hatred to Great Britain. Still I hope it will not come to that; but that the proposition will be carried, and justice be done ourselves in a peaceable way. As to the guarantee of the French Islands, whatever doubts may be entertained of the moment at which we ought to interpose, yet I have no doubt but that we ought to interpose at a proper time, and declare both to England and France that these islands are to rest with France, and that we will make a common cause with the latter for that object. As to the naval armament, the land armament, and the marine fortifications, which are in question with you, I have no doubt they will all be carried. Not that the *monocrats* and *papermen* in Congress want war; but they want armies and debts; and though we may hope that the sound part of Congress is now so augmented as to insure a majority in cases of general interest merely, yet I have always observed that in questions of expense, where members may hope either for offices or jobs for themselves or their friends, some few will be debauched, and that is sufficient to turn the decision where a majority is at most but small. I have never seen a Philadelphia paper since I left it, till those you enclosed me; and I feel myself so thoroughly weaned from the interest I took in the proceedings there while there, that I have never had a wish to see one, and believe that I never shall take another newspaper of any sort. I find my mind totally absorbed in my rural occupations.

"Accept sincere assurances of affection, &c."

"*Monticello*, Dec. 28, 1794.

"DEAR SIR: I have kept Mr. Jay's letter a post or two, with an intention of considering attentively the observations it contains; but I have really so little stomach for any thing of that kind that I have not resolution enough even to endeavor to understand the observations. I therefore return the letter, not to delay your answer to it, and beg you in answering for yourself, to assure him of my respects and thankful acceptance of Chalmers' Treatise, which I do not possess, and if you possess yourself of the scope of his reasoning, make any answer to it you please for me. If it had been on the rotation of my crops, I would have answered myself, lengthily perhaps, but certainly *con gusto.*

"The denunciation of the democratic societies is one of the extraordinary acts of boldness of which we have seen so many from the faction of monocrats. It is wonderful indeed, that the President should have permitted himself to be the organ of such an attack on the freedom of discussion, the freedom of writing, printing and publishing. It must be a matter of rare curiosity to get at the modifications of these rights proposed by them, and to see what line their ingenuity would draw between democratical societies, whose avowed object is the nourishment of the republican principles of our Constitution and the Society of the Cincinnatti, a self-created one, carving out for itself hereditary distinctions, lowering over our Constitution eternally, meeting together in all parts of the Union periodically, with closed doors, accumulating a capital in their separate treasury, corresponding secretly and regularly, and of which society the very persons denouncing the democrats are themselves the fathers, founders, and high officers. Their sight must be perfectly dazzled by the glittering of crowns and coronets, not to see the extravagance of the proposition to suppress the friends of general freedom; while those who wish to confine that freedom to the few, are permitted to go on in their principles and practices. I here put out of sight the persons whose misbehavior has been taken advantage of to slander the friends of popular rights; and I am happy to observe that, as far as the circle of my observation and information extends, every body has lost sight of them, and views the abstract attempt on their natural and constitutional rights in all its nakedness. I have never heard of a single expression or opinion which did not condemn it as an inexcusable aggression. And with respect to the transactions against the excise law, it appears to me that you are all swept away in the torrent of governmental opinions, or that we do not know what these transactions have been. We know of none which, according to the definitions of the law, have been any thing more than riotous. There was indeed a meeting to consult about a separation. But to consult on a question does not amount to a determination of that question in the affirmative, still less to the acting on such a determination; but we shall see, I suppose, what the court lawyers and courtly judges, and would-be ambassadors will make of it. The excise law is an infernal one. The first error was to admit it by the Constitution; the second to act on that admission; the third and last will be to make it the instrument of dismembering the Union and setting us all afloat to choose what part of it we will adhere to. The information of our militia, returned from the westward, is uniform, that though the people there let them pass quietly, they were objects of their laughter, not of their fear; that one thousand men could have cut off their whole force in a thousand places of the Alleghany; that their detestation of the excise law is universal, and has now associated to it a detestation of the government; and that separation which perhaps was a very distant and problematical event is now near and certain, and determined in the mind of every man. I expected to have seen some justification of arming one part of the society against another; of declaring a civil war the moment before the meeting of that body which has the sole right of declaring war; of being so patient of the kicks and scoffs of our enemies, and rising at a feather against our friends; of adding a million to the public debt, and deriding us with recommendations to pay it if we can, &c., &c. But the part of the speech which was to be taken as a justification of the armament, reminded me of parson Saunders' demonstration why *minus* into *minus* makes *plus*. After a parcel of shreds of stuff from Æsop's Fables and Tom Thumb, he jumps all at once into his *ergo*, *minus* multiplied into *minus* makes *plus*. Just so the fifteen thousand men enter after the fables in the speech.

"However, the time is coming when we shall fetch up the leeway of our vessel. The changes in your house I see are going on for the better, and even the Augean herd over your heads are slowly purging off their impurities. Hold on then, my dear friend, that we may not shipwreck in the meanwhile. I do not see in the minds of those with whom I converse, a greater affliction than the fear of your retirement; but this must not be, unless to a more splendid and more efficacious post. There I should rejoice to see you; I hope I may say I shall rejoice to see you. I have long had much in my mind to say to you on that subject; but double delicacies have kept me silent. I ought perhaps to say, while I would not give up my own retirement for the empire of the universe, how I can justify wishing one whose happiness I have so much at heart as yours, to take the front of the battle which is fighting for *my security*. This would be easy enough to be done, but not at the heel of a lengthy epistle. Adieu."

The immediate occasion of the resignation of Mr. Jefferson was the fate which befel his last official report to Congress on the commerce and navigation of the United States in their relations to foreign governments, with suggestions upon the measures which it would be expedient to adopt to improve and extend the same. This report asserts the doctrine of Free Trade, and yet entertains the contingencies of a Protective Tariff.

He begins by considering the value of the articles of our export to the different countries with whom we exchange commodities; and then proceeds to investigate the restrictions which other nations have imposed upon our trade; whence he branches out into an appeal to Congress, to devise and adopt the most eligible modes for their modification, counteraction, or removal. He then suggests as two of the most eligible methods: *first,* Negotiations for commercial treaties on the basis of reciprocity; and *second,* Legislative enactments imposing counteracting restrictions upon the trade of those nations which will not treat on the first-named condition.

Commercial regulations he deemed preferable, because he contended that an unshackled and free trade was the most profitable, reasonable and just; and that the United States ought to hold in special favor any nation which would, by commencing the system, set a good example for others to follow; and in the same spirit to resist with rigorous counteracting duties, the commerce and navigation of those countries that pertinaciously adhered to the system of prohibitions, high duties, or vexatious exactions. An obvious train of powerful argument is adduced to sustain this just position, and recommend to national patronage the navigation interest of the country; urging with a fervor commensurate to the great importance of the question, the adoption of the system of *national reciprocity*—opposing tariff to tariff—duty against duty; but at all times giving a decided preference to free and unrestrained trade, universally guaranteed from all shackles by commercial treaties and arrangements.

In support of this report Mr. Madison introduced a series of resolutions in the House, which called forth a long and animated debate. The hostility of the majority of the Representatives against the report was so intense and so evident, that the resolutions were never put to the vote; and thus the matter ended in a virtual defeat of the Secretary of

State. This report was made on the 16th of December; and immediately after the termination of the debate, on the 31st of the same month, Mr. Jefferson sent in his resignation. His intention was expressed to Washington in the following language:

"*Philadelphia*, December 31, 1793.

"SIR: Having had the honor of communicating to you, in my letter of the last of July, my purpose of retiring from the office of Secretary of State, at the end of the month of September, you were pleased, for particular reasons, to wish its postponement to the close of the year. That term being now arrived, and my propensity to retirement becoming daily more and more irresistible, I now take the liberty of resigning the office into your hands. Be pleased to accept my sincere thanks for all the indulgences which you have been so good as to exercise toward me in the discharge of its duties. Conscious that my need of them has been great, I have still ever found them greater, without any other claim on my part than a firm support of what has appeared to be right and a thorough disdain of all means which were not as open and honorable as their object was pure. I carry into my retirement a lively sense of your goodness, and shall continue gratefully to remember it

'With my serious prayers for your life, health, and tranquillity, I pray you accept the homage of the great and constant respect and attachment with which I have the honor to be, &c."

But it is doubtless true that the many and bitter dissensions which had occurred in the Cabinet between Jefferson and Hamilton, had at length rendered it impossible for them to act together to any extent. In vain had Washington endeavored to harmonize their disputes. How earnestly he desired this result may be inferred from the following extract from the letter which he addressed to each member of his Cabinet:

"My earnest wish and my fondest hope, therefore, is, that instead of wounding suspicions and irritating charges, there may be liberal allowances, mutual forbearances, and temporising yielding on all sides. Under the exercise of these, matters will go on smoothly, and, if possible, more prosperously. Without them every thing must rub, the wheels of government will clog, our enemies will triumph, and by throwing their weight into the disaffected scale, may accomplish the ruin of the goodly fabric we have been erecting,

"I do not mean to apply this advice, or these observations, to any particular person or character. I have given them in the same general terms to other officers of the government, because the disagreements which have arisen from difference of opinions, and the attacks which have been made upon almost all the measures of government, and most of its executive officers, have for a long time past filled me with painful sensations, and cannot fail, I think, of producing unhappy consequences at home and abroad."

That Mr. Jefferson was to blame for a large share of the difficulties and disputes which embarrassed the Cabinet, is unquestionable. His personal hatred of Mr. Hamilton inflamed his feelings and beclouded his judgment. In this state of mind he often opposed good measures, simply because they were defended and approved by his rival. He also aggravated the existing evils by making charges against Hamilton which were dictated by personal spite; which were unfounded in truth; and which compelled his foe to retort, and to defend himself with acrimony. As an instance of this, we may cite the accusation made by Mr. Jefferson, that Mr. Hamilton had corrupted members of the legislature and had rewarded his friends by dealing out the financial secrets of the Treasury. This charge had been first made by Mr. Jefferson in a letter to Washington, dated May 23d, 1792.* A complaint of such severity and importance as this, should have been sustained by something like proof; and if it had been true, the evidence in support of it would have been accessible. If Jefferson had possessed no proof, he should not have made the charge; and the fact that he adduced no evidence and cited no particulars, evinces clearly that he could not do so. Had he possessed the ability he certainly would not have wanted the inclination.

But, unfortunately for the sincerity and veracity of Mr. Jefferson, while there is a total absence of proof in support of his assertion, there is direct evidence in existence of its falsity.

Among the most intimate and esteemed friends of Mr. Hamilton was Colonel Lee, well known for his many brilliant exploits during the Revolution. He had been closely associated with Mr. Hamilton at the head-quarters of the army, during the period when the latter was Washington's private secretary. He was a person whom Hamilton would have gladly

* See Writings of G. Washington, by Sparks: Vol. x. Appendix, p. 504. Jefferson repeats the charge in another letter to Washington, dated Sept. 9, 1792. See Writings of Washington: Vol. x. Appendix, p. 517. The letter of May 23d, 1792, with a very slight change of form, was the letter Washington addressed to Hamilton, July 29th, 1702. See Washington's Writings: Vol. x. p. 249. Compare Hamilton's answer to the queries contained in that letter,—Hamilton's Works: Vol. iv. pp. 247, 248.

served on any possible occasion, by any means in his power. Immediately before Hamilton made his report to Congress in reference to the public credit, in December, 1789, Colonel Lee addressed certain queries to Mr. Hamilton in reference to the policy and measures which he intended to recommend, for the purpose of using the information thus obtained in private financial operations. Here was an instance in which Mr. Hamilton could have obliged one of his best friends, and could have also used the secrets of the Treasury in strengthening his supporters in Congress, had he desired to do so. His answer to Col. Lee, dated December 1st, 1789, immediately before his report was made to Congress, is as follows:

"My Dear Friend: I received your letter of the 16th inst. I am sure you are sincere when you say that you would not subject me to an impropriety; nor do I know there would be any in answering your queries. But you remember the saying with regard to Cæsar's wife. I think the spirit of it applicable to every man concerned in the administration of the finances of a country; with respect to the conduct of such men, *suspicion* is ever eagle-eyed, and the most innocent things may be misrepresented. Be assured of the affectionate friendship of yours, &c."*

Now although the evidence which proves that Mr. Hamilton refused to reveal treasury secrets to Col. Lee, does not absolutely show that he did not reveal them to others, it proves, in the absence of all testimony to the contrary, that the same spirit would actuate him consistently in all his official transactions; and the inference is legitimate and just, that he never did thus violate the dictates of honor and duty. If this be true, then the conclusion is unavoidable, that Mr. Jefferson made false charges against his rival; charges which he had no reason whatever to believe to be true; and consquently that those dissensions in the Cabinet, which resulted in part from the propagation of these slanders, were to some extent attributable to the conduct of Mr. Jefferson. This censure becomes more just when it is remembered that this ungrounded and unproven accusation is frequently repeated by him against Hamilton, both in his letters and in his Ana. That his longer connection with the Cabinet of Washington was impossible under such circumstances, and in the midst of such jealousies and recriminations, is not singular

* See Works of Hamilton, by his Son: Vol. v., p. 446.

Even the hostile feelings which had gradually grown up between Mr. Jefferson and the President were such as to render their further connection unpleasant. The *National Gazette* had been established by Mr. Jefferson; and its leading articles continually and bitterly attacked Washington, Hamilton, and their measures. In many of these articles the style of Jefferson was clearly detected; and their abuse of the President was most execrable. A literary adventurer named Freneau was used by him as his chief tool in the conduct of this paper. Mr. Jefferson was fully aware of the chagrin inflicted by the attacks of that man upon Washington. In his Ana he thus speaks of the complaints made by Washington to him in person, in a private interview:

"He adverted to a piece in Freneau's paper of yesterday; he said he despised all their attacks on him personally, but that there never had been an act of the government, not meaning in the executive line only, but in any line, which that paper had not abused. He had also marked the word republic thus (V) where it was applied to the French republic. He was evidently sore and warm, and I took his intention to be that I should interpose in some way with Freneau, perhaps withdraw his appointment of translating clerk to my office. But I will not do it. *His paper has saved our Constitution,* which was galloping fast into monarchy, and has been checked by no one means so powerfully as *that paper.* It is well and universally known, that it has been that paper which has checked the career of the monocrats; and the President, not sensible of the designs of the party, has not, with his usual good sense and sang froid, looked on the efforts and effects of this free press, and seen that though some bad things have passed through it to the public, yet the good have preponderated immensely."

After Mr. Jefferson's return to Monticello, it is certain that his residence became for several years the head-quarters of those who were opposed to the administration of Washington, and that all the democratic measures which were proposed in Congres were undertaken after his advice and approval had been obtained. He had a share in directing the attacks of the opposition journals, and he made with his own hand draughts of the bills, resolutions and reports which were offered to Congress by his confederates. His most intimate friends and associates at this period were Messrs. Madison, Monroe and Giles. It was at this period of his retirement that he wrote his famous letter to Mr. Mazzei, his Italian friend, in which he is charged with having traduced Washington. This letter was not intended for the public eye; but unfortunately it was translated into Italian in Florence, thence into French, and afterward published in the *Moniteur*. It was subsequently retranslated into English, and published both in England and the United States. The portion of this letter which refers to politics is as follows:

"The aspect of our politics has wonderfully changed since you left us April 24, 1796. In place of that noble love of liberty and republican government which carried us triumphantly through the war, an Anglican monarchical and aristocratical party has sprung up, whose avowed object is to draw over us the substance, as they have already done the forms, of the British government. The main body of our citizens, however, remain true to their republican principles; the whole landed interest is republican, and so is a great mass of talents. Against us are *the executive*, the judiciary, two out of three branches of the legislature, all the officers of the government, all who want to be officers, all timid men who prefer the calm of despotism to the boisterous sea of liberty; British merchants and Americans trading on British capitals, speculators and holders in the banks and public funds, a contrivance invented for the purposes of corruption, and for assimilating us in all things to the rotten as well as the sound parts of the British model. It would give you a fever were I to name to you the apostates who have gone over to these heresies, men who were Samsons in the field and Solomons in the council, but who have had their heads shorn by the harlot England. In short, we are likely to preserve the liberty we have obtained only by unremitting labors and perils. But we shall preserve it; and our mass of weight and wealth on the good side is so great, as to leave no danger that force will ever be attempted against us. We have only to awake and snap the liliputian cords with which they have been entangling us during the first sleep which succeeded our labors. I begin to feel the effects of age. My health has suddenly broken down, with symptoms which give me to believe I shall not have much to encounter of the *tedium vitæ.* While it remains, however, my heart will be warm in its friendships, and among these, will always foster the affections, with which I am, dear sir, your friend and servant, &c."

This letter has long been the theme of dispute between the friends and enemies of Mr. Jefferson. The former deny that Washington was referred to in it by the author, in any way. The latter assert the contrary. Timothy Pickering states, on the authority of Dr. Stuart, that Washington, after the termination of his second and last administration, called its author personally to account for the injury thus done him; and that Mr. Jefferson appeased the just resentment of Washington by some great act of apology and humiliation, the precise nature and degree of which never became known. The full and accurate truth in reference to this affair cannot now be recovered; for the lapse of time, and the careful removal of many sources of information, have effectually covered it forever with the mantle of oblivion.

Mr. Jefferson appears in a more pleasing and amiable light when viewed upon his estate, engaged in the harmless and agreeable occupation of agriculture. The celebrated French traveler, the Duke de Liancourt, thus describes the sage and politician of Monticello at this period: "His conversation is of the most agreeable kind, and he possesses a stock of information not inferior to that of any other man. In Europe he would hold a distinguished rank among men of letters, and as such he has already appeared there. At present he is employed with activity and perseverance in the management of his farms and buildings, and he orders, directs and pursues, in the minutest detail, every branch of business relating to them. The author of this sketch found him in the midst of harvest, from which the scorching heat of the sun does not prevent his attendance. His negroes are nourished, clothed, and treated as well as his white servants could be. As he cannot expect any assistance from the two small neighboring towns, every article is made on his farm; his negroes are cabinet-makers, carpenters, masons, bricklayers, &c. The children he employs in a nail manufactory, which yields already a considerable profit. The young and old negresses spin for the clothing of the rest. He animates them by rewards and distinctions; in fine, his superior mind directs the management of his domestic concerns with the same abilities, activity and regularity, which he evinced in the conduct of public affairs, and which he is calculated to display in every situation in life."

CHAPTER XII.

MR. JEFFERSON ELECTED VICE-PRESIDENT—HIS RELATIONS TO THE PRESIDENT—THE NEW CABINET—DISPUTES WITH THE FRENCH GOVERNMENT—AMERICAN ENVOYS SENT TO PARIS—THEIR RECEPTION THERE—MR. JEFFERSON'S POLITICAL CREED—INDIGNATION IN THE UNITED STATES AGAINST FRANCE—NAPOLEON BONAPARTE SUCCEEDS TO THE FRENCH DIRECTORY, AND MAKES A TREATY WITH THE UNITED STATES—TERMINATION OF MR. ADAMS' ADMINISTRATION—THE APPROACHING ELECTION—DR. LOGAN'S PRIVATE MISSION TO FRANCE.

Mr. Jefferson's retirement from public office continued during the space of three years. In October, 1796, John Adams was elected President, and Mr. Jefferson Vice-President of the United States. The former received seventy-one votes, the latter sixty-eight. In spite of his prodigious devotion to the cultivation of Lucerne and potatoes, Mr. Jefferson at once accepted the proffered dignity. In February, 1797, he prepared to leave Monticello for Philadelphia, where the Federal Government was then located. Previous to this period he had not been on very friendly terms with the President elect: but on December 28th, he addressed him a conciliatory letter, and immediately on his arrival at Philadelphia paid his respects to Mr. Adams in person. The next day Mr. Adams returned the visit. Their former friendly feelings were again revived, a circumstance which augured favorably for the harmony of the ensuing administration. The Cabinet of Mr. Adams consisted of Timothy Pickering as Secretary of State, Mr. Wolcott as Secretary of the Treasury, Mr. McHenry as Secretary of War, and Mr. Lee as Attorney-General. The relative strength of parties in the legislature stood fifty-two in favor of the administration and forty-eight against it. The President and Cabinet were Federal, the Vice-President alone was Democratic. This antagonism was not of much consequence, inasmuch as Mr. Jefferson's duties consisted merely in presiding over the deliberations of the Senate. He was not admitted to the consultations of the Cabinet. In his letters to James Sullivan, Eldredge Gerry, Mr. Madison, Colonel Burr and General Gates, of the year 1797, he expresses his great disappointment that such an invitation had not been extended to him.

The letter addressed by Mr. Jefferson to the new President, already referred to, is as follows:

"*Monticello*, Dec. 28, 1796.

"DEAR SIR: The public and the public papers, have been much occupied lately in placing us in a point of opposition to each other. I confidently trust we have felt less of it ourselves. In the retired canton where I live, we know little of what is passing. Our last information from Philadelphia is of the 16th inst. At that date the issue of the late election seems not to have been known as a matter of fact. With me, however, its issue was never doubted. I knew the impossibility of your losing a single vote north of the Delaware; and even if you should lose that of Pennsylvania in the mass, you would get enough south of it to make your election sure. I never, for a single moment, expected any other issue, and though I shall not be believed, yet it is not the less true, *that I never wished any other.* My neighbors, as my compurgators, could aver this fact, as seeing my occupations and my attachment to them. It is possible, indeed, that even you may be *cheated of your succession by a trick worthy the subtlety of your arch friend of New York*, who has been able to make of your real friends tools for defeating their and your just wishes. Probably, how ever, he will be disappointed as to you; and my inclinations put me out of his reach. I leave to others the sublime delights of riding in the storm, better pleased with a sound sleep and a warmer birth below it, encircled with the society of my neighbors, friends, and fellow-laborers of the earth, rather than with spies and sycophants. Still, I shall value highly the share I may have had in the late vote, as a measure of the share I hold in the esteem of my fellow-citizens. In this point of view, a few votes less are but little sensible, while a few more would have been in their effect very sensible and oppressive to me. I have no ambition to govern men. It is a painful and thankless office. And never since the day you signed the treaty of Paris, has our horizon been so overcast. I devoutly wish you may be able to shun for us this war, which will destroy our agriculture, commerce and credit. If you do, the glory will be all your own. And that your administration may be filled with glory and happiness to yourself, and advantage to us, is the sincere prayer of one, who, though in the course of our voyage, various little incidents have happened or been contrived, to separate us, yet retains for you the solid esteem of the times when we were working for our independence, and sentiments of sincere respect and attachment."

No one can carefully peruse this singular document without perceiving that its author therein utters sentiments unworthy of his talents and his patriotism. He is not consistent or true to his own party and professions; for how could he say that he "*never wished for any other issue*" than the election of Mr. Adams, whom he knew to be an ultra-federalist, and yet claim the least pretense to consistency? The truth is, Mr. Jefferson was extremely desirous of conciliating the President elect, in order that he might be invited to share the deliberations of the Cabinet; and to attain that end, he was willing to make concessions which true moral courage would have condemned and disdained.

Congress had been convened under the new administration for the 15th of May. The chief questions which agitated the country during the ensuing session were the spoliations of France on American commerce, the insulting treatment of the American envoys at Paris, and the anticipations of a furious conflict with that nation. Mr. Jefferson was opposed to a war with the French government and people. Indeed it must be said in justice to him, that though he hated England with an unappeasable hatred, yet he was opposed to any rupture even with that country. Mr. Pinkney, the minister sent by Mr. Adams to Paris as successor to Mr. Monroe, was refused an audience by the Directory, then acting under the influence of the artful and rapacious Talleyrand. Mr. Adams' Cabinet was divided upon the policy which it became the United States to adopt under these circumstances. A portion of them, including Mr. Pickering, thought that national self-respect forbade the appointment of any other emissary to France until an apology had been made. Another portion thought that, rather than venture on the hazards which would ensue upon a final rupture with that country, the President should once more try the effect of proffered negotiation. With these advisers Mr. Adams acquiesced; and three envoys were sent to France. These were General Pinckney, of South Carolina; Mr. Marshall, of Virginia; and Mr. Gerry, of Massachusetts. Their appointment was confirmed by the Senate. They entered on their mission, and the nation awaited the result with intense interest.

During this interval of suspense Mr. Jefferson was not idle. Though a member of, he was heartily opposed to, the existing administration. He endeavored to break it down both by his personal acts and his correspondence; and as the great name of Washington was still the chief support of the party in power, he did not scruple to assail even him. On the 17th of June he addressed a letter to Aaron Burr, in which the following language occurs:

"I had always hoped that the popularity of the late President being once withdrawn from active effect, the natural feelings of the people toward liberty would restore the equilibrium between the executive and legislative departments, which had been destroyed by the superior weight and effect of that popularity; and that their natural feelings of moral obligation would discountenance the ungrateful predilection of the executive in favor of Great Britain. But unfortunately, the preceding measures had already alienated the nation, who were the object of them, had excited reaction from them, and this reaction has, on the minds of our citizens, an effect which supplies that of the Washington popularity.

"But will that region ever awake to the true state of things? Can the Middle, Southern, and Western States hold on till they awake? These are painful and doubtful questions; and if, in assuring me of your health, you can give me a comfortable solution of them, it will relieve a mind devoted to the preservation of our republican government in the true form and spirit in which it was established, but almost oppressed with apprehensions that fraud will at length effect what force could not, and that what with currents and counter-currents, we shall, in the end, be driven back to the land from which we launched twenty years ago."

In the same spirit of censure and apprehension he wrote to Governor Rutledge, on the 24th of June, as follows:

"This is, indeed, a most humiliating state of

things; but it commenced in 1793. Causes have been adding to causes, and effects accumulating on effects, from that time to this. We had in 1793 the most respectable character in the universe. What the neutral nations think of us now, I know not; but we are low indeed with the belligerents. Their kicks and cuffs prove their contempt. If we weather the present storm, I hope we shall avail ourselves of the calm of peace to place our foreign connections under a new and different arrangement. We must make the interest of every nation stand surety for their justice; and their own loss to follow injury to us, as effect follows its cause. As to every thing except commerce, we ought to divorce ourselves from them all. But this system would require time, temper, wisdom, and occasional sacrifice of interest; and how far all these will be ours, our children may see, but we shall not. The passions are too high at present to be cooled in our day. You and I have formerly seen warm debates and high political passions. But gentlemen of different politics would then speak to each other, and separate the business of the Senate from that of society. It is not so now. Men who have been intimate all their lives cross the street to avoid meeting, and turn their heads another way, lest they should be obliged to touch their hats. This may do for young men, with whom passion is enjoyment. But it is afflicting to peaceable minds. Tranquillity is the old man's milk. I go to enjoy it in a few days, and to exchange the roar and tumult of bulls and bears for the prattle of my grandchildren, and senile rest. Be these yours, my dear friend, through long years, with every other blessing, and the attachment of friends as warm."

In the beginning of this year, 1797, Mr. Jefferson was elected President of the American Philosophical Society, of which body, for twenty years, he had been a member. He was highly gratified by this distinction; for during his whole life, in the midst of political conflicts, and all the rude scenes of public life and ambition, he greatly appreciated the value of scientific pursuits, and of those institutions which promoted their success.

It was at the same period that Mr. Jefferson addressed a letter to Mr. Gerry, in which he carefully embodied his political creed. As this document contains the fullest exposition of his political views which is to be found among his writings, it possesses a much more than transient importance. We therefore insert it here, as being an instrument of authority on the subject of which it treats.

"In confutation of these, and all future calumnies," says Mr. J., "by way of anticipation, I shall make to you a profession of my political faith; in confidence that you will consider every future imputation on me of a contrary complexion, as bearing on its front the mark of falsehood and calumny.

"I do then, with a sincere zeal, wish an inviolable preservation of our present Federal Constitution, according to the true sense in which it was adopted by the States, that in which it was advocated by its friends, and not that which its enemies apprehended, who therefore became its enemies; and I am opposed to monarchising its features by the forms of its administration, with a view to conciliate a first transition to a President and Senate for life, and from that to an hereditary tenure of these offices, and thus to worm out the elective principle. I am for preserving to the States the powers not yielded by them to the Union, and to the Legislature of the Union its constitutional share in the division of powers; and I am not for transferring all the powers of the States to the general government, and all those of that government to the Executive branch. I am for a government rigorously frugal and simple, applying all the possible savings of the public revenue to the discharge of the national debt; and not for a multiplication of officers and salaries, merely to make partisans, and for increasing, by every device, the public debt, on the principle of its being a public blessing. I am for relying for internal defense on our militia solely, till actual invasion, and for such a naval force only as may protect our coasts and harbors from such depredations as we have experienced; and not for a standing army in time of peace, which may overawe the public sentiment; nor for a navy, which by its own expenses and the eternal wars in which it will implicate us, will grind us with public burdens, and sink us under them. I am for free commerce with all nations; political connection with none; and little or no diplomatic establishment. And I am not for linking ourselves by new treaties with the quarrels of Europe; entering that field of slaughter to preserve their balance, or joining in the confederacy of kings to war against the principles of liberty. I am for freedom of religion, and against all maneuvres to bring about the legal ascendancy of one sect over another; for freedom of the press, and against all violations of the Constitution to silence by force, and not by reason, the complaints or criticisms, just or unjust, of our citizens, against the conduct of their agents. And I am for encouraging the progress of science in all its branches; and not for raising a hue and cry against the sacred name of philosophy, for awing the human mind by stories of raw-head and bloody bones, to a distrust of its own vision; and to repose implicitly on that of others; to go backward instead of forward to look for improvement; to believe that government, religion, morality, and every other science were in the highest perfection in ages of the darkest ignorance, and that nothing can ever be devised more perfect than what was established by our forefathers. To these, I will add, that I was a sincere well-wisher to the success of the French revolution, and still wish it may end in the establishment of a free and well-ordered republic, but I have not been insensible under the atrocious depredations they have committed on our commerce. The first object of my heart is my own country. In that is embarked my family, my fortune and my own existence. I have not one farthing of interest, nor one fibre of attachment out of it, nor a single motive of preference of any one nation to another, but in proportion as they are more or less friendly to us. But, though deeply feeling the injuries of France, I did not think war the surest means of redressing them. I did believe that a mission, sincerely disposed to preserve peace, would obtain for us a peaceable and honorable settlement and retribution; and I appeal to you to say, whether this might not have been obtained, if either of your colleagues had been of the same sentiment with yourself."

The new American envoys to Paris were received by the Directory with studied coldness and contempt. On the 19th of March, 1798, the President informed Congress that the dispatches received from their envoys afforded no ground to hope that their mission would be successful. He recommended that the country be put in a state of defense by providing military stores and an efficient revenue. He had also withdrawn the instructions which had been given to the custom-house officers to restrain armed vessels from leaving our ports, except in certain particular cases. On the 8th of April the Senate resolved to publish the dispatches of the American envoys; and these revealed, among other things, a disgraceful attempt on the part of Talleyrand to sell the friendly dispositions of the Directory and of himself to the United States on the payment of a large sum of money.

General indignation now pervaded the whole country against the French people and government. A provisional army was at once authorized of twenty thousand men. A tax on stamps and a direct tax on lands were immediately imposed, for the purpose of supporting the expenses of an anticipated war. The foundations of the American navy were then laid; vigorous measures seemed to characterize the administration, and resolute purposes to inflame the people. Mr. Jefferson gives the following picture, in a letter to Mr. Madison, of the state of the public mind at this crisis:

"The popular movement in the Eastern States i checked, as we expected, and war addresses are showering in from New Jersey and the great trading towns. However, we will trust that a nearer view of war and a land tax will oblige the great mass of the people to attend; at present the war-hawks talk of septembrizing, deportation, and the examples of quelling sedition set by the French executive. All the firmness of the human mind is now in a state of requisition." And on May the 3d: "The spirit kindled up in the towns is wonderful. These and New Jersey are pouring in their addresses, offering life and fortune;" and he says that the President's answers are "more thrasonic than the addresses." He regards all hope of peace as then destroyed, and supposes that the President's threats are not confined to France, but are extended to his fellow-citizens. He states that the French citizens, taking alarm at his alien bill, were going off, and among them, Volney, whom be believes to have been the principal object of the bill.

To another correspondent, a young lawyer in Fredericksburg, who had informed him of Mr. Luther Martin's attack on him, ne writes a few days afterward: "At this moment all the passions are boiling over, and one who keeps himself cool and clear of the contagion, is so far below the point of ordinary conversation, that he finds himself insulated in every society. However, the fever will not last; war, land tax and stamp tax are sedatives which must cool its ardor."—"It is our duty still to endeavor to avoid war; but if it actually shall take place, no matter by whom brought on, we must defend ourselves."

In June Messrs. Pinckney and Marshall returned home from France; Mr. Gerry yet remained. The two former were received with great demonstrations of popular respect. The future relations of the country toward France continued to engage the public mind, and to occupy the deliberations of the Cabinet until the succeeding 25th of February, when Mr. Adams nominated Messrs. Ellsworth, of Connecticut, Henry, of Virginia, and Murray, of Maryland, as ministers to France. Mr. Henry declined the appointment. The negotiations of the new envoys were more successful than those of their predecessors. They had also a different power to deal with than the imbecile and vacillating Directory. The strong arm of Napoleon had seized the reins of government, and his towering genius then directed her destinies. A treaty on liberal and equitable principles was soon adjusted between him and the American representatives, and the evils of an apprehended war were averted from both countries.

Immediately after these events a new subject of interest absorbed the popular attention. This was the general election, which was about to take place. The errors which Mr. Adams had committed, his own personal unpopularity, and the growing strength of the democratic party, were silently but effectually working the overthrow of the faction in power. The death of Washington, which occurred at this period, had shorn the Federal party of a great portion of its strength and popularity. Every thing presaged the coming supremacy of the Republicans.

Mr. Jefferson thus speaks to Mr. Madison of the approaching presidential election. "As the conveyance is confidential, I can say something on a subject which, to those who do not know my real dispositions respecting it, might seem indelicate. The Federalists begin to be very seriously alarmed about their election next fall. Their speeches in private, as well as their public and private demeanor to me, indicate it strongly." He then details the probable votes of most of the States, and thus concludes: "Still these are the ideas of the Republicans only in these three States, and we must make great allowance for their sanguine views. Upon the whole, I consider it as rather more doubtful than the last election, in which I was not deceived in more than a vote or two."

On the 12th of May he writes to the same correspondent: "The Federalists have not been able to carry a single strong measure in the lower House the whole session. When they met it was believed they had a majority of twenty; but many of these were new and moderate men, and soon saw the true character of the party to which they had been well disposed while at a distance. The tide, too, of public opinion sets so strongly against the federal proceedings, that this melted off their majority, and dismayed the heroes of the party. The Senate alone remained undismayed to the last. Firm to their purpose, regardless of public opinion, and more disposed to coerce than to court it, not a man of the majority gave way in the least."

Both parties were fully aware of the magnitude of the interests at stake, and prepared themselves to make prodigious exertions to secure an ultimate triumph.

One of the chief obstacles to the popularity of Mr. Jefferson at this crisis was the fact, that he was charged by popular rumor with having sent Dr. Logan of Philadelphia on a private mission of conciliation to Paris, after the defeat of the Embassy of Pinckney and Marshall. It was supposed that Mr. Jefferson's attachment to France, against which the United States were then incensed and indignant, had induced him to dispach this agent thither secretly in order to avert hostilities. It was proved that Mr. Jefferson furnished Logan with a certificate of his citizenship and character, together with a passport. Dr. Logan was treated by the French as he deserved, with contempt, and his mission utterly failed. When the facts became known, the public mind was incensed against Logan for his unauthorized and unwelcome interference, and Mr. Jefferson received a share of the general odium, as having been his patron. The latter however denied most positively that he had commissioned Logan to undertake his ill-starred expedition. The Federal party as vehemently asserted the contrary.

CHAPTER XIII.

POPULAR EXCITEMENT PREVIOUS TO THE ELECTION OF 1801—RESULT OF THE POPULAR VOTE—JEFFERSON'S LETTER TO BURR—ELECTION IN THE HOUSE OF REPRESENTATIVES—THE EQUALITY OF VOTES BETWEEN JEFFERSON AND BURR—INFLUENCE OF ALEXANDER HAMILTON—ELECTION OF JEFFERSON TO THE PRESIDENCY—HIS INAUGURAL ADDRESS—LETTER TO ELDREDGE GERRY—MR. JEFFERSON'S CABINET—HIS LETTER TO THOMAS PAINE—MR. LIVINGSTON APPOINTED MINISTER TO FRANCE—WAR BETWEEN THE UNITED STATES AND TRIPOLI—ITS INCIDENTS AND RESULTS—MR. JEFFERSON'S FIRST MESSAGE TO CONGRESS—MEASURES OF THE ADMINISTRATION—NEGOTIATIONS RESPECTING LOUISIANA.

As the period of the election approached, the excitement throughout the nation became more general and intense. The struggle between the party about to be driven from power, and the party about to to secure it, was bitter and violent. Never perhaps in the history of the country was a destructive conflict and collision so imminent as at this crisis of the national history. The election took place in November. Jefferson and Burr were the candidates of the Republicans; John Adams and Charles C. Pinckney were the candidates of the Federalists. The votes given to Jefferson and Burr were those of New York, twelve; of Pennsylvania, eight out of fifteen; of Maryland, five out of ten; of Virginia, twenty-one; of Kentucky, four; of North Carolina, eight out of twelve; of Tennessee, three; of South Carolina, eight; of Georgia, four. The Republicans thus received seventy-three out of one hundred and thirty-eight votes. The Federalists received sixty-five votes, one of which was given to Mr. Jay, and the balance to Messrs. Adams and Pinckney. Mr. Hamilton, being convinced of the unfitness of Mr. Adams for a second term of office, from the unpopularity with which he had covered the Federal party during his first administration, was opposed to his re-election; and was the means of preventing the votes of South Carolina from being given to Mr. Adams, in consequence of the preparation of a pamphlet which clearly set forth the fatal defects and blunders of that officer. But by a malicious and crafty trick of Burr, the contents of that pamphlet were prematurely published and perverted in such a manner, that it was made instrumental in the defeat not only of Mr. Adams, in South Carolina, but also of Mr. Pinckney; a result which was utterly hostile to the wishes of Mr. Hamilton, as well as of a large majority of the Federal party, who earnestly desired to promote the election of Mr. Pinckney.

At the popular election the number of votes obtained by the Republicans was equally divided between Jefferson and Burr. According to the arrangement existing at that time, the candidate who received the largest number of votes became President, and the second on the list became Vice-President. But in the present instance Jefferson and Burr being equal, the election was thrown into the House of Representatives. Previous, however, to the occurrence of this event, the prevalent rumor was that Mr. Jefferson had received a majority over Mr. Burr. On the 15th of December, while he himself was under that impression, Jefferson wrote a letter to Burr, in which he gives him to understand that he regretted deeply that he would not be able to offer him a place in his Cabinet. Says he: "I feel most sensibly the loss we sustain of your aid in our new administration. It leaves a chasm in my arrangements which cannot be adequately filled up. I had endeavored to compose an administration whose talents, integrity, names and dispositions should at once inspire unbounded confidence in the public mind, and insure a perfect harmony in the conduct of the public business." And yet Mr. Jefferson declares in his Diary, in reference to this same man, that very soon after his acquaintance with Mr. Burr, his conduct had inspired him with distrust.* This inconsistency is one out of many evidences which might be adduced to show that Mr. Jefferson was a supple politician, who, with very great craft, made

* Vide Jefferson's Correspondence. Vol. V., p. 520.

himself all things to all men. This peculiarity of his character and of his talents furnishes to some extent the explanation of his constant attainment of office through the whole course of his life.

After the result of the election had become known, the popular excitement became still more intense. The Republicans were overwhelmed with terror lest by some means the election in the House might be turned by the Federalists to the ultimate defeat of their opponents. The Republicans determined that if the Federalists used their majority in Congress to defeat the popular will, either in preventing an election, or by choosing different persons from those already designated by the majority of the nation, the attempt should be crushed by force. The republican governors both of Virginia and Pennsylvania were prepared to march a military force to Washington, in order to overturn the usurpers, undo what they might have done, and refer the matter back again directly to the people.

We will not follow all the details of this memorable conflict, which shook the nation to its centre. The balloting began in the House on the 11th of February, 1801. Thirty-five ballots were given without any change or variation. These occupied six days; during which period the scene presented was a singular one. The issue being uncertain, terror began to pervade the public mind. This was the period of anarchy, respecting which Burr afterward declared that, had he been disposed to overturn the government, like Cromwell or Bonaparte, he could have done it with the greatest ease, by marching at the head of five hundred soldiers into the house, dissolving the Assembly by force, and assuming the reins of authority. The position and relative strength of parties were such, that the ballotings bid fair to become endless, the Democratic delegates voting uniformly in such a ratio that a tie existed between Jefferson and Burr; and the Federalists, unable to elect their own candidates, seemed indisposed to confer any of their votes upon either of the candidates of the rival party. The state of affairs was daily becoming more desperate and perilous.

At this crisis the magnanimity and patriotism of Alexander Hamilton saved the country. Finding that the posture of affairs was becoming more dangerous from day to day, in consequence of treasonable and violent measures of redress which began to be suggested both by certain portions of the Federal party and of the Democratic, he resolved to use his great influence with the Federalists to put an end to the confusion, and secure a competent majority to his ancient and implacable foe, Mr. Jefferson, in opposition to Mr. Burr, whom he regarded as an unprincipled man. Hamilton was willing to forget his private wrongs to promote the welfare of his country. In a letter to a senator of this date he says: *If there be a man in the world I ought to hate, it is Jefferson. With Burr I have always been personally well. But the public good must be paramount to every private consideration.*" To a member of the House he writes as follows: "*To contribute to the disappointment and mortification of Mr. Jefferson, would be on my part only to retaliate for unequivocal proofs of enmity; but in a case like this, it would be base to listen to personal considerations.*"

Mr. Hamilton used his influence in accordance with these principles; and on the thirty-sixth ballot, which occurred on the 17th of February, Mr. Jefferson received the votes of ten states out of the sixteen. These were New York, New Jersey, Pennsylvania, Virginia, North Carolina, Georgia, Tennessee, Kentucky, Vermont and Maryland. Four states—New Hampshire, Massachusetts, Connecticut and Rhode Island—voted for Mr. Burr; and South Carolina and Delaware voted blank ballots. So little appreciation had Mr. Jefferson of the real power which put him in his high place, that he wrote as follows to Mr. Monroe on the 15th of February:

"If they could have been permitted to pass a law

for putting the government into the hands of an officer, they certainly would have prevented an election. But we thought it best to declare openly and firmly, one and all, that the day such an act passed, the Middle States would arm, and that no such usurpation, even for a single day, should be submitted to. This first shook them, and they were completely alarmed at the resource for which we declared, to wit, a convention, to reorganize the government, and to amend it. The very word convention gives them the horrors; as in the present democratical spirit of America, they fear they should lose some of the favorite morsels of the Constitution. Many attempts have been made to obtain terms from me. I have declared to them unequivocally, that I would not receive the government on capitulation; that I would not go into it with my hands tied."

The following extract from his Inaugural Address will give a correct idea of the policy and principles according to which he had determined to administer the government:

"Friends and fellow-citizens: Called upon to undertake the duties of the first executive office of our country, I avail myself of the presence of that portion of my fellow-citizens which are here assembled, to express my grateful thanks for the favor with which they have been pleased to look toward me, to declare a sincere consciousness that the task is above my talents, and that I approach it with those anxious and awful presentiments, which the greatness of the charge, and the weakness of my powers, so justly inspire. A rising nation, spread over a wide and fruitful land, traversing all the seas with the rich produce of their industry; engaged in commerce with nations, who feel power and forget right; advancing rapidly to destinies beyond the reach of mortal eye; when I contemplate these transcendant objects, and see the honor, the happiness, and the hopes of this beloved country, committed to the issue and the auspices of this day, I shrink from the contemplation, and humble myself before the magnitude of the undertaking. Utterly indeed should I despair, did not the presence of many whom I here see, remind me that in the other high authorities provided by our Constitution, I shall find resources of wisdom, of virtue, and of zeal, on which to rely under all difficulties. To you then, gentlemen, who are charged with the sovereign functions of legislation, and to those associated with you, I look with encouragement for that guidance and support which may enable us to steer with safety the vessel in which we are all embarked amidst the conflicting elements of a troubled world.

"During the contest of opinion through which

we have passed, the animation of discussions and exertions has sometimes worn an aspect which might impose on strangers unused to think freely, and to speak and to write what they think; but this being now decided by the voice of the nation, announced according to the rules of the Constitution, all will of course arrange themselves under the will of the law, and unite in common efforts for the common good. All too will bear in mind this sacred principle, that though the will of the majority is in all cases to prevail, that will to be rightful must be reasonable; that the minority possess their equal rights, which equal laws must protect, and to violate would be oppression. Let us then, fellow-citizens, unite with one heart and one mind; let us restore to social intercourse that harmony and affection, without which liberty and even life itself are but dreary things; and let us reflect that having banished from our land that religious intolerance under which mankind so long bled and suffered, we have yet gained little if we countenance a political intolerance as despotic, as wicked, and capable of as bitter and bloody persecutions. During the throes and convulsions of the ancient world, during the agonizing spasms of infuriated man, seeking through blood and slaughter his long lost liberty, it was not wonderful that the agitation of the billows should reach even this distant and peaceful shore—that this should be more felt and feared by some and less by others, and should divide opinions as to measures of safety; but every difference of opinion, is not a difference of principle. We have called by different names, brethren of the same principle. We are all Republicans—all Federalists. If there be any among us who would wish to dissolve this Union, or to change its republican form, let them stand undisturbed as monuments of the safety with which error of opinion may be tolerated where reason is left free to combat it. I know, indeed, that some honest men fear that a republican government cannot be strong; that this government is not strong enough. But would the honest patriot, in the full tide of successful experiment, abandon a government which has so far kept us free and firm, on the theoretic and visionary fear that this government, the world's best hope, may by possibility want energy to preserve itself? I trust not. I believe this, on the contrary, the strongest government on earth. I believe it the only one where every man, at the call of the law, would fly to the standard of the law, and would meet invasions of the public order as his own personal concern. Sometimes it is said that man cannot be trusted with the government of himself. Can he then be trusted with the government of others? Or have we found angels in the form of kings to govern him? Let history answer the question. Let us then, with courage and confidence, pursue our own Federal and Republican principles; our attachment to union and representative government. Kindly separated by nature, and a wide ocean, from the exterminating havoc of one quarter of the globe; too high minded to endure the degradations of the others; possessing a chosen country, with room enough for descendants to the thousandth and thousandth generation; entertaining a due sense of our equal right to the use of our own faculties, to the acquisition of our own industry, to honor and confidence from our fellow-citizens, resulting not from birth but from our actions, and their sense of them; enlightened by a benign religion, professed indeed and practiced in various forms, yet all of them inculcating honesty, truth, temperance, gratitude, and the love of man; acknowledging and adoring an over-ruling Providence, which by all its dispensations proves that it delights in the happiness of man here, and his greater happiness hereafter; with all these blessings, what more is necessary to make us a happy and prosperous people? Still one thing more, fellow-citizens; a wise and frugal government, which restraining men from injuring one another, shall leave them otherwise free to regulate their own pursuits of industry and improvement, and shall not take from the mouth of labor the bread it has earned. This is the sum of good government; and this is necessary to close the circle of our felicities.

"About to enter, fellow-citizens, on the exercise of duties which comprehend every thing dear and valuable to you, it is proper you should understand what I deem the essential principles of our government, and consequently those which ought to shape its administration. I will compress them within the narrowest compass they will bear, stating the general principle, but not all its limitations. Equal and exact justice to all men, of whatever state or persuasion, religious or political; peace, commerce and honest friendship with all nations; entangling alliances with none; the support of the State governments in all their rights, as the most competent administration for our domestic concerns, and the surest bulwark against anti-republican tendencies; the preservation of the general government in its whole constitutional vigor, as the sheet-anchor of our peace at home and safety abroad; a jealous care of the right of election by the people; a mild and safe corrective of abuses, which are lopped by the sword of revolution where peaceable remedies are unprovided; absolute acquiescence in the decisions of the majority, the vital principle of republics, from which is no appeal but to force, the vital principle and immediate parent of despotism; a well-disciplined militia, our best reliance in peace, and for the first moments of war, till regulars may relieve them; the supremacy of the civil over the military authority; economy in the public expense, that labor may be lightly burdened; the honest payment of our debts, and sacred preservation of the public faith; encouragement of agriculture, and of commerce as its handmaid; the diffusion of information and arraignment of all abuses at the bar of public reason; freedom of religion, freedom of the press, and freedom of the person under protection of the habeas corpus; and trial by juries impartially selected. These principles form the bright constellation which has gone before us, and guided our steps through an age of revolution and reformation. The wisdom of all our sages, and blood of our heroes, have been devoted to their attainment; they should be the creed of our political faith; the text of civic instruction; the touchstone by which to try the services of those we trust; and, should we wander from them in moments of error or of alarm, let us hasten to retrace our steps, and regain the road which alone leads to peace, liberty and safety."

Further light may be obtained in reference to the feelings and purposes of the new President from the following extract from a letter to Eldredge Gerry, dated March 29, 1801:

"I thought, on your return, that if you had come forward boldly, and appealed to the public by a full statement, it would have had a great effect in your favor personally, and that of the republican cause, then oppressed almost unto death. But I judged from a tact of the southern pulse. I suspect that of the north was different, and decided your conduct, and perhaps it has been as well. If the revolution of sentiment has been later, it has perhaps been not less sure. At length it has arrived. What with the natural current of opinion, which has been setting over to us for eighteen months, and the immense impetus which was given to it from the 11th to the 17th of February, we may now say that the United States, from New York southwardly, are as unanimous in the principles of '76, as they were in '76. The only difference is, that the leaders who remain behind are more numerous and bolder than the apostles of toryism in '76. The reason is, that we are now justly more tolerant than we could safely have been then, circumstanced as we were. Your part of the Union, though as absolutely republican as ours, had drunk deeper of the delusion, and is therefore slower in recovering from it. The ægis of government, and the temples of religion and of justice, have all been prostituted there, to toll us back to the times when we burnt witches. But your people will rise again. They will awake like Samson from his sleep, and carry away the gates and posts of the city. You, my friend, are destined to rally them again under their former banners, and when called to the post, exercise it with firmness and with inflexible adherence to your own principles. The people will support you, notwithstanding the howlings of the ravenous crew from whose jaws they are escaping. It will be a great blessing to our country, if we can once more restore harmony and social love among its citizens. I confess, as to myself, it is almost the first object of my heart, and one to which I would sacrifice every thing but principle. *With the people* I have hopes of effecting it. But their coryphæi are iucurables. I expect little from them.

"I was not deluded by the eulogiums of the public papers in the first moments of change. If they could have continued to get all the loaves and fishes, that is, if I would have gone over to them, they would continue to eulogize. But I well knew that the moment that such removals should take place, as the justice of the preceding administration ought to have executed, their hue and cry would be set up, and they would take their old stand. I shall disregard that also. Mr. Adams's last appointments, when he knew he was naming counselors and aids for me, and not for himself, I set aside as far as depends on me. Officers who have been guilty of gross abuses of office, such as marshals packing juries, &c., I shall now remove, as my predecessor ought in justice to have done. The instances will be few, and governed by strict rule, not party passion. The right of opinion shall suffer no invasion from me. Those who have acted well have nothing to fear, however they may have differed from me in opinion; those that have done ill, however, have nothing to hope; nor shall I fail to do justice, lest it should be ascribed to that difference of opinion. A coalition of sentiments is not for the interest of the printers. They, like the clergy, live by the zeal they can kindle, and the schisms they can create. It is the contest of opinion in politics, as well as religion, which makes us take great interest in them, and bestow our money liberally on those who furnish aliment to our appetite. The mild and simple principles of the Christian philosophy would produce too much calm, too much regularity of good, to extract from its disciples a support for a numerous priesthood, were they not to sophisticate it, ramify it, split it into hairs, and twist its texts till they cover the divine morality of its author with mysteries, and require a priesthood to explain them. The Quakers seem to have discovered this. They have no priests, therefore no schisms. They judge of the text by the dictates of common sense and common morality."

In the formation of his cabinet Mr. Jefferson selected the following persons: Mr. Madison was made Secretary of State; Mr. Gallatin, Secretary of the Treasury; General Dearborn of Massachusetts, Secretary of War; Robert Smith of Maryland was appointed Secretary of the Navy; and Levi Lincoln of Massachusetts, Attorney-General.

It was at this period that Mr. Jefferson addressed the following important letter to Thomas Paine, the author of the Age of Reason. It indicates his high esteem for the character and even for some of the sentiments of that celebrated man:

"Dear Sir: Your letters of October the 1st, 4th, 6th and 16th, came duly to hand, and the papers which they covered were, according to your permission, published in the newspapers, and in a pamphlet, and under your own name. These papers contain precisely our principles, and I hope they will be generally recognized here. The return of our citizens from the frenzy into which they had been wrought partly by ill conduct in France, partly by artifices practiced on them, is almost entire, and will, I believe, become quite so. But these details, too minute and long for a letter, will be better developed by Mr. Dawson, the bearer of this, a member of the late Congress, to whom I refer you for them. He goes in the *Maryland*, a sloop of war, which will wait a few days at Havre to receive his letters, to be written on his arrival at Paris. You expressed a wish to get a passage to this country in a public vessel. Mr. Dawson is charged with orders to the captain of the *Maryland* to receive and accommodate you with a passage back, if you can be ready to depart at such short warning. Robert R. Livingston is appointed minister plenipotentiary to the republic of France, but will not leave this till we receive the ratification of the convention by Mr. Dawson. I am in hopes you will find us returned generally to sentiments worthy of former times. In these it will be your glory to have steadily labored, and with as much effect as any man living. That you may long live to continue your useful labors, and to reap their reward in the thankfulness of nations, is my sincere prayer. Accept assurances of my high esteem and affectionate attachment."

One of the first acts of the new administration was to appoint Chancellor Livingston, of New York, minister to France. It was on this occasion tnat Mr. Jefferson, in his instructions to him, asserted the great democratic principle that "free ships make free goods;" and while he admitted that the prevalent practice of nations was on the contrary doctrine, he held that a reform should take place on the subject. He contended that a ship sailing on the high seas was solely within the jurisdiction of the nation to which it belonged, and he denied the reasonableness of the exception for contraband. He desired Mr. Livingston to coöperate as far as he could in establishing the principle abroad.

In May, 1801, Mr. Jefferson dispatched Commodore Dale with a squadron of three frigates and a sloop-of-war to the Mediterranean against the bashaw of Tripoli, who had declared war against the United States, and had commenced piratical operations against our commerce. The squadron arrived off Tripoli in August, immediately blockaded it, and captured a polacre of fourteen guns. Many engagements ensued at successive periods subsequently. The *Enterprise* under Captain Sterret, was victorious in an action with a Tripolitan corsair off Malta. Commodore Murray, in the frigate *Constitution*, was attacked off Tripoli by a formidable array of gun-boats, and compelled them to retire with immense loss. The frigate *Philadelphia*, Captain Bainbridge, ran upon a rock when surrounded by the enemy's boats, and his crew of three hundred men were compelled to surrender The vessel herself was afterward retaken from the enemy by Captain Stephen Decatur. The Americans now formed a coalition with Hamet, a deposed brother of the reigning bashaw, for the purpose of reinstating him on the throne. The probability of this result brought the bashaw to terms; a favorable peace was concluded by Colonel Lear; and the American prisoners, who had been treated with the most horrid barbarity, were released.

Congress assembled on the first Monday in December, and Mr. Jefferson sent to them his written message, instead of delivering an oral speech, as had previously been the custom. The following is an extract from the letter which accompanied the message:

"The circumstances under which we find ourselves at this place rendering inconvenient the mode heretofore practiced, of making by personal address the first communications between the legislative and executive branches, I have adopted that by message, as used on all subsequent occasions through the session. In doing this I have had principal regard to the convenience of the legislature, to the economy of their time, to their relief from the embarrassment of immediate answers on subjects not yet fully before them, and to the benefits thence resulting to the public affairs. Trusting that a procedure founded on these motives will meet their approbation, I beg leave through you, sir, to communicate the inclosed message, with the documents accompanying it, to the honorable the Senate, and pray you to accept for yourself and them the homage of my high respect and consideration." The reason, however, which weighed with him probably more than any other was, that a speech savored of the forms of royalty. But he well knew that this motive would be fully understood and properly appreciated by those whose favor and approbation he was most desirous of obtaining.

In this message Mr. Jefferson spoke of the various subjects which were then of prominent importance to the nation—including the census, the army, navy, taxation, the importance of the militia, agriculture, commerce, manufactures, navigation, the judiciary system, and a revision of the laws of naturalization.

During the year 1802 many changes and reforms were introduced into the government of the country, in most of which the Executive acquiesced. The

Republican party had a small majority in both Houses, and were enabled to carry their measures. The two great subjects of party conflict were the repeal of the internal taxes, and of the law which had been passed creating a new set of Federal courts.

In 1801 Spain had ceded Louisiana to France. This event excited the indignation and disgust of the citizens of the United States, inasmuch as the possession of Louisiana gave France the control of the port of New Orleans, which was the only outlet between the Western States and the Atlantic. In April, 1802, Mr. Jefferson addressed a letter to Mr. Livingston in Paris, in which he showed the evils which would ensue from the possession of this port and the surrounding country by France, and the infinite causes of irritation which would ensue between the two countries. He directed Mr. Livingston to commence negotiations with the French government, in reference to the final adjustment of this important matter, and the ultimate disposal of Louisiana in such a way that, by ceding or selling that territory to the United States, the interests of both countries might be secured, and the dangers of impending conflict between them might be happily averted

CHAPTER XIV.

THE SETTLEMENT OF THE YAZOO CLAIMS IN ALABAMA AND MISSISSIPPI—THE PURCHASE OF LOUISIANA FROM FRANCE—LETTER OF MR. JEFFERSON ON THE SUBJECT TO GENERAL GATES—REPEAL OF THE BANKRUPT LAW—MR. JEFFERSON'S VIEWS ON THE UNITED STATES BANK—DEATH OF MRS. EPPES—MR. JEFFERSON'S GUN-BOAT SYSTEM—RESULTS OF HIS FIRST ADMINISTRATION—MR. JEFFERSON'S MOTIVES AND EXCUSES FOR A SECOND ELECTION—HIS LETTER TO ALEXANDER I., CZAR OF RUSSIA.

An important measure connected with the administration in 1803, was the passage of a law which provided for the settlement of various claims to lands located in that vast tract of country extending from the western borders of South Carolina and Georgia to the Mississippi River. This country now constitutes the States of Alabama and Mississippi. Until the year 1803, the title of the Indians to this territory remained undisputed. Then South Carolina demanded that portion of it lying along the southern boundary of Tennessee, by virtue of her original charter. Georgia also claimed the whole of it, under her own charter. The United States afterward became the claimant, by the right of conquest and the treaty of peace.

Commissioners had been appointed by the United

States to adjust the claim with Georgia, and also to satisfy the demands of the settlers. Some of the latter held their titles from grants made by the State of Georgia, and some from grants obtained from the United States. The former claimants endeavored to obtain a recognition and settlement of their rights from the United States, and were known by the epithet of the Yazoos. The greatest foe of these claimants was John Randolph of Roanoke, who rendered himself celebrated by his fierce, powerful, and sarcastic eloquence against their demands. The conflict raged during eleven years, until at length it was finally settled in 1814, on the recommendation made by the commissioners, by the purchase of the rights of the Yazoo claimants by the United States for five millions of dollars.

The negotiation with France for the purchase of Louisiana was attended with equal and more immediate success. The American ministers in Paris not only succeeded in negotiating for New Orleans and the Floridas, but were able to effect a purchase of the whole of Louisiana, which contained a territory equal in extent to the whole previous territorial possessions of the United States.

By this treaty of purchase eleven millions, two hundred and fifty thousand dollars were to be paid to France, in six per cent. stock, three months after the delivery of the possession of the country; and certain claims held by American citizens against France, which were about equal to three and a half millions, were to be assumed by the United States. This territory was to be admitted to the confederacy as soon as it complied with the requirements of the Constitution. This acquired territory contained about a million of square miles, and had about ninety thousand civilized inhabitants in addition to the savages who still roamed over it.

Mr. Jefferson was highly gratified at the conclusion of this treaty. It completed the supremacy of the United States throughout the southern peninsula, and gave compactness and unity to the territorial confines of the confederacy. In a letter to General Gates, he thus refers to this subject. It is dated at Washington, July 11, 1803.

Dear General: I accept with pleasure, and with pleasure reciprocate your congratulations on the acquisition of Louisiana; for it is a subject of mutual congratulation, as it interests every man of the nation. The territory acquired, as it includes all the waters of the Missouri and Mississippi, has more than doubled the area of the United States, and the new part is not inferior to the old in soil, climate, productions, and important communications. If our legislature dispose of it with the wisdom we have a right to expect, they may make it the means of tempting all our Indians on the east side of the Mississippi to remove to the West, and of condensing instead of scattering our population. I find our opposition is very willing to pluck feathers from Monroe, although not fond of sticking them into Livingston's coat. The truth is, both have a just portion of merit; and were it necessary, or proper, it would be shown that each has rendered peculiar services."

In another letter to Judge Breckenridge, he thus follows up his ideas of exultation at this bright achievement of his administration:—"Objections are raising to the eastward against the vast extent of our boundaries, and propositions are made to exchange Louisiana, or a part of it, for the Floridas. But, as I have said, we shall get the Floridas without, and I would not give one inch of the waters of the Mississippi to any nation; because I see, in a light very important to our peace, the exclusive right to its navigation, and the admission of no nation into it, but as into the Potomac or Delaware, with our consent and under our police. These federalists see in this acquisition the formation of a new confederacy, embracing all the waters of the

Mississippi, on both sides of it, and a separation of its eastern waters from us."

One of the virtues of the character of Mr. Jefferson, consisted in the simplicity of his mind, which influenced him to avoid ostentation, pomp, ceremony and vain parade, and inclined him to give a preference to every mode of performing an action which combined the greatest convenience, and involved the least display. An application having been made to him by some of the citizens of Boston, in August, 1803, to ascertain the date of his birth, in order to celebrate his birthday, he declined to communicate the information in a letter to Levi Lincoln, couched in the following words: "With respect to the day on which they wish to fix their anniversary, they may be told, that disapproving myself of transferring the honors and veneration for the great birthday of our republic to any individual, or of dividing them with individuals, I have declined letting my own birthday be known, and have engaged my family not to communicate it. This has been the uniform answer to every application of the kind."

Another noteworthy feature of the first administration of Mr. Jefferson was the repeal of the bankrupt law which had been first enacted in one of the late years of Mr. Adams' administration. This law, which had authorized the discharge of a debtor from all his preceding debts on the consent of a *majority* of his creditors, had been regarded as an invidious privilege granted to the mercantile community, especially in the Southern States, where the agricultural interest was of more real value and importance to the community than the commercial.

At this period a proposition was made in Congress to create a branch of the United States Bank in New Orleans. Mr. Jefferson embraced this opportunity to repeat his first objections to that colossal institution, in the following language:

"This institution is one of the most deadly hostility existing against the principles and forms of our Constitution. The nation is, at this time, so strong and united in its sentiments, that it cannot be shaken at this moment. But suppose a series of untoward events should occur, sufficient to bring into doubt the competency of a republican government to meet a crisis of great danger, or to unhinge the confidence of the people in the public functionaries; an institution like this, penetrating by its branches every part of the Union, acting by command and in phalanx, may in a critical moment upset the government. I deem no government safe which is under the vassalage of any self-constituted authorities, or any other authority than that of the nation, or its regular functionaries. What an obstruction could not this bank of the United States, with all its branch banks, be in time of war? It might dictate to us the peace we should accept, or withdraw its aids. Ought we then to give further growth to an institution so powerful, so hostile?"

These general considerations are then followed by cogent arguments *ad hominem.* "That it is hostile we know, 1. From a knowledge of the principles of the persons composing the body of directors in every bank, principal, or branch; and those of most of the stockholders. 2. From their opposition to the measures and principles of the government, and to the election of those friendly to them; and 3. From the sentiments of the newspapers they support. Now, while we are strong, it is the greatest duty we owe to the safety of our Constitution, to bring this powerful enemy to a perfect subordination under its authorities. The first measure would be to reduce them to an equal footing only with other banks, as to the favors of the government. But in order to be able to meet a general combination of the banks against us, in a critical emergency, could we not make a beginning toward an independent use of our own money, toward holding our own deposits in all the banks where it is received, and letting the treasurer give his draft or note, for payment at any particular place, which in a well-conducted government ought to have as much credit as any private draft, or bank-note or bill, and would give us the same facilities which we derive from the banks?"

In the spring of 1804 Mr. Jefferson suffered a severe domestic bereavement in the death of Mrs. Eppes, one of his daughters. On this occasion the wife of ex-President Adams addressed him a letter of condolence, to which Mr. Jefferson responded in a similar spirit of friendship and conciliation. This correspondence became the cause of the renewal of the friendship which had formerly existed between Mr. Jefferson and Mr. Adams, and continued uninterruptedly during many years, until death put an end to the existence of both on the same anniversary of the birthday of the nation's liberties. To Governor Page Mr. Jefferson writes, in reference to this calamity:

"Others," he says, "may lose of their abundance, but I of my wants have lost even the half of all I had. My evening prospects now hang on the slender thread of a single life. Perhaps I may be destined to see even this last cord of parental affection broken. The hope with which I had looked forward to the moment when, resigning public cares to younger hands, I was to retire to that domestic comfort from which the last great step is to be taken, is fearfully blighted."

On the reassembling of Congress, on the 5th of November, Mr. Jefferson sent in his opening message. The chief peculiarity of this message is, that he therein recommends the adoption of the system of gun-boats for the protection of the harbors. These gun-boats he termed floating-batteries; and he estimated that two hundred and fifty of them would effectually defend the fifteen harbors and the coasts of the United States. These he termed a cheap marine; and Congress was induced to pass an appropriation of sixty thousand dollars, for the purpose of testing the feasibility of the plan. The matter excited much discussion at the time, and the gun-boats were generally opposed and condemned by the officers of the navy. An opportunity was eagerly waited for to test the availability of this new arm of the service; and it was not long before such an opportunity was afforded. As these boats were sailing along the coast a violent storm arose, when some of them were driven ashore, some were swamped, and the whole of them destroyed or rendered entirely unfit for service. The gun-boats were thus proved to be utterly unable to resist even the pacific perils of the deep; and their total ruin cast a torrent of popular ridicule on the Executive, who had sc strenuously insisted on their superior availability and merit.

During the first administration of Jefferson, which now terminated, the public debt had been reduced more than twelve millions; the territorial area of the United States had been doubled; many expensive revenue offices had been abolished; the taxes had been greatly diminished; a war with France and Spain had been skillfully and honorably averted; the Tripolitans had been conquered; successful war had been made on Tunis and Algiers; and internal prosperity, wealth, and improvement had prodigiously increased. The first administration of Mr. Jefferson, therefore, terminated in a halo of popularity and splendor, which rendered his re-election inevitable; which made him for a brief period the idol of the nation, and the possessor of a degree of adulation second in intensity only to that which had become the permanent and unchanging inheritance of Washington.

He commenced his second administration on the 4th of March, 1805. The causes which induced him to accept a re-election, which resulted in a much greater majority than he had obtained on the first, are stated by Mr. Jefferson himself in the following letter to Mr. Gerry:

"I sincerely regret that the unbounded calumnies

of the Federal party have obliged me to throw myself on the verdict of my country for trial, my great desire having been to retire at the end of the present term, to a life of tranquillity; and it was my decided purpose when I entered into office. They force my continuance. If we can keep the vessel of state as steadily in her course for another four years, my earthly purposes will be accomplished, and I shall be free to enjoy, as you are doing, my family, my farm, and my books." When it is considered that Mr. Jefferson was a zealous and primitive dissenter from the unlimited re-eligibility of the executive; and that he espoused with ardor short terms of office, and had originally intended to hold the office but four years, it must be deeply lamented that he suffered the clamor of enemies to divert him from establishing a precedent of so much vital consequence to the purity and duration of our free institutions. The reasons he adduces for this dereliction are such as might with equal force be alleged for a continuance in the office for life. How much of real glory he lost by missing this opportunity of putting the seal of sincerity and the test of consistency on his original professions, can only be estimated by a full and just consideration of the difficulty attending the sacrifice of ambition to principle; of resisting the temptation of personal vanity for the enduring future applause of mankind.

Devoted to science, and at all times intent on improvements in literature and knowledge, as well as politics and government, Mr. Jefferson now projected the expedition of Lewis and Clarke to the Columbia River, for the purpose of exploring and ascertaining the geography, natural history, climate, riches, resources, and peculiarities of the new purchase of the Territory of Louisiana.

It was at this period that Mr. Jefferson addressed a letter to the Emperor Alexander I. of Russia, in behalf of the principle of neutral rights, which he earnestly desired might be duly secured by the treaties which were about to be formed by Napoleon with the powers of Europe, at the general pacification which was then anticipated. In this remarkable letter, after speaking of his gratification at seeing advanced to the government of so extensive a portion of the earth, and at so early a period of his life, a sovereign whose ruling desire was the happiness of his people, and whose philanthropy was extended to "a distant and infant nation, unoffending in its course and unambitious in its views," he further compliments the emperor on his efforts toward the pacification of Europe, and reminds him of the common interest which the United States and the northern nations of Europe have in preserving neutral rights. He suggests that the emperor and Napoleon have it in their power, at the approaching pacification, to render eminent services to nations in general, by incorporating into the act of pacification a correct definition of the rights of neutrals on the high seas, and "that these rights thus defined could be enforced, if further sanction were necessary, by an exclusion of the nation violating them from all commerce with the rest."

"Having taken," he says, "no part in the past or existing troubles of Europe, we have no part to act on its pacification. But as principles may then be settled in which we have a deep interest, it is a great happiness for us that they are placed under the protection of an umpire, who, looking beyond the narrow bounds of an individual nation, will take under the cover of his equity the rights of the absent and unrepresented. It is only by a happy concurrence of good characters and good occasions, that a step can now and then be taken to advance the well-being of nations. If the present occasion be good, I am sure your majesty's character will not be wanting to avail the world of it. By monuments of such good offices may your life become an epoch in the history of the condition of men, and may He who called it into being, for the good of the human family, give it length of days and success, and have it always in his holy keeping."

This communication was addressed by Mr. Jefferson directly to the Autocrat, and not to his Minister of Foreign Affairs, through the American Secretary of State, as diplomatic usage would have required. In pursuing this course, the President designed to carry out and illustrate the supposed simplicity of republican forms, in every department of his administration, from the most dignified to the most minute.

CHAPTER XV.

THE CONSPIRACY OF AARON BURR—THE NATURE OF HIS ENTERPRISE—MR. RANDOLPH'S RESOLUTION IN CONGRESS—ARREST OF COL. BURR—INCIDENTS OF THE TRIAL—ELOQUENCE OF WM. WIRT—JEFFERSON'S PREJUDICES AGAINST BURR—THE EMBARGO LAW—MR. JEFFERSON'S LAST MESSAGE TO CONGRESS—ADDRESSES SENT TO MR. JEFFERSON ON HIS RETIRING—ADDRESS OF THE LEGISLATURE OF VIRGINIA—INAUGURATION OF MR. MADISON—MR. JEFFERSON'S FINAL RETURN TO MONTICELLO—HIS FEELINGS ON THIS OCCASION.

THE most important event connected with the second administration of Mr. Jefferson was the conspiracy and trial of Aaron Burr. This celebrated man had lost the confidence of the Democratic party which had previously placed him in the office of Vice-President, in consequence of his supposed intrigues with the Federalists. He endeavored to regain official rank and influence by obtaining the post of Governor of New York. In that State many of his former opponents among the Federalists, influenced by hatred to the administration of Jefferson, were disposed to give Burr their assistance. The latter would have been elected had it not been for the determined opposition of Alexander Hamilton, who regarded Burr as a dangerous and unscrupulous adventurer, and exerted himself to defeat him. The consequence of this opposition was the unfortunate duel, in which Hamilton became the victim of the insatiable vengeance of his foe. This deed forever blasted the prospects of Burr in New York, and compelled or induced him to turn his enterprising and crafty mind to the elaboration of other schemes of ambition and aggrandizement. Then it was that Burr formed his gigantic plans of conquest and glory in the far South-West. Then it was that he resolved to concentrate all his great powers on the establishment of a splendid empire, composed of the extreme southern territories of the United States, combined with a conquered portion of the ancient realms of Montezuma. Nor was Burr unfitted to the accomplishment of these lofty and aspiring aims. His military talents were of a high order, and he could lead his armed hosts to battle and direct their movements with the skill of a great commander. His talents for political intrigue were consummate and unrivaled; being the most crafty, skillful and far-reaching tactician in the country. As a conqueror, as a legislator, and as a ruler, Burr could boast no inconsiderable resemblance in the universality and extent of his talents, to Napoleon Bonaparte.

Burr's first object was the invasion of Mexico. A large part of his materials for this expedition he expected to obtain in the South-Western States and Territories. He found however that the attachment of the people there to the Union, could not be moved; and consequently he prepared to march first to Mexico, and achieve his first triumphs there. By this time the American government had obtained satisfactory information of the culpable nature of his movements; if not that they were treasonable, at least that they were illegal, as being of a warlike nature against a country with which the United States were then at peace. General Wilkinson was ordered immediately to proceed to New Orleans, and to take every possible means to defeat the expedition. On the 27th of November, Mr. Jefferson issued a proclamation cautioning all citizens against joining the enterprise; and orders were then issued to the United States troops, stationed at different points along the Ohio and Mississippi, to seize the boats and stores, and arrest the members of the expedition.

On the 16th of January Mr. Randolph moved in Congress that the President be called on to impart such information respecting Burr's movements as might then be in the possession of the government. On the 22d of that month the call of the resolution was complied with. He stated in substance that information had been received that some boats filled with adventurers, perhaps three or four hundred in number, had passed the Falls of the Ohio for the purpose of meeting the rendezvous appointed at the mouth of Cumberland River; that Burr himself had descended the Cumberland on the 22d of December with two boats; that General Wilkinson had made ample preparations to defend New Orleans, and that orders had been issued for the arrest of the chief conspirator.

In accordance with these orders, Dr. Bolman and Mr. Swartwout, two of Burr's principal aids, were arrested at New Orleans. On the 31st of December Burr himself passed Fort Massac with ten boats. But as he approached New Orleans he found the preparations made by General Wilkinson so extensive and efficient that he discovered the utter futility of his plans. He then proceeded to the Tombigbee, having landed with a single companion on the banks of the Mississippi on the 13th of January. His ultimate destination was then unknown; but he was detected and arrested by the emissaries of the government in February, 1807. He was immediately conveyed on horseback to Richmond, Virginia, to be tried by the Federal court, held by Chief Justice Marshal, assisted by Justice Griffin.

Burr reached Richmond on the 26th of March. The court admitted him to bail in the sum of ten thousand dollars, which was immediately entered for him by members of the Federal party. Mr. Hay prosecuted for the government, assisted by William Wirt. Able counsel represented the defendant, the chief of whom was the celebrated Luther Martin. It was on this memorable occasion that the stately, imposing, and resplendent eloquence of Wirt shone forth with unrivaled magnificence, in strains of power and pathos which will be admired, quoted, and read with rapture till the end of time. Even the stern and iron heart of Burr himself trembled, and his eagle eye quailed beneath the overwhelming torrent of scathing invective, argument, and declamation, with which that great orator and ornament of the American bar reviewed the events developed by his bold, ambitious, and desperate career.

After a trial of three weeks, and prodigious exertions of counsel on both sides, Burr was acquitted, on the ground that the offense, if any, had not been committed within the jurisdiction of the court. It was Mr. Jefferson's purpose to commence a second prosecution, in which the plea to the jurisdiction should be evaded and the charges tried entirely on the merits; but the purpose was afterward abandoned. Burr immediately sailed for England, where it was supposed he designed to obtain means for the purpose of carrying on his ambitious plans more successfully. In this purpose he signally failed; both in England and France he was reduced almost to the verge of starvation; and he ultimately returned to New York, a ruined and disgraced outcast.

The chief charge against Burr in his trial was that of treason against the United States. That Mr. Jefferson himself did not believe in the justice of this charge at the time it was made, is evident from the following letter to Mr. Bowdoin, dated April 2d, 1807:

"No better proof of the good faith of the United States could have been given, than the vigor with which we have acted, and the expense incurred, in suppressing the enterprise meditated lately by Burr, against Mexico. Although at first he proposed a separation of the western country, and on that ground received encouragement and aid from Yrujo, according to the usual spirit of his government toward us, yet he very early saw that the fidelity of the western country was not to be shaken, and *turned himself wholly toward Mexico.* And so popular is an enterprise on that country, in this, that we had only to lie still, and he would have had followers enough to have been in the city of Mexico in six weeks."

Mr. Jefferson evidently hated Burr personally,

for in a letter to Mr. Hay, the prosecuting officer, he terms him "an impudent, Federal bull-dog." Jefferson also became highly incensed against Chief Justice Marshall, whom he falsely and basely charged with endeavoring to protect and shield the defendant.

The effects of the Berlin and Milan Decrees of Napoleon, and of the Orders in Council on the part of England, now began to be felt as serious aggressions on the commerce and revenue of the United States. The licentious and preposterous doctrines of blockade, proclaimed by France, and the retaliation of so monstrous a violation of the laws of nations by England, soon inflicted the most fatal wounds upon neutral commerce, insulting and degrading to the national character, at the same time that it cut up its resources, plundered its wealth, and mutilated its marine. Impressment was added to robbery and confiscation, our flag being unable to protect the persons of our citizens from the power of insolent England, or secure their property from the rapacity of libertine France, Unhappily for this country and its national character, the feuds engendered by the collisions between those two countries among our citizens, during the French revolution, had enlisted the Democratic and Federal parties under the banners of the two European belligerents.

It was known that Mr. Jefferson was partial to France and hated England; and as he always preferred peace to war, a disposition to negotiate for a redress of wrongs of this heinous character, was construed by some into a pusillanimous submission to the despotism of France; and by the adverse party, into a degrading acquiescence in the wrongs of England. The Democrats called for a war with Great Britain; the Federalists, and those who opposed French tyranny, demanded war against France. Mr. Jefferson desired peace, and disregarding the clamors of both, proceeded to negotiation. In a letter to Lafayette in 1807, he thus pictures our distressful and embarrassing situation:—

"I enclose you a proclamation, which will show you the critical footing on which we stand at present with England. Never since the battle of Lexington, have I seen this country in such a state of of exasperation as at present. And even that did not produce such unanimity. The Federalists themselves coalesce with us as to the object, although they will return to their old trade of condemning every step we take toward obtaining it. 'Reparation for the past, and security for the future,' is our motto. Whether these will be yielded freely, or will require resort to non-intercourse, or to war, is yet to be seen. We have actually near two thousand men in the field, covering the exposed parts of the coast, and cutting off supplies from the British vessels."

The attack made on the frigate Chesapeake by the British admiral, and the Order of the British Council prohibiting all commerce between America and the ports of her enemies in Europe, unless their cargoes were first landed in England and duties there paid on re-exportation, which threatened the total ruin of American commerce, induced Mr. Jefferson to recommend an embargo law. This law was passed by Congress on the 22d of December, 1807.

This was the last important act of Mr. Jefferson's political life. His administration was now drawing to a close, after forty years of public service, and twenty of party turmoil. He had now attained the age of sixty-five, and if the enjoyment of power had not produced satiety, the charms of retirement must at least have promised the delight of novelty. His annual message to Congress this year, 1808, spoke of this event in a strain of unaffected modesty, dignified feeling, and patriotic eloquence, every way creditable to his head and heart. "Availing myself of this, the last occasion which will occur of addressing the two houses of the legislature at their meeting, I cannot omit the expression of my sincere gratitude for the repeated proofs of confidence manifested to me by themselves and their predecessors, since my call to the administration, and the many indulgences experienced at their hands. The same grateful acknowledgments are due to my fellow-citizens generally, whose support has been my great encouragement under all embarrassments. In the transaction of their businesss I cannot have escaped error—it is incident to our imperfect nature. But I may say with truth my errors have been of the understanding, not of intention, and that the advancement of their rights and interests has been the constant motive for every measure. On these considerations I solicit their indulgence. Looking forward with anxiety to their future destinies, I trust, that in their steady character, unshaken by difficulties, in their love of liberty, obedience to law, and support of public authorities, I see a sure guarantee of the permanence of our republic; and retiring from the charge of their affairs, I carry with me the consolation of a firm persuasion, that Heaven has in store for our beloved country, long ages to come of prosperity and happiness."

It was on the 7th of November that Mr. Jefferson sent in to Congress his last annual address, containing many items of interest connected with the state of the country, and the past measures of his administration. Among other statements he informs them that the yearly receipts of the Treasury were then eighteen millions of dollars; that two millions and a half of the national debt had been discharged; and that nearly fourteen millions remained as surplus in the treasury. During the six years preceding, thirty millions of the national debt had been liquidated.

At the general election in October, James Madison had been chosen as the successor of Mr. Jefferson. At the expiration of the term of the latter, he received addresses of esteem and respect from the legislatures of Vermont, New Jersey, Pennsylvania, Maryland, Georgia, New York and Virginia. The address of the legislature of Virginia proceeded from the polished pen of William Wirt; and was couched in the following language

"SIR: The General Assembly of your native State cannot close their session without acknowledging your services in the office which you are just about to lay down, and bidding you a respectful and affectionate farewell.

"We have to thank you for the model of an administration conducted on the purest principles of republicanism; for pomp and state laid aside; patronage discarded; internal taxes abolished; a host of superfluous officers disbanded; the monarchic maxim that 'a national debt is a national blessing,' renounced, and more than thirty-three millions of our debt discharged; the native right to near one hundred millions of acres of our national domain extinguished; and without the guilt or calamities of conquest, a vast and fertile region added to our country, far more extensive than her original possessions, bringing along with it the Mississippi and the port of Orleans, the trade of the West to the Pacific Ocean, and in the intrinsic value of the land itself, a source of permanent and almost inexhaustible revenue. These are points in your administration which the historian will not fail to seize, to expand, and to teach posterity to dwell upon with delight. Nor will he forget our peace with the civilized world, preserved through a season of uncommon difficulty and trial; the good-will cultivated with the unfortunate aborigines of our country, and the civilization humanely extended among them; the lesson taught the inhabitants of the coast of Barbary, that we have the means of chastising their piratical encroachments, and awing them into justice; and that theme, which, above all others, the historic genius will hang upon with rapture, the liberty of speech and the press preserved inviolate, without which genius and science are given to man in vain.

"In the principles on which you have administered the government, we see only the continuation and the maturity of the same virtues and abilities which drew upon you in your youth the resentment of Dunmore. From the first brilliant and happy moment of your resistance to foreign tyranny until the present day, we mark with pleasure and with gratitude the same uniform and consistent character—the same warm and devoted attachment to liberty and the republic, the same Roman love of your country, her rights, her peace, her honor, her prosperity.

"How blessed will be the retirement into which you are about to go! How deservedly blessed will it be! For you carry with you the richest of all rewards, the recollection of a life well spent in the service of your country, and proofs the most decisive of the love, the gratitude, the veneration of your countrymen.

"That your retirement may be as happy as your life has been virtuous and useful; that our youth may see, in the blissful close of your days, an additional inducement to form themselves on your model, is the devout and earnest prayer of your fellow-citizens who compose the General Assembly of Virginia."

M.:. Jefferson's second term of office as President of the United States, terminated on March 4th, 1809. He remained to witness the inauguration of his successor, and sat on his right hand during the delivery of his address. Several days afterward he left Washington, and journeyed by slow and easy stages to Monticello, where he arrived in the middle of March. Thus after forty years of political turmoil, agitation and labor, this great statesman and politician retired at last to the quiet and seclusion of private life. His feelings on this occasion may be inferred from the following letter to M. Dupont de Nemours, in Paris:

"Within a few days I retire to my family, my books and farms; and having gained the harbor myself, I shall look on my friends still buffeting the storm, with anxiety, indeed, but not with envy. Never did a prisoner, released from his chains, feel such relief as I shall on shaking off the shackles of power. Nature intended me for the tranquil pursuits of science, by rendering them my supreme delight. But the enormities of the times in which I have lived, have forced me to take a part in resisting them, and to commit myself on the boisterous ocean of political passions. I thank God for the opportunity of retiring from them without censure, and carrying with me the most consoling proofs of public approbation."

He gives the following account of his journey:—

"I had a very fatiguing journey, having found the roads excessively bad, although I have seen them worse. The last three days I found it better to be on horseback, and traveled eight hours through as disagreeable a snow-storm as I was ever in. Feeling no inconvenience from the expedition but fatigue, I have more confidence in my *vis vitæ* than I had before entertained. The spring is remarkably backward."

Having been welcomed home by the citizens of his county, he addressed them in the following strain of attachment and affection:—

"Returning to the scenes of my birth and early life, to the society of those with whom I was raised, and who have been ever dear to me, I receive, fellow-citizens and neighbors, with inexpressible pleasure, the cordial welcome you are so good as to give me. Long absent on duties which the history of a wonderful era made incumbent on those called to them, the pomp, the turmoil, the bustle and splendor of office, have drawn but deeper sighs for the tranquil and irresponsible occupations of private life, for the enjoyment of an affectionate intercourse with you, my neighbors and friends; and the endearments of family love, which nature has given us all, as the sweetener of every hour. For these I gladly lay down the distressing burden of power, and seek, with my fellow-citizens, repose and safety under the watchful cares, the labors and perplexities of younger and abler minds. The anxieties you express to administer to my happiness, do, of themselves, confer that happiness; and the measure will be complete, if my endeavors to fulfill my duties in the several public stations to which I have been called, have obtained for me the approbation of my country. The part which I have acted on the theatre of public life, has been before them; and to their sentence I submit it: but the testimony of my native county, of the individuals who have known me in private life, to my conduct in its various duties and relations, is the more grateful, as proceeding from eye-witnesses and observers—from triers of the vicinage. Of you, then, my neighbors, I may ask in the face of the world, 'Whose ox have I taken, or whom have I defrauded? Whom have I oppressed, or of whose hand have I received a bribe to blind mine eyes therewith?' On your verdict I rest with conscious security. Your wishes for my happiness are received with just sensibility, and I offer sincere prayers for your own welfare and prosperity."

CHAPTER XVI.

MR. JEFFERSON'S HABITS OF LIFE IN HIS RETIREMENT—INCIDENTS OF HIS RESIDENCE AT MONTICELLO—THE MECKLENBURG DECLARATION OF INDEPENDENCE—MR. JEFFERSON'S PECUNIARY DIFFICULTIES—THE PLAN OF A LOTTERY—PUBLIC CONTRIBUTIONS TO HIS RELIEF—HIS LAST SICKNESS—HIS DEATH—ESTIMATE OF HIS CHARACTER—HIS RELIGIOUS OPINIONS—DEFECTS OF HIS CHARACTER—HIS WANT OF SINCERITY AND TRUTHFULNESS—HIS FALSE CHARGES AGAINST MR. HAMILTON—EVIDENCE OF THEIR FALSEHOOD—HIS SECRET OPPOSITION TO THE FEDERAL CONSTITUTION—NOVEL AND ABSURD GROUNDS OF HIS OPPOSITION—CHIEF DIFFERENCE BETWEEN JEFFERSON AND HAMILTON—CONCLUSION.

MR. JEFFERSON was sixty-six years of age when he retired, for the last time, from public life to the quietude and seclusion of his estate at Monticello. His property consisted of nearly seven thousand acres of land, and was worked by a hundred and thirteen slaves. He also possessed four thousand acres at Poplar Forest, on which there were eighty-five slaves. But although he was a large landed proprietor, his estates were not very productive; and the profuse hospitality which during many years he exercised at Monticello, very perceptibly diminished his resources from year to year. He had also a passion for building; and being deprived of the income which for eight years he had been in the habit of receiving as President, he gradually became involved in pecuniary difficulties. He thus describes his avocations in a letter of this date, to his illustrious friend Koskiusco:

"In the bosom of my family, and surrounded by my books, I enjoy a repose to which I have been long a stranger. My mornings are devoted to correspondence. From breakfast to dinner I am in my shops, my garden, or on horseback among my farms; from dinner to dark I give to society and recreation with my neighbors and friends; and from candle light to early bedtime I read. My health is perfect, and my strength considerably reinforced by the activity of the course I pursue; perhaps it is as great as usually falls to the lot of near sixty-seven years of age. I talk of plows and harrows, seeding and harvesting, with my neighbors, and of politics, too, if they choose, with as little reserve as the rest of my fellow-citizens, and feel at length the blessing of being free to say and do what I please, without being responsible for it to any mortal. A part of my occupation, and by no means the least pleasing, is the direction of the studies of such young men as ask it. They place themselves in the neighboring village, have the use of my library and counsel, and make a part of my society. In advising the course of their reading, I endeavor to keep their attention fixed on the main objects of all science, the freedom and happiness of man." He concludes by adverting to his pecuniary difficulties, and says he has to pass such a length of time in a thraldom of mind never before known to him. "But for this," he says, "his happiness would have been perfect." Among those who thus profited by his counsels in the way spoken of, were Mr. Rives, the late Minister to France, and Francis W. Gilmer, late Professor of Law in the University of Virginia.

His workshops were those of carpenters, blacksmiths, wheelwrights and nailsmiths. Mr. Jefferson was fond of exercising himself in mechanical employments. He had a small apartment adjoining his bed-room, in which there was a complete assortment of tools, in the use of which he had acquired much practical skill, and which at once enabled him to take exercise within doors, to find an agreeable relaxation for his mind, to repair any of his various instruments in physical science, and to execute any little scheme of the moment in the way of furniture or experiment. He had many very respectable workmen among his slaves, whose expertness had been greatly improved, both by his instructions and the diversified occupation which he afforded them. The carriage in which he ordinarily rode, his garden-seats, even some of his household furniture, were the joint work of himself and his slaves. His favorite exercise, however, was riding on horseback, and he never was unprovided with handsome horses. It was the only thing in which he was lavish of money for his exclusive gratification; and the four which he purchased for his carriage when he was elected President, cost him two thousand dollars.

Thus year after year of the retirement of this celebrated man glided quietly away; yet occasionally diversified by pleasing and novel incidents. One of these was the correspondence which took place between Mr. Jefferson and Mr. John Adams. Another was the epistolary intercourse which occurred between him and the illustrious Madame de Stael. His correspondence with Mr. Adams elicited new and strange information in reference to the Mecklenburg Declaration of Independence, from which it has been charged that Mr. Jefferson derived the chief ideas of his own draft of the American Declaration. This subject has been fiercely contested on both sides. The coincidences of expression between these two documents are so remarkable as to *justify* the full conviction, that the one was in a great measure derived from the other. That the reader may judge for himself on this subject, we here insert this rare and interesting document, as well as Mr. Adams' letter to Mr. Jefferson on the subject:

"*Quincy*, 22d of June, 1819.

"DEAR SIR: May I enclose you one of the greatest curiosities, and one of the deepest mysteries that ever occurred to me; it is in the *Essex Register* of June the 5th, 1819. It is entitled, from the *Raleigh Register*, 'Declaration of Independence.' How is it possible that this paper should have been concealed from me to this day! Had it been communicated to me in the time of it, I know, if you do not know, that it would have been printed in every whig newspaper upon the continent. You know that if I had possessed it, I would have made the Hall of Congress echo and re-echo with it fifteen months before your Declaration of Independence. What a poor, ignorant, malicious, short-sighted, crapulous mass is Tom Paine's Common Sense in comparison with this paper. Had I known it, I would have commented upon it from the day you entered Congress till the fourth of July, 1776.

"The genuine sense of America at that moment was never so well expressed before or since. Richard Caswell, William Hooper, and Joseph Hughes, the then representatives of North Carolina in Congress, you know as well as I; and you know that the unanimity of the States finally depended on the vote of Joseph Hewes, and was finally determined by him; and yet history is to ascribe the American Revolution to Thomas Paine. *Sat verbum sapienti.*

"I am, dear sir, your invariable friend," &c.

The Mecklenburg Declaration is as follows:

"May 20th, 1775. That whoever directly or indirectly abets, or in any way, form, or manner, countenances the unchartered and dangerous invasion of our rights, as claimed by Great Britain, is an enemy to this country, to America, and to the inherent and undeniable rights of man.

"That we, the citizens of Mecklenburg county, do hereby *dissolve the political bands which have connected us with the mother conntry*, and hereby *absolve ourselves from all allegiance to the British crown*, and abjure all *political connection*, contact or association with that nation, who have wantonly trampled on our rights and liberties, and inhumanly shed the blood of American patriots at Lexington.

"That we do hereby declare ourselves a free and independent people; *are, and of right ought to be*, a sovereign and self-governing association, under the control of no power, other than that of our God, and the general government of Congress; to the maintenance of which independence, we solemnly pledge to each other, our mutual co-operation, *our lives, our fortunes, and our most sacred honor.*

"That as we acknowledge the existence and control of no law nor legal officer, civil or military, within this county, we do hereby ordain and adopt as a rule of life, all, each, and every of our former laws; wherein, nevertheless, the crown of Great Britain never can be considered as holding rights, privileges, immunities, or authority therein.

"That it is further decreed, that all, each, and every military officer in this county, is hereby reinstated in his former command and authority, he acting conformably to the regulations. And that every member present of this delegation shall henceforth be a civil officer, viz. a justice of the peace, in the character of a committee man, to issue process, hear, and determine all matters of controversy, according to said adopted laws; and to preserve peace, union, and harmony in said county, and to use every exertion to spread the love of country and fire of freedom throughout America, until a more general and organized government be established in this province."

Another agreeable incident connected with these retired and unobtrusive years of Mr. Jefferson's life, was the visit which he received from General La Fayette, when making his tour through the United

States. There was the utmost cordiality between them while together; yet Mr. Jefferson, with his prevalent duplicity, speaks in a letter to Mr. Madison of La Fayette's "*canine thirst for popularity.*" How much real esteem and regard Mr. Jefferson could have entertained for a person of whom he speaks in such terms, it is not difficult to determine.

In 1824 Mr. Jefferson began to see his wishes and labors in reference to the University of Virginia approaching a successful termination. The buildings were very near their completion, and an able corps of professors had been procured. Mr. Jefferson was chosen President of the Board of Trustees, and he aided the new Institution with generous gifts of books, money, services and influence. He framed the laws for the government of the University. These laws he made entirely too democratic; and the consequence was that the students soon proved themselves utterly unfit for self-government, and their insubordination nearly brought the institution to the verge of ruin. Severe measures became necessary, and the ringleaders were expelled by the faculty, among whom was one of Mr. Jefferson's own nephews. The necessary amendments to the constitution and laws of the University were made; and subsequently greater rigor secured greater order and propriety of behavior.

The last event in the life of Mr. Jefferson which attracted public attention was one of a painful and distressing nature. Together with the failure of his health, and his sufferings from a chronic disease of the bladder, his pecuniary difficulties had been increasing for many years. His vast tracts of land had long been expensive and comparatively unprofitable. His debts had largely increased. He had been relieved, immediately after his retirement from the Presidency, by a loan of ten thousand dollars secured on his property. He realized in his experience the evils which attended the employment of overseers and slaves. The proceeds of his estates rarely covered the expenses. He was also so imprudent and unfortunate as to endorse for his friend, Governor Nicholas, to the amount of twenty thousand dollars; and for this sum, by the insolvency of Mr. Nicholas, he became responsible.

In order to relieve his pressing pecuniary difficulties, a plan was devised by his friends to obtain an act of the Legislature of Virginia, authorizing the disposal of a part of his property by lottery. He himself prepared a petition to that effect, to be presented to that body. The legislature acquiesced, and passed the act; but the enemies of Mr. Jefferson embraced the opportunity to utter the most severe and sarcastic strictures upon him. He thus writes to Mr. Madison in reference to the subject in February, 1826.

"You will have seen in the newspapers some proceedings in the legislature, which have cost me much mortification. My own debts had become considerable, but not beyond the effect of some lopping off of property, which would have been little felt, when our friend Nicholas gave me the *coup de grace.* Ever since that, I have been paying twelve hundred dollars a year interest on his debt, which, with my own, was absorbing so much of my annual income, as that the maintenance of my family was making deep and rapid inroads on my capital, and had already done it. Still, sales at a fair price, would leave me competently provided. Had crops and prices, for several years, been such as to maintain a steady competition of substantial bidders at market, all would have been safe. But the long succession of years of stunted crops, of reduced prices, the general prostration of the farming business, under levies for the support of manufacturers, &c., with the calamitous fluctuations of value in our paper medium, have kept agriculture in a state of abject depression, which has peopled the western States by silently breaking up those on the Atlantic, and glutted the land market, while it drew off its bidders. In such a state of things, property has lost its character of being a resource for debts.

High land in Bedford, which, in the days of our plethory, sold readily for from fifty to one hundred dollars the acre, (and such sales were many then,) would not now sell for more than from ten to twenty dollars, or one quarter or one fifth of its former price. Reflecting on these things, the practice occurred to me of selling, on fair valuation, and by way of lottery, often resorted to before the Revolution, to effect large sales, and still in constant usage in every State, for individual as well as corporation purposes. If it is permitted in my case, my lands here alone, with the mills, &c., will pay every thing, and leave me Monticello and a farm free. If refused, I must sell every thing here, perhaps considerably in Bedford, move thither with my family, where I have not even a log-hut to put my head into, and whether ground for burial will depend on the depredations which, under the form of sales, shall have been committed on my property. The question then with me was, *ultrum horum?*"

In conclusion he makes the following pathetic appeal:

"But why afflict you with these details? Indeed, I cannot tell, unless pains are lessened by communication with a friend. The friendship which has subsisted between us, now half a century, and the harmony of our political principles and pursuits, have been sources of constant happiness to me through that long period. And if I remove beyond the reach of attention to the university, or beyond the bourne of life itself, as I soon must, it is a comfort to leave that institution under your care, and an assurance that it will not be wanting. It has also been a great solace to me, to believe that you are engaged in vindicating to posterity the course we have pursued for preserving to them, in all their purity, the blessings of self-government, which we had assisted, too, in acquiring for them. If ever the earth has beheld a system of administration conducted with a single and steadfast eye to the general interest and happiness of those committed to it, one which, protected by truth, can never know reproach, it is that to which our lives have been devoted. To myself you have been a pillar of support through life. Take care of me when dead, and be assured that I shall leave with you my last affections."

Mr. Jefferson's Memorial to the Legislature attracted public attention to his difficulties, and various plans were suggested for his relief. It was thought desirable by his friends that his property and his mansion, to which he had given celebrity, should remain in his possession; and to secure this end it was proposed to suspend the proceedings in relation to the lottery, and commence a subscription throughout the United States, for the purpose of collecting a hundred thousand dollars—the sum which his exigencies demanded. Nearly nine thousand were raised in New York, five thousand in Philadelphia, three thousand in Baltimore, and smaller sums elsewhere throughout the country. The whole amounted to eighteen thousand dollars; but the progress of the contributions was stopped by Mr. Jefferson's last illness and death.

During the month of June, 1826, he suffered severely from an attack of dysentery, which became worse from day to day. On the first of July he was confined to his bed. He was attended by Dr. Dunglison, who felt convinced that the attack would prove fatal. During his last illness, a visitor was announced. Mr. Jefferson supposed that it was a clergyman of Charlottesville, Mr. Hatch, whose name had been mentioned. Under this impression, Mr. Jefferson said: "Is that Mr. Hatch? He is a very good man, and I am glad to see him as a neighbor, but not as a clergyman." In truth, Mr. Jefferson declined all religious sympathy during his last hours, having long previously made up his mind in reference to those subjects, and not desiring his views in the midst of feebleness and suffering to be assailed and disturbed.

On the 3d of July, he continued to sink. Near the middle of the night he asked the hour; and on being told that it was near one o'clock, he expressed his joy. The spirit of the aged statesman yearned to survive, to see once more the anniversary of that glorious day, in whose immortal incidents, just half a century before, he himself had played so important and so honorable a part. At last about two o'clock on the morning of the fourth of July, while millions of freemen were exulting in the dawn of that welcome anniversary, the spirit of Thomas Jefferson quietly and calmly burst the bands which bound it to its earthly tenement, and sped away to other spheres. On the same day one of his most illustrious associates, rivals, and friends, paid the same great debt to nature, in a distant commonwealth. John Adams and Thomas Jefferson, both signers of the Declaration of Independence, and both Ex-Presidents of the United States, expired on the 4th of July, 1826. Mr. Jefferson was eighty-three years of age.

Mr. Jefferson's funeral was simple and unostenta tious. It took place on the afternoon of the day after his death. His remains were deposited in a small grave-yard on the side of the mountain at Monticello. A granite obelisk, eight feet high, marks the last resting-place of this celebrated man; and on it are inscribed the following words, which were found, in his own hand-writing, among his papers, and designated by himself as designed for his tomb:

HERE LIES BURIED
THOMAS JEFFERSON.
AUTHOR OF THE DECLARATION OF INDEPENDENCE,
OF THE STATUTE OF VIRGINIA FOR RELIGIOUS FREEDOM,
AND FATHER OF THE UNIVERSITY OF VIRGINIA.

The character and merits of Mr. Jefferson have long been the subject of violent controversy. By his admirers he has been elevated to the highest eminence in human virtue, while his opponents have gone to an equally absurd extreme. The truth is, that his character possessed many great merits and some great defects. He was, unquestionably, a man of a large, powerful, and capacious intellect. His views on every subject were marked by depth, sagacity, and originality. As a lawyer he was learned and acute. As a writer he was clear, strong, and convincing. He possessed little imagination, and little love or appreciation of the beautiful. He was very adroit in the management of men and parties. This is evinced by the success with which he attained all the various offices in the gift of the people. He began with the lowest, and ascended to the highest. First, he was a Justice of the Peace, then a Member of the Legislature, then Speaker of the House, then Governor of the State, then member of the Continental Congress, then Minister to France, then Secretary of State, then Vice-President, then President; and was then even re-elected, in spite of his own frequent protestations against the unrepublican tendency of long tenures of office. Mr. Jefferson was in truth the prince of American *politicians*, both in respect to the skill with which he managed party politics and party forces, and with respect to the success which attended his ambitious labors.

His services to his country, as long as they appertained to the establishment of her liberties and the formation of her government, were of the first order. As the author of the Declaration of Independence his name will live forever, and be associated with the brightest and noblest page of American history. His religious opinions and his views of Christianity will be best learned from his own language. Says he:

"I have to thank you for your pamphlets on the subjects of *Unitarianism*, and to express my gratification with your efforts for the revival of primitive Christianity in your quarter. No historical fact is better established than that the doctrine of one God, pure and uncompounded, was that of the early ages of Christianity; and was among the efficacious doctrines which gave it triumph over the Polytheism of the ancients, sickened with the absurdities of their own theology. Nor was the unity of the Supreme Being ousted from the Christian creed by the force of reason, but by the sword of civil government, wielded at the will of the fanatic Athanasius. The hocus-pocus phantasm of a God, like another Cerberus, with one body and three heads, had its birth and growth in the blood of thousands and thousands of martyrs. And a strong proof of the solidity of the primitive faith, is its restoration, as soon as a nation arises which vindicates to itself the freedom of religious opinion, and its external divorce from the civil authority. The pure and simple unity of the Creator of the universe is now all but ascendant in the Eastern States; it is dawning in the West, and advancing toward the South; and I confidently expect that the present generation will see Unitarianism become the general religion of the United States. The Eastern presses are giving us many excellent pieces on the subject; and Priestley's learned writings on it are, or should be, in every hand. In fact, the Athanasian paradox that one is three, and three but one, is so incomprehensible to the human mind, that no candid man can say he has any idea of it; and how can he believe what presents no idea? He who thinks he does, only deceives himself. He proves, also, that man once surrendering his reason, has no remaining guard against absurdities the most monstrous, and, like a ship without a rudder, is the sport of every wind. With such persons, gullability, which they call faith, takes the helm from the hand of reason, and the mind becomes a wreck." In another place he says:—"The doctrines of Jesus are simple, and tend all to the happiness of man.

"1. That there is one only God, and he all perfect.

"2. That there is a future state of rewards and punishments.

"3. That to love God with all thy heart, and thy neighbor as thyself, is the sum of religion. These are the great points on which he endeavored to reform the religion of the Jews." He then compares these with the doctrines of Calvin, and adds: "Now, which of these is the true and charitable Christian? He who believes and acts on the simple doctrines of Jesus, or the impious dogmatists, as Athanasius and Calvin? Verily, I say these are the false shepherds foretold us to enter not by the door into the sheepfold, but to climb up some other way. They are mere usurpers of the Christian name, teaching a counter religion made up of the *deleria* of crazy imaginations, as foreign from Christianity as is that of Mahomet. Their blasphemies have driven thinking men into infidelity, who have too hastily rejected the supposed author himself, with the horrors so falsely imputed him. Had the doctrines of Jesus been preached always as pure as they came from his lips, the whole civilized world would now have been Christians. I rejoice that in this blessed country of free inquiry and belief, which has surrendered its creed and conscience to neither kings nor priests, the genuine doctrine of one only God is reviving, and I trust that there is not a young man now living in the United States who will not die a Unitarian."

The chief defect in the character of Mr. Jefferson, was his want of sincerity and truthfulness. This charge may be substantiated by many unanswerable proofs. Thus for instance he proclaimed himself the advocate of popular rights; he defended the dignity, purity, and honesty of the masses; and pretended that they were more worthy of confidence, and were safer depositaries of power, than the higher and more exclusive ranks. Yet in spite of these declarations, Mr. Jefferson was in reality the most aristocratic of men. In his heart he despised the multitude; he placed no confidence in their judgment; and held both them and their character in contempt. As an evidence of this we may adduce the following extract from a letter addressed to one of his most intimate friends:

"The *Political Progress* is a work of value, and of a singular complexion. The author's eye seems to be a natural achromatic, divesting every object of the glare of color. The former work of the same title possessed the same kind of merit. They disgust one, indeed, by opening to his view the ulcerated state of the human mind. But to cure an ulcer, you must go to the bottom of it, which no author does more radically than this. The reflections into which it leads us are not very flattering to the human species. In the whole animal kingdom, I recollect no family but man, steadily and systematically employed in the destruction of itself. Nor does what is called civilization produce any other effect than to teach him to pursue the principle of the *bellum omnium in omnia*, on a greater scale, and, instead of the little contests between tribe and tribe, to comprehend all the quarters of the earth in the same work of destruction. If to this we add, that as to other animals, the lions and tigers are mere lambs compared with man as a destroyer, we must conclude that Nature has been able to find in man alone a sufficient barrier against the too great multiplication of other animals, and of man himself, an equilibrating power against the fecundity of generation. While in making these observations, my situation points my attention to the welfare of man in the physical world, yours may perhaps present him as equally warring in the moral one."

The utter inconsistency of these sentiments with those more publicly professed by the great apostle of popular infallibility, justice, and humanity, will clearly appear to every impartial reader.

But it was when the personal feelings of Mr. Jefferson were enlisted against any of his associates and rivals, that his statements in reference to them, their character and measures were the most unfair and untrue. There are many instances of these mistatements in existence, which clearly prove that, from the nature of the case, he must have been fully aware of the falsity of his assertions. Perhaps the most remarkable examples of this description are to be found in his declarations against the man whom of all others he most sincerely hated, and whom he most bitterly reviled. This was Alexander Hamilton, the illustrious and powerful head of the Federal party

Thus Mr. Jefferson asserted in the most distinct and authoritative manner, without adducing any proof whatever of the truth of the charge, that Hamilton considered a public debt as a public blessing; and in a letter to Gen Washington, dated 9th September, 1792, ("Writings of Washington," by Sparks, Vol. x., p. 17, Appendix,) he says: "My whole correspondence while in France, and every word, and letter, and act on the subject since my return, prove that no man is more ardently intent to see the public debt soon and sacredly paid off than I am. This exactly marks the difference between Colonel Hamilton's views and mine, that I wish the debt paid off to-morrow; *he wishes it never to be paid, but always to be a thing wherewith to corrupt and manage the legislature.*"

Here is a distinct and positive charge of the most serious character; and it is to be regretted that such is the propensity of mankind to believe injurious imputations without asking for their proof, that it is very generally believed and very frequently alleged, even until this day. The evidence that this charge was wholly unfounded, and that Mr. Jefferson knew it to be so when he made it, is as follows: Mr. Hamilton, in his "Report on Public Credit," dated January 9, 1790, (Vol. 3, "Hamilton's Works," p. 40,) proposes that "reserving out of the residue of those duties, &c., the surplus, together with the product of other duties, be applied to the payment of the interest on the new loan by an appropriation co-extensive with the duration of the debt." On page 41 he says: "Persuaded as the Secretary is, that the proper funding of the present debt will render it a public blessing, yet he is so far from acceding to the position in the latitude in which it is sometimes laid down, that 'public debts are public blessings'—a position inviting to prodigality, and liable to dangerous abuse—that he ardently wishes to see it incorporared as a fundamental maxim in the system of public credit of the United States, that the creation of debt should always be accompanied with the means of its extinguishment. This he regards as the true secret of rendering public credit immortal." He then proceeds to propose that certain revenues "shall be appropriated to continue so vested until the whole debt shall be discharged.'

This Report, which was published and commented upon throughout the United States, must have been read by Mr. Jefferson; and as it was long anterior to the date of the letter referred to, it may be safely asserted that he knew such to be the principle of the measures of financial administration constantly recommended by Hamilton.

In further proof of the falsehood of this charge see "Hamilton's Report on Estimates," dated August 5, 1790. It will be found there that he urges that a surplus in the treasury of one million should be applied to the payment of the public debts. In his

Report on Manufactures, dated December 5, 1791, he says: "And as the vicissitudes of nations beget a perpetual tendency to the accumulation of debt, there ought to be, in every government, a perpetual, anxious, and unceasing effort to reduce that which at any time exists as fast as practicable, consistently with integrity and good faith." This most urgent admonition was published long before the date of Mr. Jefferson's letter.*

Another evidence of the insincerity of Mr. Jefferson was the fact that, while he pretended to approve of the Federal Constitution, he was in reality opposed to it. Thus he writes in a letter to John Adams, November 18, 1787: "How do you like our new Constitution? I confess there are things in it, which stagger all my dispositions to subscribe to what such an assembly had proposed. * * * Indeed I think all the good in this new Constitution might have been couched in three or four new articles to be added to the good, old and venerable fabric, which should have been preserved, even as a religious relic."

* See Hamilton's "Report on the public debt," dated November 30, 1792, pp. 338, 339; and at p. 346, referring to the proceeds of the public debt, Hamilton says: "Whenever they can be brought into public use, their action will be important aid, materially accelerating the ultimate redemption of the entire debt."

And again he says to A. Donald, February 7th, 1788: "I wish with all my soul that the nine first conventions may accept the Constitution, because this will secure to us the good it contains, which I think great and important. But I equally wish that the four latest conventions, whichever they be, may refuse to execute it, till a Declaration of Rights be annexed." The reason of this wish was because the first clause of Article 7th of the Constitution provided that "the ratification of the conventions of nine States shall be sufficient for the establishment of this Constitution *between the States so ratifying the same.*"

The whole number was thirteen. Jefferson wished that nine should ratify, and that five should refuse. This would have included New York as refusing; and thus he proposed to postpone the Union, and run the risk of establishing separate confederacies!

Elsewhere in his private correspondence, Mr. Jefferson may be said to have objected to the Federal Constitution on another ground, and one in the highest degree novel and singular. It was on the general principle asserted in a letter to James Madison, dated September 6, 1789, at Paris. "The question whether one generation of men has a right to bind another, seems never to have been started either on this side or our side of the water. Yet it is a question of such consequence as not only to merit discussion, but place also among the fundamental principles of every government. The course of reflection in which we are immersed here, on the elementary principles of society, has presented this question to my mind, and that no such obligation can be transmitted, *I think very capable of proof.*"

Mr. Jefferson arrives at this conclusion: "That neither the representatives of a nation, nor the whole nation itself assembled, can validly engage debts beyond what they may pay in their own time; that is to say within thirty-four years from the date of the engagement."

He concludes his course of reasoning thus: "That no society can make a *perpetual constitution*, or even a perpetual law." Consequently all constitutions must be adopted or renewed every thirty-five years; and if not, it follows that the society goes into a state of anarchy and dissolution. These are the sober and deliberately expressed opinions of this wise and practical statesman!

Additional proofs of the falsity of many of Mr. Jefferson's statements, in reference to his political and personal enemies, may be found in a work published in 1832, by Henry Lee of Virginia, in which that writer clearly exposes the error of many of Mr. Jefferson's declarations in reference to Gen.

Henry Lee, of the Revolution, as contained in his published Memoirs, his Anas, and his correspondence. For the remarkable and unanswerable evidences, contained in that work, of the unfounded and calumnious assertions of Mr. Jefferson on many subjects, we refer the reader to its pages.*

Yet nothing human is perfect; and no inconsiderable excuse may be found for this error of Mr. Jefferson in the fact, that he was himself fiercely persecuted, slandered, and misrepresented by many of his personal and political opponents; and that his severest strictures were but retaliations on them of the wrongs and the injustice which he supposed them to have inflicted on himself. Whatever may be his relative merit and demerit, it is certain that, as long as the American confederacy shall survive the shocks of time, and as it grows greater and more powerful, the name and the services of Thomas Jefferson will continue to live fresh and fadeless in the memories and the gratitude of millions of prosperous and intelligent freemen!

The chief difference between the political opinions of Jefferson and Hamilton—the great Democrat

* See "Observations on the writings of Thomas Jefferson; with particular reference to the attack they contain on the Memory of the late General Henry Lee, by H. Lee, of Virginia. New York. Published by Charles de Behr. 1832." See particularly pp. 41, 45, 51, 107, and 201

and the great Federalist of American history—may be thus briefly stated: In establishing the form of government, and in administering it, these statesmen were guided by principles as opposite as the poles. Hamilton preferred practice to theory; that is, he thought it wiser to adopt those elements of the British government which, while they accorded with the spirit of true liberty, possessed the additional advantage of the prosperous and favorable experience of the past in their support. Mr. Jefferson, on the contrary, discarded every thing which had appertained to European governments, and insisted on carrying out a full and independent theory of his own, which embodied his whole conception of what a free, popular, and democratic government should be. Mr. Hamilton wished to leave room for future legislation, adapted to the developing wants and resources of the country. Mr. Jefferson insisted upon realizing at once and immediately his ideal of a free government, whether that ideal proved in itself practicable and beneficial or not. Mr. Hamilton looked partly to the past for guidance. Mr. Jefferson regarded all the past as wrong, as perversion, as injustice and outrage upon the rights of man, and looked only to the future. Hamilton was cautious of losing all by grasping too much. Jefferson wished to realize his full rights at the outset, forgetful of the wise maxim, that nothing human is at the same time both begun and perfected. Hamilton was conservative; Jefferson was radical. Hamilton penned the Constitution, Jefferson interpreted it; just as Homer wrote the Iliad, and Aristotle afterward inferred from its matchless numbers the great rules and canons of poetical composition. But whether Hamilton or Jefferson understood the Constitution best, may be as readily determined as the question, who was the greater poet, the author or the critic of the Iliad.

APPENDIX.

No. I.

A DECLARATION BY THE REPRESENTATIVES OF THE UNITED STATES OF AMERICA, IN GENERAL CONGRESS ASSEMBLED, AS FIRST WRITTEN AND AFTERWARD AMENDED.*

When, in the course of human events, it becomes necessary for one people to dissolve the political bands which have connected them with another, and to assume among the powers of the earth the separate and equal station to which the laws of nature and of nature's God entitle them, a decent respect to the opinions of mankind requires that they should declare the causes which impel them to the separation.

We hold these truths to be self-evident: that all men are created equal; that they are endowed by their Creator with (inherent and †) inalienable rights; that among these are life, liberty, and the pursuit of happiness; that to secure these rights, governments are instituted among men, deriving their just powers from the consent of the governed; that whenever any form of government becomes destructive of these ends, it is the right of the people to alter or abolish it, and to institute new government, laying its foundation on such principles, and organizing its powers in such form,

* The parts struck out are enclosed in brackets. The additions are placed in foot-notes.

† Certain inalienable rights.

as to them shall seem most likely to effect their safety and happiness. Prudence, indeed, will dictate that governments long established should not be changed for light and transient causes; and accordingly all experience hath shown that mankind are more disposed to suffer while evils are sufferable, than to right themselves by abolishing the forms to which they are accustomed. But when a long train of abuses and usurpations [begun at a distinguished period and] pursuing invariably the same object, evinces a design to reduce them under absolute despotism, it is their right, it is their duty to throw off such government, and to provide new guards for their future security. Such has been the patient sufferance of these colonies; and such is now the necessity which constrains them to [expunge*] their former systems of government. The history of the present king of Great Britain is a history of [unremitting†] injuries and usurpations, [among which appears no solitary fact to contradict the uniform tenor of the rest, but all have‡] in direct object the establishment of an absolute tyranny over these states. To prove this, let facts be submitted to a candid world [for the truth of which we pledge a faith yet unsullied by falsehood.]

He has refused his assent to laws the most wholesome and necessary for the public good.

He has forbidden his governors to pass laws of immediate and pressing importance, unless suspended in their operation till his assent should be obtained; and, when so suspended, he has utterly neglected to attend to them.

He has refused to pass other laws for the accommodation of large districts of people, unless those people would relinquish the right of representation in the legislature, a right inestimable to them, and formidable to tyrants only

* Alter. † Repeated injuries. ‡ All having in direct object.

He has called together legislative bodies at places unusual, uncomfortable, and distant from the depository of their public records, for the sole purpose of fatiguing them into compliance with his measures.

He has dissolved representative houses repeatedly [and continually] for opposing with manly firmness his invasions on the rights of the people.

He has refused for a long time, after such dissolutions, to cause others to be elected, whereby the legislative powers, incapable of annihilation, have returned to the people at large for their exercise, the state remaining, in the mean time, exposed to all the dangers of invasion from without and convulsions within

He has endeavored to prevent the population of these states; for that purpose obstructing the laws for naturalization of foreigners, refusing to pass others to encourage their migrations hither, and raising the conditions of new appropriations of lands.

He has [suffered*] the administration of justice [totally to cease in some of these states†] refusing his assent to laws for establishing judiciary powers.

He has made [our] judges dependent on his will alone for the tenure of their offices, and the amount and payment of their salaries.

He has erected a multitude of new offices, [by a self-assumed power] and sent hither swarms of new officers to harass our people and eat out their substance.

He has kept among us in times of peace standing armies [and ships of war] without the consent of our legislatures.

He has affected to render the military independent of, and superior to, the civil power.

He has combined with others to subject us to a jurisdic

* Obstructed. † By refusing his assent to laws.

tion foreign to our constitutions and unacknowledged by our laws, giving his assent to their acts of pretended legislation for quartering large bodies of armed troops among us; for protecting them by a mock trial from punishment for any murders which they should commit on the inhabitants of these states; for cutting off our trade with all parts of the world; for imposing taxes on us without our consent; for depriving us* of the benefits of trial by jury; for transporting us beyond seas to be tried for pretended offenses; for abolishing the free system of English laws in a neighboring province, establishing therein an arbitrary government, and enlarging its boundaries, so as to render it at once an example and fit instrument for introducing the same absolute rule into these [states ;†] for taking away our charters, abolishing our most valuable laws, and altering fundamentally the forms of our governments; for suspending our own legislatures, and declaring themselves invested with power to legislate for us in all cases whatsoever.

He has abdicated government here [withdrawing his governors, and declaring us out of his allegiance and protection.‡]

He has plundered our seas, ravaged our coasts, burnt our towns, and destroyed the lives of our people.

He is at this time transporting large armies of foreign mercenaries to complete the works of death, desolation, and tyranny, already begun with circumstances of cruelty and perfidy § unworthy the head of a civilized nation.

He has constrained our fellow-citizens taken captive on the high seas to bear arms against their country, to become the executioners of their friends and brethren, or to fall themselves by their hands.

* In many cases. † Colonies

‡ By declaring us out of his protection and waging war against us.

§ Scarcely paralleled in the most barbarous ages and totally.

He has* endeavored to bring on the inhabitants of our frontiers the merciless Indian savages, whose known rule of warfare is an undistinguished destruction of all ages, sexes, and conditions [of existence].

[He has incited treasonable insurrections of our fellow-citizens, with the allurements of forfeiture and confiscation of our property.

He has waged cruel war against human nature itself, violating its most sacred rights of life and liberty in the persons of a distant people who never offended him, captivating and carrying them into slavery in another hemisphere, or to incur miserable death in their transportation thither. This piratical warfare, the opprobrium of infidel powers, is the warfare of the Christian king of Great Britain. Determined to keep open a market where men should be bought and sold, he has prostituted his negative for suppressing every legislative attempt to prohibit or to restrain this execrable commerce. And that this assemblage of horrors might want no fact of distinguished dye, he is now exciting those very people to raise in arms among us, and to purchase that liberty of which he has deprived them, by murdering the people on whom he also obtruded them: thus paying off former crimes committed against the liberties of one people, with crimes which he urges them to commit against the lives of another.]

In every stage of these oppressions we have petitioned for redress in the most humble terms; our repeated addresses have been answered only by repeated injuries.

A prince whose character is thus marked by every act which may define a tyrant is unfit to be the ruler of a† people [who mean to be free. Future ages will scarcely believe that the hardiness of one man adventured, within the short

* Excited domestic insurrections among us, and has

† Free.

compass of twelve years only, to lay a foundation so broad and so undisguised for tyranny over a people fostered and fixed in principles of freedom.]

Nor have we been wanting in attentions to our British brethren. We have warned them from time to time of attempts by their legislature to extend [a*] jurisdiction over [these our states.†] We have reminded them of the circumstances of our emigration and settlement here, [no one of which could warrant so strange a pretension; that these were effected at the expense of our own blood and treasure, unassisted by the wealth or the strength of Great Britain; that in constituting indeed our several forms of government, we had adopted one common king, thereby laying a foundation for perpetual league and amity with them; but that submission to their parliament was no part of our constitution, nor ever in idea, if history may be credited: and,] we‡ appealed to their native justice and magnanimity [as well as to§] the ties of our common kindred to disavow these usurpations which [were likely to ||] interrupt our connection and correspondence. They too have been deaf to the voice of justice and of consanguinity, [and when occasions have been given them, by the regular course of their laws, of removing from their councils the disturbers of our harmony, they have, by their free election, re-established them in power. At this very time too, they are permitting their chief magistrate to send over not only soldiers of our common blood, but Scotch and foreign mercenaries to invade and destroy us. These facts have given the last stab to agonizing affection, and manly spirit bids us to renounce forever these unfeeling brethren. We must endeavor to

* An unwarrantable jurisdiction. † Us. ‡ Have.

§ And we have conjured them by the ties.

|| Would inevitably interrupt.

forget our former love for them, and hold them as we hold the rest of mankind, enemies in war, in peace friends. We might have been a free and a great people together; but a communication of grandeur and of freedom, it seems, is below their dignity. Be it so, since they will have it. The road to happiness and to glory is open to us too. We will tread it apart from them, and*] acquiesce in the necessity which denounces our (eternal) separation! †

We, therefore, the representatives of the United States of America in General Congress assembled, do in the name, and by the authority of the good people of these [states, reject and renounce all allegiance and subjection to the kings of Great Britain and all others who may hereafter claim by, through, or under them; we utterly dissolve all political connection which may heretofore have subsisted between us and the people or parliament of Great Britain; and finally we do assert and declare these colonies to be free and independent states,] and that as free and independent states, they have full power to levy war, conclude peace, contract alliances, establish commerce, and to do all other acts and things which independent states may of right do.‡

* We must therefore acquiesce.

† And hold them as we hold the rest of mankind, enemies in war, in peace friends.

‡ We, therefore, the representatives of the United States of America in General Congress assembled, appealing to the supreme Judge of the world for the rectitude of our intentions, do in the name and by the authority of the good people of these colonies, solemnly publish and declare that these united colonies are, and of right ought to be, free and independent states; that they are absolved from all allegiance to the British crown, and that all political connection between them and the state of Great Britain is, and ought to be, totally dissolved; and that, as free and independent states, they have full power to levy war, conclude peace, contract alliances, establish commerce, and to do all other acts and things which independent states may of right do.

And for the support of this declaration, we mutually pledge to each other our lives, our fortunes, and our sacred honor.*

No. II.

LETTERS OF JOHN RANDOLPH IN RELATION TO MR. JEFFERSON'S ELECTION TO THE PRESIDENCY.

Chamber of the House of Representatives,
Wednesday, February 11th, 1801.

Seven times we have ballotted—eight States for J.—six for B.—two, Maryland and Vermont, divided. Voted to postpone for an hour the process; now, half-past four, resumed—result the same.

The order against adjourning, made with a view to Mr. Nicholson, who was ill, has not operated. He left his sick bed—came through a snow storm—brought his bed, and has prevented the vote of Maryland from being given to Burr. Mail closing.

Yours with perfect love and esteem,

J. R., Jr.

Thursday morning, February 12th.

My Dear Sir:

We have just taken the n neteenth ballot. The result has invariably been eight States for J., six for B., two divided. We continue to ballot with the interval of an hour. The rule for making the sittings permanent seems

* And for the support of this declaration, with a firm reliance on the protection of Divine Providence, we mutually pledge to each other our lives, our fortunes, and our sacred honor.

now to be not so agreeable to our Federal gentlemen. No election will, in my opinion, take place. By special permission the mail will remain open until four o'clock. I will not close this letter until three. If there be a change I shall notify it, if not I shall add no more to the assurance of my entire affection.

JOHN RANDOLPH, JR.

Chamber of the House of Representatives,
February 14*th*, 1801.

After endeavoring to make the question before us depend upon physical construction, our opponents have begged for a dispensation from their own regulation, and without adjourning we have *postponed*, (like able casuists) from *day* to *day*, the ballotting. In half an hour we shall recommence the operation. The result is marked below.

We have ballotted thirty-one hours. Twelve o'clock, Saturday noon, eight for J., six for B., two divided. Again at one, not yet decided. Same result. Postponed till Monday twelve o'clock.

JOHN RANDOLPH, JR.

Chamber of the Representatives,
February 17*th*.

On the thirty-sixth ballot, there appeared, this day, ten States for Thomas Jefferson—four (New England) for A. Burr, and two blank ballots, (Delaware and South Carolina.) This was the second time that we ballotted to-day.

The four Burr-ites of Maryland, put blanks into the box of that State. The vote was, therefore, unanimous. Mr. Morris, of Vermont, left his seat, and the result was, therefore, Jeffersonian. Adieu, Tuesday, two o'clock, P. M.

J. R., JR.

I need not add that Mr. J. was declared duly elected.

No. III.

JEFERSON'S NOTE ON MR. BAYARD.

The following vindication of Mr. Jefferson for a note in in his *ana* concerning the late Mr. Bayard of Delaware, was written by Mr. Madison, and was first published in the National Gazette of February 5th, 1831:

25th January, 1831.

Mr. Editor: The National Gazette of January 1st, contained a publication, edited since in pamphlet form, from two sons of the late Mr. Bayard; its object being to vindicate the memory of their father against certain passages in the writings of Mr. Jefferson.

The filial anxiety which prompted the publication was natural and highly commendable. But it is to be regretted, that in performing that duty, they have done great injustice to the memory of Mr. Jefferson, by the hasty and limited views taken of the evidence deducible from the sources to which they had appealed.

The first passage on which they found their charges is in the following words:

"*February* 12, 1801.—Edward Livingston tells me, that Bayard applied, to-day or last night, to General Smith, and represented to him the expediency of coming over to the States who vote for Burr, that there was nothing in the way of appointment which he might not command, and particularly mentioned the Secretaryship of the Navy. Smith asked him if he was authorized to make the offer. He said he was authorized. Smith told this to Livingston, and to Wilson Carey Nicholas, who confirms it to me." [See Mr. Jefferson's Memoirs, Vol. IV. p. 515.]

From this statement it appears, that Mr. Jefferson was told by Mr. Livingston, that he had it from General Smith, that Mr. Bayard had applied to him [General Smith,] with an offer of a high appointment, if he would come over from the Jefferson party, and join that of the rival candidate for the presidency. It appears that this information of Mr. Livingston was confirmed to Mr. Jefferson by Mr. W. C. Nicholas, who also said he had it from General Smith. It appears that the communication thus made to Mr. Jefferson, was reduced by him to writing on the day on which it was made; and that the incident which was the subject of it, took place on the morning of the same day, or at furthest on the night before. It is found also, that what was in this case reduced to writing, made no part of what was first reduced to writing on the 15th of April, 1806, [see Vol. IV. p. 521] but that it was then expressly referred to, as having been reduced to writing at the time.

Opposed to this memorandum of Mr. Jefferson is first—the declaration of Mr. Livingston on the floor of the Senate of the United States, after a lapse of about twenty-nine years, "that as to the precise question put to him, [touching the application of Mr. Bayard to General Smith,] he must say that after having taxed his recollection, as far as it could go, on so remote a transaction, he had no remembrance of it;" implying that he might have had a conversation with Mr. Jefferson relating to the remote transaction, not within the scope of the precise question. Second—the declaration of General Smith in the same place, and after the same lapse of time, "that he had not the most distant recollection that Mr. Bayard had ever made such a proposition to him," adding, "that he never received from any man any such proposition"

On comparing these declarations, made after an interval of so many years, with the statement of Mr. Jefferson reduced to writing at the time, it is impossible to regard hem as proof, that communications were not made to him by Mr. Livingston and Mr. W. C. Nicholas, which he [Mr. Jefferson,] understood to import, that Mr. Bayard had made to General Smith the application as stated. And if Mr. Jefferson was under that impression, however erroneous it might be, his subsequent opinion and language in reference to Mr. Bayard, are at once accounted for, without any resort to the imputations in the publication.

That there has been great error somewhere is apparent; that respect for the several parties requires it to be viewed as involuntary, must be admitted; that being involuntary, it must have proceeded from misapprehensions or failures of memory; that there having been no interval for the failure of the memory of Mr. Jefferson, the error, if with him, must be ascribed to misapprehension. The resulting question therefore is, between the probability of misapprehensions by Mr. Jefferson of the statements made to him at the time by Mr. Livingston and Mr. Nicholas, and the probability of misapprehensions or failures of memory in some one or more of the other parties; and the decision of this question must be left to an unbiased and intelligent public.

The other passage is at page 521, Volume IV. of the Memoir, and is as follows, under date of April 15, 1806. Referring to a previous conversation with Colonel Burr, he says—

"I did not commit these things to writing at the time, but I do it now, because in a suit between him [Col. Burr] and Cheetham, he had a deposition of Mr. Bayard taken, which seems to have no relation to the suit, nor to any other object than to calumniate me. Bayard pretends to have addressed to me during the pending of the presidential election in February, 1801, through General Samuel Smith, certain conditions on which my election might be obtained, and that General Smith, after conversing with me, gave answers for me. This is absolutely false. No proposition of any kind was ever made to me on that occasion by General Smith, nor any answer authorized by me; and this fact General Smith affirms at this moment."

The reply given to this memorandum by the authors of the publication is a reference to the depositions of Mr. Bayard and General Smith, in the cause of Gillespie and Smith.

It appears that Mr. Jefferson, attending merely to the matter of Mr. Bayard's deposition, did not distinguish between the suit of Burr and Cheetham, and that of Gillespie and Smith; in the latter of which the deposition of General Smith as well as that of Mr. Bayard was taken.

The part of the deposition of Mr. Bayard referred to by Mr. Jefferson is as follows:

"I [Mr. Bayard] told him [General Smith] I should not be satisfied, nor agree to yield, till I had the assurance from Mr. Jefferson himself; but that if he, General Smith, would consult Mr. Jefferson, and bring the assurance from him, the election should be ended. The general made no difficulty in consulting Mr. Jefferson; and proposed giving me his answer the next morning. The next day upon our meeting, General Smith informed me that he had seen Mr. Jefferson and stated to him the points mentioned; and was authorized by him to say that they corresponded with his views and intentions; and that we [Mr. B., &c.] might confide in him accordingly. The opposition of Vermont, &c. &c. was immediately withdrawn, and Mr. Jefferson was made President by the vote of ten States."

Here it is explicitly stated, by the authority of General

Smith, that an assurance in the nature of a pledge was authorized by Mr. Jefferson to be given to Mr. Bayard, that he [Mr. Jefferson] would conform to the conditions on which his election was to be obtained.

The terms used by Mr. Jefferson in denouncing the fact deposed by Mr. Bayard are accounted for, by the odious light in which it presented itself, by his consciousness that he had never authorized it, by the impressions unfavorable to Mr. Bayard which had been made upon him, by the information, as he understood it, given him by Mr. Livingston and Mr. Nicholas; and especially by the denial of the fact by General Smith at the moment.

Certain it is, that there is a direct contrariety between the deposition of Mr. Bayard, and the memorandum of Mr. Jefferson, involving a question between General Smith and Mr. Bayard on the one hand, and between Mr. Jefferson and General Smith on the other.

That Mr. Bayard understood General Smith to have borne an authorized pledge from Mr. Jefferson, is attested by the fact that he proceeded forthwith to execute the purpose of which such a pledge was the condition.

Passing to the deposition of General Smith, given twelve days after that of Mr. Bayard, and on the same day on which the memorandum of Mr. Jefferson is dated, let it be seen what light is furnished by that document.

The assertion of Mr. Jefferson in the memorandum is, that no proposition was ever made to him on that occasion by General Smith, nor any answer authorized by him; and this fact General Smith affirms at this moment.

In accordance with this assertion of Mr. Jefferson, and confirmation by General Smith, is the passage in the deposition of General Smith which declares "that he knew of no bargains or agreements, which took place at the time of the ballotting;" and the other passage which states "that he [M. Jefferson] had told me [General Smith] that any opinion he should give at this time might be attributed to improper motives. That to me [General Smith] he had no hesitation in saying that as to the public debt, &c. &c. he had not changed his opinion, &c. &c." This was so far from authorizing any use of what he said that might be attributed to improper motives, that it was expressed as between themselves, and consequently with a view to guard against any such use.

The passage in the deposition of General Smith on which particular reliance seems to be placed, as contradicting the statements of Mr. Jefferson, is the following:

"He [Mr. Bayard] then stated that he had it in his power (and was so disposed) to terminate the election, but he wished information as to Mr. Jefferson's opinions on certain subjects, and mentioned (I think) the same three points already alluded to, as asked by Colonel Parker and General Drayton, [viz.: respecting the navy, commerce, and public debt,] and received from me the same answer in substance (if not in words) that I had given to General Drayton. He added a fourth, to wit: What would be Mr. Jefferson's conduct as to the public officers? He said he did not mean confidential officers, but by way of elucidating his question, he added, such as Mr. Latimer of Philadelphia, and Mr. M'Lane of Delaware. I answered that I never had heard Mr. Jefferson say any thing on that subject. He requested that I would inquire, and inform him the next day. I did so. And the next day (Saturday) told him that Mr. Jefferson had said that he did not think that such officers ought to be dismissed on political grounds only, except in cases where they had made improper use of their offices, to force the officers under them to vote contrary to their judgment. That as to Mr. M'Lane, he had already been spoken to in his behalf by Major Eccleston, and from the character given him by that gentleman, he considered him a meritorious officer; of course that he would not be displaced, or ought not to be displaced. I further added, that Mr. Bayard might rest assured (or words to that effect) that Mr. Jefferson would conduct as to those points, agreeably to the opinions I had stated as his. Mr. Bayard then said, we will give the vote on Monday, and we separated."

Here it is to be observed, that General Smith does not say that he had made any proposition to Mr. Jefferson, or that he should communicate to Mr. Bayard the conversation then held with Mr. Jefferson.

The expression having most the aspect of a pledge is, "he [Mr. Jefferson] considered him [Mr. M'Lane] a meritorious officer; of course that he would not be displaced, or ought not to be displaced, &c."

It cannot be denied that the phrase admits the construction that "of course, &c." was a continuation of what was said by Mr. Jefferson, not the inference of General Smith. But to construe the expression as conveying a pledge from Mr. Jefferson is forbidden—1. By the declaration of General Smith in the same deposition, "that he [General Smith] knew of no bargains or agreements which took place at the time of the ballotting;" 2. By the caution of Mr. Jefferson, as stated by General Smith, in expressing even his opinions at a time when they might be attributed to improper motives; 3. By the confirmation given by General Smith to Mr. Jefferson's denial of the fact, that any proposition of any kind was ever made to him on any occasion by General Smith, or any answer authorized by him [Mr. Jefferson].

It is true that Mr. Bayard, as already observed, must have understood General Smith in this conversation as meaning that he was authorized by Mr. Jefferson to say, "that the points mentioned (the conditions made by Mr. Bayard) corresponded with his [Mr. Jefferson's] views and intentions." But whether this discrepancy is to be explained by misapprehensions at the time, or by the lapse of nearly five years, the explanation cannot invalidate the positive denial of Mr. Jefferson, that any such authority was given to General Smith, and his affirmance of the denial at the moment when it was put into the memorandum by Mr. Jefferson.

It can never be admitted that the authority of the deliberate statement of Mr. Jefferson is impaired by its being without the sanction of an oath. Apart from its intrinsic sufficiency, no one can doubt that such a sanction would readily have been added on any occasion calling for it; and with the greater confidence, as the fact sworn to would have been reduced to writing at the time—an advantage always duly estimated in cases depending on the accuracy of recollection.

The situation of Mr. Jefferson during the critical period of the presidential contest in the House of Representatives, was equally marked by its peculiarity and its importance. He saw the whole government in a state of convulsion; he saw the danger of an absolute interregnum in its executive branch, the consequences of which could not be foreseen; he saw what he regarded as the will of the people about to be trampled upon, and the party whose ascendancy he believed to be of vital importance to the cause of republican government, attempted to be broken down; and he saw at the same time, no escape from all these dangers, but in pledges which might be stigmatized as an ambitious intrigue, and a purchase of success at the expense of those principles and feelings which he had avowed and held inviolable. Happily the course of circumstances fulfilled his patriotic wishes without the sacrifice which the accomplishment of them had seemed to require.

The situation of Mr. Bayard was also peculiar and trying. He was justly struck with horror at the prospect of an interregnum in the government so full of evils, and so fatal in its example; and he was scarcely less alarmed at the danger which threatened what he held to be a vital policy of his country. But holding at the same time, in his hands, the event on which every thing depended, he availed himself of the opportunity of terminating the crisis in a manner wh ch prevented the calamity which he most dreaded, and provided, as he believed, an adequate security against the other.

Before dismissing the subject, a word may be proper with respect to the charge in the publication against Mr. Jefferson, of leaving the memorandum referring to Mr. Bayard's deposition, for posthumous use, when the means of refuting it might be lost.

The suit of Gillespie and Smith, which led to the deposition of Mr. Bayard, is said to have been a fictitious one, instituted for the purpose of obtaining and perpetuating testimony against the purity of Mr. Jefferson's conduct during the presidential election in 1801. The cause, it is understood, was never brought to trial; and it is inferred from the resort to the source which furnished the copies of the depositions of Mr. Bayard and General Smith, that the depositions were never published. Of their existence, however, (and in a custody supposed by Mr. Jefferson to be unfriendly,) and of the passage in that of Mr. Bayard, testifying that he [Mr. Jefferson,] had authorized General Smith to accede for him to certain conditions on which his election to the presidency might be obtained, Mr. Jefferson, it seems, was apprized from some friendly quarter. With this knowledge of a shaft that might posthumously inflict a deep wound on his reputation, could he do less than provide a shield against it, by recording with his own hand the falsity of the charge, and the affirmance of its falsity at the moment of his doing so, by the individual named as the authority for the charge? What is now before the public proves that a weapon was in reserve, by which a posthumous assault on his reputation might be made. And if there be unfairness in the case, let candor pronounce on which side it is chargeable; on that of Mr. Jefferson, or that, not of the (doubtless involuntary) deponents, but of the parties to the suit which rendered the precaution necessary

No. IV.

THE SOLEMN DECLARATION AND PROTEST OF THE COMMONWEALTH OF VIRGINIA, ON THE PRINCIPLES OF THE CONSTITUTION OF THE UNITED STATES OF AMERICA, AND ON THE VIOLATIONS OF THEM. WRITTEN BY MR. JEFFERSON.

We, the General Assembly of Virginia, on behalf, and in the name of the people thereof, do declare as follows:

The states in North America which confederated to establish their independence on the government of Great Britain, of which Virginia was one, became, on that acquisition, free and independent states, and as such authorized to constitute governments, each for itself, in such form as it thought best.

They entered into a compact, (which is called the Constitution of the United States of America,) by which they agreed to unite in a single government as to their relations with each other, and with foreign nations, and as to certain other articles particularly specified. They retained at the same time, each to itself, the other rights of independent government, comprehending mainly their domestic interests.

For the administration of their federal branch, they agreed to appoint, in conjunction, a distinct set of functionaries, legislative, executive, and judiciary, in the manner settled in that compact; while to each, severally, and of course, remained its original right of appointing, each for itself, a separate set of functionaries, legislative, executive, and judiciary, also, for administering the domestic branch of their respective governments.

These two sets of officers, each independent of the other, constitute thus a *whole* of government, for each state separately; the powers ascribed to the one, as specifically made federal, exercised over the whole the residuary powers retained to the other, exercisable exclusively over its particular state, foreign herein, each to the others, as they were before the original compact.

To this construction of government and distribution of its powers, the commonwealth of Virginia does religiously and affectionately adhere, opposing, with equal fidelity and firmness, the usurpation of either set of functionaries on the rightful powers of the other.

But the federal branch has assumed, in some cases, and claimed in others, a right of enlarging its own powers by constructions, inferences, and indefinite deductions from those directly given, which this Assembly does declare to be usurpations of the powers retained to the independent branches, mere interpolations into the compact, and direct infractions of it.

They claim, for example, and have commenced the exercise of a right to construct roads, open canals, and effect other internal improvements within the territories and jurisdictions exclusively belonging to the several states, which this Assembly does declare has not been given to that branch by the constitutional compact, but remains to each state among its domestic and unalienated powers, exercisable within itself and by its domestic authorities alone.

This Assembly does further disavow and declare to be most false and unfounded, the doctrine that the compact, in authorizing its federal branch to lay and collect taxes, duties, imposts and excises to pay the debts and provide for the common defense and general welfare of the United States, has given them thereby a power to do whatever *they* may think, or pretend, would promote the general welfare, which construction would make that, of itself, a complete government, without limitation of powers; but that the plain sense and obvious meaning were, that they might levy the taxes necessary to provide for the general welfare, by the various acts of power therein specified and delegated to them, and by no others.

Nor is it admitted, as has been said, that the people of these states, by not investing their federal branch with all the means of bettering their condition, have denied to themselves any which may effect that purpose; since, in the distribution of these means, they have given to that branch those which belong to its department, and to the states have reserved separately the residue which belong to them separately. And thus by the organization of the two branches taken together, have completely secured the first object of human association, the full improvement of their condition, and reserved to themselves all the faculties of multiplying their own blessings.

Whilst the General Assembly thus declares the rights

retained by the states, rights which they have never yielded, and which this state will never voluntarily yield, they do not mean to raise the banner of disaffection, or of separation from their sister states, co-parties with themselves to this compact. They know and value too highly the blessings of their Union as to foreign nations and questions arising among themselves, to consider every infraction as to be met by actual resistance. They respect too affectionately the opinions of those possessing the same rights under the same instrument, to make every difference of construction a ground of immediate rupture. They would, indeed, consider such a rupture as among the greatest calamities which could befall them; but not the greatest. There is yet one greater, submission to a government of unlimited powers. It is only when the hope of avoiding this shall become absolutely desperate, that further forbearance could not be indulged. Should a majority of the co-parties, therefore, contrary to the expectation and hope of this assembly, prefer, at this time, acquiescence in these assumptions of power by the federal member of the government, we will be patient and suffer much, under the confidence that time, ere it be too late, will prove to them also the bitter consequences in which that usurpation will involve us all. In the meanwhile, we will breast with them, rather than separate from them, every misfortune, save that only of living under a government of unlimited powers. We owe every other sacrifice to ourselves, to our federal brethren, and to the world at large, to pursue with temper and perseverance the great experiment which shall prove that man is capable of living in society, governing itself by laws self-imposed, and securing to its members the enjoyment of life, liberty, property and peace; and further to show, that even when the government of its choice shall manifest a tendency to degeneracy, we are not at once to despair but that the will and the watchfulness of its sounder parts will reform its aberrations, recall it to original and legitimate principles, and restrain it within the rightful limits of self-government. And these are the objects of this Declaration and Protest.

Supposing then, that it might be for the good of the whole, as some of its co-states seem to think, that the power of making roads and canals should be added to those directly given to the federal branch, as more likely to be systematically and beneficially directed, than by the independent action of the several states, this commonwealth, from respect to these opinions, and a desire of conciliation with its co-states, will consent, in concurrence with them, to make this addition, provided it be done regularly by an amendment of the compact, in the way established by that instrument, and provided also, it be sufficiently guarded against abuses, compromises, and corrupt practices, not only of possible, but of probable occurrence.

And as a further pledge of the sincere and cordial attachment of this commonwealth to the union of the whole, so far as has been consented to by the compact called "The Constitution of the United States of America," (construed according to the plain and ordinary meaning of its language, to the common intendment of the time, and of those who framed it;) to give also to all parties and authorities, time for reflection and for consideration, whether, under a temperate view of the possible consequences, and especially of the constant obstructions which an equivocal majority must ever expect to meet, they will still prefer the assumption of this power rather than its acceptance from the free-will of their constituents; and to preserve peace in the meanwhile, we proceed to make it the duty of our citizens, until the legislature shall otherwise and ultimately decide, to acquiesce under those acts of the federal branch of our government which we have declared to be usurpations, and against which, in point of right, we do protest as null and void, and never to be quoted as precedents of right.

No. V.

JEFFERSON'S ESTIMATE OF FEDERALISM AND DEMOCRACY.*

JEFFERSON says "That at the formation of our government, many had formed their opinions on European writings and practices, believing the experience of old countries, and especially of England, oppressive as it was, to be a safer guide than mere theory. The doctrines of Europe were, that men in numerous associations cannot be restrained within the limits of order and justice but by forces physical and moral, wielded over them by authorities independent of their will. Hence their organization of kings, hereditary nobles, and priests. Still further to constrain the brute force of the people, they deem it necessary to keep them down by hard labor, poverty, and ignorance, and to take from them, as from bees, so much of their earnings, as that unremitting labor shall be necessary to obtain a sufficient surplus barely to maintain their privileged orders in splendor and idleness, to fascinate the eyes of the people, and excite in them an humble adoration and submission, as to an order of superior beings. Although few among us had gone all these lengths of opinion, yet many had advanced, some more, some less, on the way. And in the Convention which formed our government, they endeavored to draw the cords of govern-

* From a letter to Judge Johnson, of South Carolina, in 1823.

ment as tight as they could obtain them, to lessen the dependence of the general functionaries on their constituents; to subject to them those of the states; and to weaken their means of maintaining the steady equilibrium which the majority of the Convention had deemed salutary for both branches, general and local. To recover, therefore, in practice the powers which the nation had refused, and to warp to their own wishes those actually given, was the steady object of the federal party. Ours, on the contrary, was to maintain the will of the majority of the Convention, and of the people themselves. We believed, with them, that man was a rational animal, endowed by nature with rights, and with an innate sense of justice; and that he could be restrained from wrong, and protected in right, by moderate powers, confided to persons of his own choice, and held to their duties by dependence on his own will. We believed that the complicated organization of kings, nobles, and priests, was not the wisest or best to effect the happiness of associated man; that wisdom and virtue were not hereditary; that the trappings of such a machinery consumed, by their expense, those earnings of industry they were meant to protect, and, by the inequalities they produced, exposed liberty to sufferance. We believed that men enjoying in ease and security the full fruits of their own industry, enlisted by all their interests on the side of law and order, habituated to think for themselves, and to follow their reason as their guide, which would be more easily and safely governed, than with minds nourished in error, and vitiated and debased, as in Europe, by ignorance, indigence and oppression. The cherishment of the people was then our principle, the fear and distrust of them that of the other party. Composed, as we were, of the laboring interests of the country, we could not be less anxious for a government of law and order than were the inhabitants of the cities, the strongholds of federalism. And whether our efforts to save the principles and form of our Constitution have not been salutary, let the present republican freedom, order, and prosperity of our country determine. History may distort truth, and will distort it for a time, by the superior efforts at justification of those who are conscious of needing it most. Nor will the opening scenes of our present government be seen in their true aspect, until the letters of the day, now held in private hoards, shall be broken up and laid open to public view. What a treasure will be found in General Washington's cabinet, when it shall pass into the hands of as candid a friend to truth as he was himself! When no longer like Cæsar's notes and memorandums in the hands of Anthony, it shall be open to the high priests of federalism only, and garbled to say so much and no more, as suits their view "

No. VI.

JEFFERSON'S OPINION OF GEORGE WASHINGTON.

"His mind was great and powerful, without being of the very first order; his penetration strong, though not so acute as that of a Newton, Bacon, or Locke; and as far as he saw, no judgment was ever sounder. It was slow in operation, being little aided by invention or imagination, but sure in conclusion. Hence the common remark of his officers, of the advantage he derived from councils of war, where, hearing all suggestions, he selected whatever was best; and certainly no general ever planned his battles more judiciously. But if deranged during the course of the action, if any member of his plan was dislocated by sudden circumstances, he was slow in a readjustment. The consequence was, that he often failed in the field, and rarely against an enemy in station, as at Boston and York. He was incapable of fear, meeting personal dangers with the calmest unconcern. Perhaps the strongest feature in his character was prudence, never acting until every circumstance, every consideration, was maturely weighed, refraining if he saw a doubt, but when once decided, going through with his purpose, whatever obstacles opposed His integrity was most pure, his justice the most inflexible I have ever known; no motives of interest or consanguinity, of friendship or hatred, being able to bias his decision. He was, indeed, in every sense of the word, a wise, a good, and a great man. His temper was naturally irritable and high-toned; but reflection and resolution had obtained a firm and habitual ascendancy over it. If ever, however, it broke its bonds, he was most tremendous in his wrath. In his expenses he was honorable, but exact; liberal in contributions to whatever promised utility; but frowning and unyielding on all visionary projects, and all unworthy calls on his charity. His heart was not warm in its affections; but he exactly calculated every man's value, and gave him a solid esteem proportioned to it. His person, you know, was fine, his stature exactly what one would wish, his deportment easy, erect and noble, the best horseman of his age, and the most graceful figure that could be seen on horseback. Although in the circle of his friends, where he might be unreserved with safety, he took a free share in conversation; his colloquial talents were not above mediocrity, possessing neither copiousness of ideas, nor fluency of words. In public, when called on for a sudden opinion, he was unready, short, and embarrassed. Yet he wrote readily, rather diffusely, in an easy and correct style. This he had acquired by conversation with the world, for his education was merely reading, writing, and common arithmetic, to which he added surveying at a later day. His time was employed in action chiefly, reading little, and that only in agriculture and English history. His correspondence became necessarily extensive, and with journalizing his agricultural proceedings occupied most of his leisure hours within doors. On the whole, his character was, in its mass, perfect; in nothing bad, in a few points indifferent; and it may truly be said, that never did nature and fortune combine more perfectly to make a man great, and to place him in the same constellation with whatever worthies have merited from man an everlasting remembrance. For his was the singular destiny and merit of leading the armies of his country successfully through an arduous war, for the establishment of its independence; of conducting its councils through the birth of a government, new in its forms and principles, until it had settled down into a quiet and orderly train; and of scrupulously obeying the laws through the whole of his career, civil and military, of which the history of the world furnishes no other example."

No. VII.

JEFFERSON'S OPINION OF PLATO.

He speaks most contemptuously of the "whimsies, the puerilities, and unintelligible jargon of this work;" and says he often asked himself how the world could have so long consented to give reputation to such nonsense. He thus accounts for Plato's influence among the moderns. "In truth he is one of the race of genuine sophists, who has escaped the oblivion of his brethren, first, by the elegance of his diction, but chiefly by the adoption and incorporation of his whimsies into the body of artificial Christianity. His foggy mind is ever presenting the semblances of objects which, half seen through a mist, can be defined neither in form nor dimension. Yet this, which should have consigned him to early oblivion, really procured him immortality of fame and reverence. The Christian priesthood, finding the doctrines of Christ leveled to every understanding, and too plain to need explanation, saw in the mysticisms of Plato, materials with which they might build up an artificial system, which might, from its indistinctness, admit everlasting controversy, give employment for their order, and introduce it to profit, power, and pre-eminence. The doctrines which flowed from the lips of Jesus himself are within the comprehension of a child; but thousands of volumes have not yet explained the Platonisms engrafted on them: and for this obvious reason, that nonsense cannot be explained."

Without denying that the sublimated speculations of Plato, in the main, merit the severe censure bestowed on them by Mr. Jefferson, another explanation may be given for the favor which this philosopher found among the earlier Christian writers, without supposing it was the result of settled design. First, on account of his pure and lofty theism, and next because his mystical fancies could be made to harmonize with some of the more subtle doctrines which the controversies of the Christian sects had engendered; and which were thus more readily received by the scholars of the age, when recommended by an authority of such celebrity

No. VIII.

JEFFERSON'S RULES FOR THE CONDUCT OF LIFE.

Mr. Jefferson wrote a letter to his namesake, Thomas Jefferson Smith, of Washington, at the instance of his father, who requested him to address something to his son which might have a salutary influence on his future life, when he could understand it. More solid advice was never conveyed in so small a compass, and no one could have a better chance for respectability or happiness who would faithfully observe these precepts. Those which respect his religious and moral character are six. 1. Adore God. 2. Reverence and cherish your parents. 3. Love your neighbor as yourself, your country more than yourself 4. Be just. 5. Be true. 6. Murmur not at the ways of Providence.

He also gives him ten canons for the regulation of his practical life They were—1. Never put off till to-morrow what you can do to-day. 2. Never trouble another for what you can do yourself. 3. Never spend your money before you have it. 4. Never buy what you do not want, because it is cheap; it will be dear to you. 5. Pride costs us more than hunger, thirst, and cold. 6. We never repent of having eaten too little. 7. Nothing is troublesome that we do willingly. 8. How much pain have cost us the evils which have never happened. 9. Take things by the smooth handle. 10. When angry, count ten before you speak; if very angry, a hundred.

He also cited to him for his imitation, the translation of one of the Psalms, beginning, "Lord, who's the happy man;" which he calls "the portrait of a good man by the most sublime of poets."

No. IX.

JEFFERSON'S CORRESPONDENCE AFTER HIS RETIREMENT.

One of the inconveniences felt by Mr. Jefferson, from the conspicuous part he had acted in public affairs, as well as from his popularity, was the number of letters with which he was importuned. This tax, in a greater or less degree, every ex-president must pay; but no one, unless perhaps General Washington, was ever called upon to pay it to the same extent as Mr. Jefferson. He sorely complains of it in a letter to Mr. Adams, dated June 27, 1822. "I do not know how far you may suffer, as I do, under the persecution of letters, of which every mail brings a fresh load. They are letters of inquiry for the most part, always of good-will, sometimes from friends whom I esteem, but much oftener from persons whose names are unknown to me, but written kindly and civilly, and to which, therefore, civility requires answers. Perhaps the better known failure of your hand in its function of writing, may shield you in greater degree from this distress, and so far qualify the misfortune of its disability. I happened to turn to my letter list some time ago, and a curiosity was excited to count those received in a single year. It was the year before last. I found the number to be one thousand two hundred and sixty-seven, many of them requiring answers of elaborate research, and all to be answered with due attention

30*

and consideration. Take an average of this number for a week or a day, and I will repeat the question suggested by other considerations in mine of the 1st. Is this life? At best it is but the life of a mill-horse, who sees no end to his circle but in death. To such a life, that of a cabbage would be a paradise."

No. X.

JEFFERSON'S LETTERS TO THE AMERICAN PHILOSOPHICAL SOCIETY.

"*Monticello*, January 28, 1797.

"GENTLEMEN: I have duly received your favor of the 7th instant, informing me that the American Philosophical Society have been pleased to name me their president. The suffrage of a body which comprehends whatever the American world has of distinction in philosophy and science in general, is the most flattering incident of my life, and that to which I am the most sensible. My satisfaction would be most complete, were it not for the consciousness that it is far beyond my titles. I feel no qualification for this distinguished post, but a sincere zeal for all the objects of our institution, and an ardent desire to see knowledge so disseminated through the mass of mankind, that it may at length reach the extremes of society, beggars and kings. I pray you, gentlemen, to testify for me, to our body, my sense of their favor, and my disposition to supply by zeal what I may be deficient in the other qualifications proper for their service, and to be assured that your testimony cannot go beyond my feelings.

"Permit me tc avail myself of this opportunity of expressing the sincere grief I feel for the loss of our beloved Rittenhouse. Genius, science, modesty, purity of morals, simplicity of manners, marked him as one of nature's best samples of the perfection she can cover under the human form. Surely, no society till ours, within the same compass of time, ever had to deplore the loss of two such members as Franklin and Rittenhouse. Franklin, our patriarch, whom philosophy and philanthropy announced the first of men; and whose name will be like a star of the first magnitude in the firmament of heaven, when the memory of those who have surrounded and obscured him, will be lost in the abyss of time.

"With the most affectionate attachment to their memory, and with sentiments of the highest respect to the society, and to yourselves personally, I have the honor to be, gentlemen,

"Your most obedient,

'And most humble servant,

"TH. JEFFERSON."

"To Messrs. Samuel Magaw, Jonathan Williams, William Burton, and John Bleakley, Secretaries of the American Philosophical Society."

"*Monticello*, Nov. 23, 1814.

SIR: I solicited on a former occasion permission from the American Philosophical Society to retire from the honor of their chair, under a consciousness that distance, as well as other circumstances, denied me the power of executing the duties of the station, and that those on whom they devolved were best entitled to the honors they confer. It was the pleasure of the society at that time, that I should remain in their service, and they have continued since to renew the same marks of their partiality. Of these I have been ever duly sensible, and now beg leave to return my thanks for them with humble gratitude. Still I have never ceased, nor can I cease to feel, that I am holding honors without yielding requital, and justly belonging to others As the period of election is now therefore approaching, I take the occasion of begging to be withdrawn from the attention of the society at their ensuing choice, and to be permitted now to resign the office of president into their hands, which I hereby do. I shall consider myself sufficiently honored in remaining a private member of their body, and shall ever avail myself with zeal of every occasion which may occur of being useful to them, retaining indelibly a profound sense of their past favors."

No. XI.

JEFFERSON'S OPINIONS OF BONAPARTE AND THE ENGLISH GOVERNMENT.

For several years the uninterrupted military successes of Napoleon Bonaparte, and the gradual enlargement of his power to a height never before attained by man, excited not merely sympathy for the nations whom he despoiled of their independence, but very lively fears for that of the United States. It seemed as if the whole civilized world was destined, sooner or later, to bow to the ascendancy of his genius and fortune; and though some hopes were entertained that he would meet with an effectual check in Spain, yet similar hopes had too often proved abortive, for these to be very lively. In a letter to Mr. Langdon of New Hampshire, Mr. Jefferson thus discloses his views on this subject. "The fear that Bonaparte will come over to us and conquer us also, is too chimerical to be genuine.

Supposing him to have finished Spain and Portugal, he has yet England and Russia to subdue. These two subdued, ancient Greece and Macedonia, the cradle of Alexander, his prototype, and Constantinople, the seat of empire for the world, would glitter more in his eye than our bleak mountains and rugged forests. Egypt too, and the golden apples of Mauritania, have for more than half a century fixed the longing eyes of France; and with Syria, you know, he has an old affront to wipe out. Then come 'Pontus and Galatia, Cappadocia, Asia, and Bithynia,' the fine countries on the Euphrates and Tigris, the Oxus and Indus, and all beyond the Hydaspes, which bounded the glories of his Macedonian rival; with the invitations of his new British subjects on the banks of the Ganges, whom, after receiving under his protection the mother country, he cannot refuse to visit. When all this is done and settled, and nothing of the old world remains unsubdued, he may turn to the new one. But will he attack us first, from whom he will get but hard knocks, and no money? or will he first lay hold of the gold and silver of Mexico and Peru, and the diamonds of Brazil. A *republican* emperor, from his affection to republics, independent of motives of expediency, must grant to ours the Cyclops' boon of being the last devoured. While all this is doing, we are to suppose the chapter of accidents read out, and that nothing can happen to cut short or to disturb his enterprises."

The following was his theory of the English government: "The real power and property in the government is the great aristocratical families of the nation. The nest of office being too small for all of them to cuddle in at once, the contest is eternal which shall crowd the other out. For this purpose they are divided into two parties, the Inns and the Outs, so equal in weight that a small matter turns the balance. To keep themselves in when they are in, every stratagem must be practiced, every artifice used which may flatter the pride, the passions, or the power of the nation. Justice, honor, faith, must yield to the necessity of keeping themselves in place. The question whether a measure is moral, is never asked; but whether it will nourish the avarice of their merchants, or the piratical spirit of their navy, or produce any other effect which may strengthen them in their places. As to engagements, however positive, entered into by the predecessors of the Ins, why they were then enemies; they did every thing which was wrong; and to reverse every thing they did must therefore be right. This is the true character of the British government in practice, however different its theory; and it presents the singular phenomenon of a nation, the individuals of which are as faithful to their private engagements and duties, as honorable, as worthy, as those of any nation on earth, and whose government is yet the most unprincipled at this day known." He then speaks of the general causes why princes should be superior to other men, and by way of illustration gives a sketch of the principal monarchs of Europe, which, in the style of broad caricature, retains enough of resemblance to the originals to be readily acknowledged.

No. XII.

JEFFERSON'S VIEWS ON THE CESSION OF LOUISIANA, IN A LETTER TO CAPTAIN LEWIS.

"*Washington*, July 15, 1803.

"DEAR SIR: I dropped you a line on the 11th inst., and last night received yours of the 8th. Last night also we received the treaty from Paris, ceding Louisiana, according to the bounds to which France had a right—price, eleven and a quarter millions of dollars, besides paying certain debts of France to our citizens, which will be from one to four millions. I received also from Mr. Lacepede at Paris, to whom I had mentioned your intended expedition, a letter, of which the following is an extract: 'Mr. Broughton, one of the companions of Captain Vancouver, went up Columbia River one hundred miles, in December, 1792. He stopped at a point which he named Vancouver, latitude 45° 27′, longitude 237° 50′ E. Here the river Columbia is still a quarter of a mile wide, and from twelve to thirty-six feet deep. It is far then to its head. From this point Mount Hood is seen, twenty leagues distant, which is probably a dependance of the Stony Mountains, of which Mr. Fiedler saw the beginning about latitude 40°, and the source of the Missouri is probably in the Stony Mountains If your nation can establish an easy communication by rivers, canals, and short portages, between New York, for example, and the city [they were building, or to be built, for the badness of the writing makes it uncertain which is meant, but probably the last] at the mouth of Columbia, what a route for the commerce of Europe, Asia and America!'

"Accept my affectionate salutations,

"THOMAS JEFFERSON."

No. XIII

JEFFERSON'S FAMILY AND DESCENDANTS.

I. One daughter—Martha Wayles Randolph, widow of the late Governor Randolph.

II. Eleven grandchildren, to wit

1. Thomas Jefferson Randolph.
2. Ellen Coolidge, wife of Joseph Coolidge of Boston.
3. Virginia Trist, wife of Nicholas P. Trist, consul at Havana.
4. Cornelia Randolph.
5. Mary Randolph.
6. James Madison Randolph, since deceased.
7. Benjamin Franklin Randolph, a physician in Albemarle.
8. Meriwether Lewis Randolph, residing in Arkansas.
9. Septimia Randolph.
10. George Wythe Randolph, midshipman in the navy.
11. Francis Eppes, the only grandchild by his daughter Maria Eppes.

III. Fourteen great-grandchildren, to wit:

The children of Thomas Jefferson Randolph—six.

The children of Ann Bankhead, deceased, the eldest daughter of Mrs. Randolph—four.

A daughter of Mrs. Coolidge.

The children of Francis Eppes—two.

A daughter of Mrs. Trist.

Since Mr. Jefferson's death, time has made its usual changes, both by deaths and births, and the number of his descendants now exceeds forty, among whom are several of the fifth generation.

No. XIV.

JEFFERSON'S OPINIONS IN REFERENCE TO THE SOCIETY OF THE CINCINNATI.*

"Having been in America during the period in which this institution was formed, and being then in a situation which gave me opportunities of seeing it in all its stages, I may venture to give M. de Meusnier materials for a succinct history of its origin and establishment. I should write its history in the following form.

"When, on the close of that war which established the independence of America, its army was about to be disbanded, the officers who, during the course of it had gone through the most trying scenes together, who, by mutual aids and good offices had become dear to one another, felt with great apprehension of mind the approach of that moment which was to separate them, never, perhaps, to meet again. They were from different States, and from distant parts of the same State. Hazard alone could therefore give them but rare and partial occasions of seeing each other. They were, of course, to abandon altogether the hope of ever meeting again, or to devise some occasion which might bring them together. And why not come together on purpose at stated times? Would not the trouble of such a journey be greatly overpaid by the pleasure of seeing each other again, by the sweetest of all consolations, the talking over the scenes of difficulty and endearment they had gone through? This, too, would enable them to know who of them should succeed in the world, who should be

* The remainder of this Appendix is taken from the "Observations of Henry Lee, of Virginia, on the Writings of Thomas Jefferson," &c. This is a very valuable work, and not generally accessible to the reader. The following extracts possess more than ordinary interest.

31

unsuccessful and to open the purses of all to every laboring brother. This idea was too soothing not to be cherished in conversation. It was improved into that of a regular association, with an organized administration, with periodical meetings, general and particular, fixed contributions for those who should be in distress, and a badge, by which not only those who had not had occasion to become personally known should be able to recognize one another, but which should be worn by their descendants, to perpetuate among them the friendship which had bound their ancestors together.

"Gen. Washington was, at that moment, oppressed with the operation of disbanding an army which was not paid; and the difficulty of this operation was increased, by some two or three States having expressed sentiments, which did not indicate a sufficient attention to their payment. He was sometimes present when his officers were fashioning in their conversations their newly proposed society. He saw the innocence of its origin, and foresaw no effects less innocent. He was at that time writing his valedictory letter to the States, which has been so deservedly applauded by the world. Far from thinking it a moment to multiply the causes of irritation, by thwarting a proposition which had absolutely no other basis but that of benevolence and friendship, he was rather satisfied to find himself aided in his difficulties by this new incident, which occupied, and at the same time, soothed, the minds of his officers. He thought too, that this institution would be one instrument the more for strengthening the federal bond, and for promoting federal ideas. The institution was formed. They incorporated into it the officers of the French army and navy, by whose sides they had fought, and with whose aid they had finally prevailed."

After stating that Gen. Washington accepted the office

of President of the society, (which he held until his death) and mentioning the opposition which its supposed tendency to divide the community into distinct orders, soon excited, he proceeds :—

"The uneasiness excited by this institution, had very early caught the notice of Gen. Washington. Still recollecting all the purity of the motives which gave it birth, he became sensible that it might produce political evils, which the warmth of those motives had masked. Add to this, that it was disapproved by the mass of citizens of the Union. This alone was reason strong enough in a country where the will of the majority is the law, and ought to be the law. He saw that the objects of the institution were too light to be opposed to considerations as serious as these ; and that it was become necessary to annihilate it absolutely. On this, therefore, he was decided. The first annual meeting at Philadelphia, was now at hand ; he went to that, determined to exert all his influence for its suppression. He proposed it to his fellow-officers, and urged it with all his powers. It met an opposition which was observed to cloud his face with an anxiety that the most distressful scenes of the war had scarcely ever produced. It was canvassed for several days, and at length it was no more a doubt what would be its ultimate fate. The order was on the point of receiving its annihilation, by a vote of a great majority of its members. In this moment their envoy arrived from France, charged with letters from the French officers, accepting with cordiality the proposed badges of union, with solicitations from others to be received into the order, and with notice that their respectable sovereign had been pleased to recognize it, and to permit his officers to wear its badges. The prospect was now changed. The question assumed a new form. After the offer made by them, and accepted by their friends, in what words could they clothe a proposition to retract it, which would not cover themselves with the reproaches of levity and ingratitude—which would not appear an insult to those whom they loved? Federal principles, popular discontent, were considerations whose weight was known and felt by themselves. But would foreigners know and feel them equally? Would they so far acknowledge their cogency, as to permit, without indignation, the Eagle and Ribbon to be torn from their breasts, by the very hands which placed them there? The idea revolted the whole society They found it necessary, then, to preserve so much of their institution as might continue to support this foreign branch, while they should prune off every other which would give offense to their fellow-citizens; thus sacrificing, on each hand, to their friends, and to their country.

The society was to retain its existence, its name, its meetings, and its charitable funds; but these last were to be deposited with their respective legislatures. The order was to be no longer hereditary. The Eagle and Ribbon were indeed retained, because they were worn, and they wished them to be worn by their friends in a country where they would not be objects of offense; but themselves never wore them. They laid them up in their bureaus, with the medals of American Independence, with those of the trophies they had taken and the battles they had won. But through all the United States no officer is seen to offend the public eye with a display of this badge. These changes have tranquillized the American States. Their citizens feel too much interest in the reputation of their officers, and value too much whatever may serve to recall to the memory of their allies the moments wherein they formed but one people, not to do justice to the circumstances which prevented the total annihilation of the order; and it would be an extreme affliction to them, if the domestic reformation which has been found necessary, if the censures of individual writers, or if any other circumstance, should discourage the wearing their badge by their allies, or lessen its reputation." He then adds, that the above is "a short and true history of the Order of the Cincinnati."

From this account then, we have the grave authority of Mr. Jefferson himself, for saying, that the Society of Cincinnati was founded exclusively on sentiments of "benevolence and friendship," was "innocent in its origin," and as far as its members could foresee, "no less innocent in its effects," was considered likely to smooth the difficulties of disbanding the army, and to strengthen the tendencies to union among the States. That as soon as unforeseen objections were entertained toward it by their fellow-citizens, "a great majority" of its members, in conformity with the advice of Gen. Washington, and in patriotic deference to the sovereignty of the public will, resolved on its immediate annihilation. That this radical measure was prevented *solely* by an accidental circumstance, which opposed to it their respect, gratitude, and attachment for the French officers, who, in compliance with their invitation, and by permission of their own government, had become members of it. That, influenced by a desire to comply with the opinions of their countrymen, and at the same time to avoid disrespect to their foreign friends, they pruned off the hereditary quality, and other objectionable parts of their institution, and preserved only so much as might support the foreign branch. That this reformation satisfied the people of the United States, who felt a pride in the estimation in which the society was held abroad, and would view, with "extreme affliction," any evidence of a decline in that flattering sentiment.

This, he says, is "the true history" of the society. It does not look like "*carving out for itself hereditary dis-*

tinctions," or "*lowering over the Constitu ion eternally.*" And as to "accumulating a capital in their separate treasury," he declares the object of that *design* (for no capital of any consequence ever was accumulated, the great majority of the officers having lived and died poor,) was to relieve the necessities of their unfortunate associates; and that the funds, should any be collected, were to be placed for that purpose in the treasuries to the several States.

As he affirms that his account of M. de Meusnier was a *true history*, it is hardly necessary to say that the one here given to Mr. Madison could not be any thing but a libel upon men whose patriotism, benevolence, friendship and modesty, throughout all its stages, he himself had solemnly attested. That he presented the genuine account to his French friend, and put the base one on Mr. Madison, you may be inclined to attribute to the predominance of familiarity over respect in their intimacy. But the fact is, that the truth was to be locked up in a foreign library, or to reach few American readers, and was intended to minister to no ulterior purpose. Whereas, the article fabricated for Mr. Madison, was for home consumption; was a thread in that web of misrepresentation which he was weaving around the character of Gen. Washington—a web of torments—which, if we believe him, were not less fierce and mighty than those which writhe and swell the figure of Canova's Hercules—when the distracted demigod—

> " Felt the envenom'd robe, and tore,
> Through pain, up by the roots Thessalian pines,
> And Lichas from the top of Œta threw,
> Into the Euboic sea."

These torments were cruelly inflicted, as they were calmly witnessed, for the purpose of bringing his own claims before the people with a better chance of success.

As this hatred and suspicion of the Cincinnati Society were evidently spurious and unfounded, you will be the less surprised to learn that the zeal expressed in the same letter, in behalf of the democratic societies, "the friends of popular rights," was not the fruit of principle but of interest. At page 345 of his fourth volume, is a letter from Mr. Jefferson of the 6th of March, 1822, in which he declines an invitation to become a member of a society whose object was "to promote civilization and improvement among the Indians." In this letter he observes—"I shall not undertake to draw a line of demarcation between private associations of laudable views and unimposing numbers, and those whose magnitude may rivalize and jeopardize the march of regular government. Yet such a line does exist. I have seen the days—they were those which preceded the Revolution—when even this last and perilous engine became necessary; but they were days which no man would wish to see a second time." He proceeds to deprecate such associations upon the ground of their being bad and prolific examples, of being "wheels within a wheel," and by reference to the excesses perpetrated by the Jacobin Clubs of France.

It would appear, therefore, that while Mr. Jefferson felt called on "as a good citizen" to discourage a society instituted for the purpose of "promoting civilization and improvement among the Indians," as setting a dangerous example, and tending "to rivalize and jeopardize the march of regular government," he pronounced Gen. Washington guilty of "an inexcusable aggression on popular rights," when he discountenanced in terms of anxious patriotism and considerate dignity, the proceedings of organized political clubs, which had nearly involved us in foreign war, in opposition to "the march of regular government," and had, as he and his whole Cabinet believed, and as a majority of the members of the legislature declared, fomented a formidable domestic insurrection.

Since, of his contradictory opinions on this subject, those expressed in his letter to Mr. Morse are said to be *conscientious*, the natural and melancholy conclusion is, that the false and scandalous ones again fall to the share of Mr. Madison.

But to go on with his letter of December, 1794. After attempting to separate these societies from their proceedings, affecting "to put out of sight the persons" whose confessed *misdemeanors* he calls *misbehavior*, he proceeds to affirm that the President's allusion to them was generally and justly considered "an abstract attempt on the natural and constitutional rights of the people."

The injustice of these expressions is much more conspicuous than their meaning. What is "an abstract attempt," on a practical subject—or on any subject? But a more important question is, what sense of equity was Mr. Jefferson guided by, when he pronounced the societies innocent, in spite of practical guilt, and Gen. Washington guilty, in spite of practical innocence? Is this judging the tree by its fruits, or men by their works?

It may be here observed, that while in his letters to Gen Washington of May the 14th and September the 7th, 1794, and that of June the 19th, 1796, the last, it appears, he ever wrote him, he was *humbugging* that confiding friend, that kind benefactor, that illustrious patriot, with professions of undiminished attachment for him, unabated love for retirement and repugnance to politics—with such expressions as "I cherish tranquillity too much to suffer political things to enter my mind at all," "it is a great pleasure to me to retain the esteem and approbation of the President," "I put away this disgusting dish of old fragments, and talk to you about my peas and clover," with "the Albany pea,"

—"the hog pea,"—"the true winter vetch,"—"the Carolina drill,"—and "the Scotch threshing-machine," he was collecting from "an extensive circle of observation and information," and transmitting to the head of the opposition in Congress the most unjust and poisonous opinions that could possibly be fabricated of the President's character and conduct. This would of itself have furnished cause sufficient for Gen. Lee, or any other sincere friend of the President, to put him on his guard, to open his eyes to the ambush from which this pretended friend and philosopher was secretly wounding him—where, too, his great and patriotic soul felt the injury the most acutely—in the love and confidence of his country.

No. XV.

JEFFERSON'S PROFESSIONS OF FRIENDSHIP AND SECRET HOSTILITY TO BURR.

To this person he continued to manifest the most respectful friendship, as will be seen by a letter of the 1st of February, 1801, just before the competition for the Presidency was to be decided by the House of Representatives, and when it was desirable not to irritate Burr or disgust his friends.

"DEAR SIR: It was to be expected that the enemy would endeavor to *sow tares* between us that they might divide us and our friends. Every consideration assures me that you will be on your guard against this, as I assure you I am strongly. I hear of one stratagem so imposing and so base, that it is proper I should notice it to you. Mr. Mumford, who is here, says he saw at New York before he left it, an original letter of mine to Judge Breckenridge, in which are sentiments highly injurious to you. He knows my hand-writing, and did not doubt that to be genuine. I inclose you a copy taken from the press copy of the only letter I ever wrote Judge Breckenridge in my life; the press copy itself has been shown to several of our mutual friends here. Of consequence the letter seen by Mr. Mumford must have been a forgery, and if it contains a sentiment unfriendly or disrespectful to you, I affirm it solemnly to be a forgery, as also if it varies from the copy enclosed. With the common trash of slander I should not think of troubling you, but the forgery of one's hand-writing is too imposing to be neglected. A mutual knowledge of each other furnishes us with the best test of the contrivances which will be practiced by the enemies of both."

The difference here in point of fact is between the statements of Mr. Mumford and the *press copy;* and as Mr. Jefferson himself affirms that, from the commencement of his acquaintance with Burr, he was in the habit of expressing to Mr. Madison his suspicious of his honesty, and perceived that he kept himself in the market, it is reasonable to suppose that he indulged the same sentiments in letters to other gentlemen, and that consequently the *press copy* was mistaken. This is the more probable, as a similar accident will hereafter be pointed out, and as he does not refer Burr to Judge Breckenridge, either for a sight of the letter itself or for a copy of it. The last sentence, however, contains the quintessence of deceit, where he tells Burr, that by reflecting on their mutual sincerity and reciprocal respect, he would furnish himself with the best possible test for detecting the poison of the mischief-making fabrications of their enemies. That is, 'if you hear any thing of me inconsistent with honor on my part, and with respect and friendship for you, you have only to feel assured that it is a base contrivance of our mutual enemies to sow tares between us. This is the reasoning I shall employ, should a similar stratagem be attempted on me.' Now only suppose that Mr. Madison had just at this time discovered to Burr one of the "habitual cautions," which he had received in regard to him!

When, however, in 1807, his friend Burr was arrested on a charge of treason, he discovered that he had all along despised him, in spite both of his own endearing professions, and of the equally cordial effusions of his *press copy*. In a letter to Mr. Giles of the 20th of April, 1807, (Vol. IV. p. 74,) he says: "Against Burr personally I never had one hostile sentiment. I never indeed thought him an honest, frank-dealing man, but considered him as a crooked gun, or other perverted machine, whose aim or shot you could never be sure of."

The contrast between these sentiments and those in the *Anas*, on the one hand, and those in his letters to Burr,—all volunteers, not answers—on the other; will be useful in enabling you to comprehend the difference of his style, when speaking *to* a man he hated, and *of* him. It justifies the inference that at the very moment he was so grossly traducing Gen. Lee to Gen. Washington, declaring that he had never "done him any other injury than that of declining his confidences," he would have been glad, had there been the least prospect of promoting his own interest by it, to encumber him with epistles and *press copies* of homage and attachment.

Of the object of the conspiracy, his conduct in regard to which is now to be compared with that pursued in quelling the Western insurrection, he gives the following account in a letter of the 2d of April, 1807, to our minister in Spain, (Vol. IV. p. 71,) "Although at first he proposed a separation of the Western country, and on that ground received encouragement and aid from Yrujo, according to the usual spirit of his government toward us, yet he very early saw that the fidelity of the Western country was not to be shaken, and turned himself wholly toward Mexico." And in the letter to Mr. Giles of the 20th, he thus describes the points of treason he expects to be established, by witnesses whose testimony he affirms "will satisfy the world, if not the Judge, of Burr's guilt"—"And I do suppose the following overt acts will be proved: 1. The enlistment of men in a regular way. 2. The regular mounting of guard round Blennerhasset's island, when they discovered Governor Tiffin's men to be on them *modo guerrino arriati*. 3. The rendezvous of Burr with his men at the mouth of Cumberland. 4. His letter to the acting Governor of Mississippi, holding up the prospect of civil war. 5. His capitulation regularly signed with the aids of the Governor, as between two independent hostile commanders."

These acts, he says, amount incontestably to treason. Yet the attack of five hundred armed men on the house of the inspector of the revenue, and a detachment of the troops of the United States—the burning the inspector's house and forcing an officer of the United States Army to march out and surrender—the shooting at the marshal with intent to kill him, while in the execution of his duty—the seizing and violating the mail of the United States on its passage to the seat of government—the arrest and intimidation of the marshal—the banishment of those citizens of Pittsburg, who were suspected of allegiance to their country—open resistance to the laws and defiance of the government—the rejection of an offered amnesty—the preparation of a force of 7,000 men to wage war against the United States, and to effect ultimately a dissolution of the Union—all these revolting outrages, in the comparative infancy of the government, when they were leveled at the peace and dignity of the nation, through the fame and feelings of President Washington, Mr. Jefferson considered as nearly harmless, as provoked by "an infernal law," and as at most merely "riotous transactions ! !"

The force with which Burr was to accomplish his designs, he estimates as follows, in a letter of the 14th of July, 1807, to Gen. La Fayette. (Vol. IV. p. 97.) "Burr had probably engaged one thousand men to follow his fortunes, without letting them know his projects, otherwise than by assuring them the government approved of them. The moment a proclamation issued undeceiving them, he found himself left with about thirty desperadoes only." This conspirator, with his gang of thirty followers, however, was too formidable to be left unpunished, whether in due course of law or not, and therefore the President of the United States descended from his station, and took the lead in hunting him down.

Accordingly, on the 2d of June, 1807, he opened a correspondence with the District Attorney of the United States, (Vol. IV. pp. 75 to 103,) which for indecency to the court, disrespect for the independence of a co-ordinate department, outrage upon the sanctity of justice, and cruelty to the prisoner, was never exceeded by the executive authority of any nation, in any age. After saying to Mr. Hay, "While Burr's case is depending before the court, I will trouble you from time to time with what occurs to me," —he proceeds to counsel him as to the management of various stages of the prosecution, inspiring him all the while with distrust of the purity of the court before which he was pleading, until the 19th of June, when he makes a suggestion, the wickedness of which cannot be adequately expressed in any language but his own. (p. 86.) "I inclose you the copy of a letter received last night, and giving singular information. I have inquired into the character of Graybell. He was an old revolutionary captain, is now a flour merchant in Baltimore, of the most respectable character, and whose word would be taken as implicitly as any man's for whatever he affirms. The letter writer also is a man of entire respectability. I am well informed that for more than a twelvemonth it has been believed in Baltimore, generally, that Burr was engaged in some criminal enterprise, and that Luther Martin knew all about it. We think you should immediately dispatch a subpœna for Graybell; and while that is on the road, you will have time to consider in what form you will use his testimony: *e. g.* shall Luther Martin be summoned as a witness against Burr, and Graybell held ready to confront him? It may be doubted whether we could examine a witness to discredit our own witness. Besides, the lawyers say that they are privileged from being forced to breaches of confidence, and that no others are. Shall we move to commit Luther Martin, as *particeps criminis* with Burr? Graybell will fix upon him suspicion of treason at least. And at any rate, his testimony will put down this unprincipled and impudent federal bull-dog, and add another proof that the most clamorous defenders of Burr are all his accomplices. It will explain why Luther Martin flew so hastily to the aid of his 'honorable friend,' abandoning his clients and their property during the session of a principal court in Maryland, now filled, as I am told, with the clamors and ruin of his clients."

You perceive from this that a *general belief*, *reported* to exist in Baltimore, of Burr's having meditated an unlawful enterprise, of *some sort or other*, and that Luther Martin *knew all about it;* with the *second hand* assertion that this knowledge could be proved by a *third person*, was cause sufficient in the humane and philosophic mind of Mr.

Jefferson to fix the stigma of treason on Luther Martin, by arresting him as *particeps criminis* with the prisoner he was defending. And if this unjust proceeding should fail of every other effect, it would at least have the happy one "of putting down this unprincipled and impudent federal bull-dog"—that is, it would silence him as an advocate for Burr—would deprive the prisoner of the assistance of the counsel on whom he peculiarly relied in a trial for his life, and thus expose him to all the violence and stratagem that the zeal of lawyers and the unbridled hate of the Executive could impart to the prosecution. Had this cruel project been fulfilled, Burr would have stood like Bothwell, his sword-arm broken and his dagger lost, while his bloodthirsty and hypocritical adversary, represented by the President, brandished his impatient blade aloft, and plunged it to the hilt in his body.

In unison with this unparalleled mixture of craft and inhumanity, more fit for the cells of the Spanish Inquisition than for an American court of justice, is his resentment at the zeal with which Mr. Martin undertook the defense of a man, who, though accused, was yet unconvicted, was under the legal presumption of innocence, had been dear to Martin as a friend, and had, moreover, a right, on the usual conditions, to his services. The whole correspondence with Mr. Hay is of this cast, diversified occasionally with promises of new witnesses, and interspersed toward the close of the trial with insinuations against the integrity of the court; leaving but one doubt as to the disposition of President Jefferson at the time, that is, whether he was more eager to hang the judge or the criminal.

No. XVI.

JEFFERSON'S STRICTURES ON WASHINGTON'S ADMINISTRATION.

SHOULD your good-nature revolt at the vindictive appearance of the examination, through the perplexities of which I am endeavoring to guide you, I have little to soothe it with, but an expression of my regret, or to relieve it by, but an appeal to your justice. If Mr. Jefferson's character is now for the first time to be displayed in its true light, and to be divested of the folds of artifice and delusion in which he disguised it, it is only because he painted in false and opprobrious colors that of others; and though it be, when thus exposed, a subject of unpleasing contemplation, it may prove a useful and instructive study. In the system of the moral world, it seems to be established by Providence, that injustice done to our neighbor should sooner or later recoil on ourselves. And naturalists tell us, that although, at first sight, the history of the lion appears more entertaining than that of all other beasts, yet that on close inspection, more vivid curiosity and agreeable wonder are excited by the structure of the spider—that sly insect, which—

> "Throned on the centre of his thin designs,
> Proud of a vast extent of flimsy lines,"

entangles and destroys the bold hornet and the blossom-loving bee.

Pursuing then the analysis of this envenomed letter to Mr. Madison, let us pass from its palpable injustice toward Gen. Washington and Gen. Lee, to the consideration of its main design, which is both concealed, and betrayed by an artifice, not unlike the trick of an Indian juggler. The object of all Mr. Jefferson's schemes and movements, of his friendships and hatreds, his slanders and praises; of that philosophy, for worship in the sanctuary of which, he would have the world believe he was predestined by nature, (Vol. IV. p. 126, et passim,) of his *mis*-quotation from the Georgics, (Vol. III. p. 337,) his "mould-board of least resistance," (p. 334;) of that retirement which was so profound, that lest it should be unnoticed, he proclaimed it in all directions, as the Irishman was to whistle when he should fall asleep; the real object of all these professions, passions, pretensions, and maneuvres, was the office of President. For this he deserted the Cabinet of Washington, against the entreaties of that illustrious man; and having got into a private station,—for this, he was now wriggling and stretching to get out of it. To Mr. Madison, whose powerful aid was indispensable, he was holding out his hand for help.

In disparaging and traducing Gen. Washington so industriously, his intention was not to supplant him; for besides that he could neither have desired nor hoped to compete with him before the people, he knew the general was now in his second and last official term. But his design was by curtailing the influence of his name and opinions, to change the course of succession, which, should that influence be left unimpaired, the sense of the nation would probably give to the Chief Magistracy—devolving it first on Adams, whom he disliked, next on Hamilton, whom he hated; whose superiority in the Cabinet he had felt and still resented; whose ready eloquence, cogent reasoning, practical views, ascendant genius, martial spirit, generous character, rebuked and foiled his own subtle sagacity, pusillanimous temper, and indirect ambition.

As it was to be supposed that Mr. Madison was apprized of Gen. Washington's wish to appoint him Secretary of State, and for that and other reasons retained a degree of kindness and respect for him, there was room to apprehend that his sense of justice would revolt at the gross and virulent detraction which Mr. Jefferson, in execution of one part of his scheme, had thought proper to hazard. Therefore, as physicians expel one poison from the body by the introduction of a more energetic one, the sage of Monticello proceeded to counteract the occurrence of remorse, by means of those never-failing agents, vanity and ambition. While urging Mr. Madison to persevere in his meritorious opposition, and foretelling that a change of men and measures was soon to take place, he encroached so far on the "double delicacy" of himself, and the simple modesty of his friend, as to insist that if he does *retire*, it must only be "to a more splendid and a more efficacious post;" for which, by the way, by an evolution peculiar to his own tactics, he had himself *retired.* The heartfelt joy this promotion of Mr. Madison over his own head would give him, may be better conceived than described; steeped as he lay in the charms of a "retirement," which he protests he "would not give up for the empire of the universe."

Nothing could be more skillful than this move. Like that of a knight at chess, it placed in check King, Queen and Castle, and all at once. It told the opposition that it was time to bring forward determinedly a candidate for the Presidency. It said to Mr. Madison, "As I have proposed you for this post, you cannot do less than support me, upon that principle of seniority and civility which would be observed were we to come together at the entrance of a drawing-room." It suppressed any scruples that a gentleman might feel at entering into an alliance founded on injustice to the father of his country, by overshadowing his judgment with clouds of vain incense and visions of future greatness through which Mr. Jefferson's election could not but appear as previous and instrumental to his own elevation, and it conformed apparently with that rural seclusion which the artless philosopher loved as dearly as he did his friend Col. Burr, and was as willing to forsake.

These advantages of the maneuver were not counterbalanced by a single inconvenience. There was not the slightest chance of Mr. Madison's superseding him; for besides that he was a man of personal modesty and of comparatively mild ambition, Mr. Jefferson was entitled by preoccupancy to the head of the opposition; to precedence, by superior age, and the high diplomatic and executive stations he had filled, to the duties of which Mr. Madison was yet a stranger. Had it been in his wish therefore to put himself before Mr. Jefferson, it would not have been in his power. Mr. Madison's situation and character at the time, in short, render it a moral certainty, that Mr. Jefferson's professing a wish to see his election, was simply an expedient to promote his own.

In tracing his correspondence up to the 19th of June, 1796, when he wrote the letter in vulgar abuse of Gen. Lee, and cruel *humbug* of Gen. Washington, I shall not stop to notice those in which he exasperates the zeal of Mr. Giles's opposition; encourages and counsels that of Mr. Madison; hails the appearance of an inconsiderable demagogue in Pennsylvania as "an acquisition upon which he congratulates republicanism;" caricatures by a most invidious criticism one of the President's messages to Congress, and by lecturing Mr. Rutledge of Carolina, on the debt of public service he had left unpaid to the nation by his retirement from political life, endeavors to provoke a reciprocation of that grateful reproach.

These I shall pass by, as subordinate stratagems in his

grand design, at once exposed by and exposing it, in order to examine his strictures on the next in succession and importance of President Washington's measures—the treaty of amity, commerce and navigation, concluded with the government of Great Britain, on the 19th of November, 1794, by our envoy Mr. Jay.

A sketch has already been attempted of our political parties, from their rise to the period at which Mr. Jefferson took his place at the head of Gen. Washington's cabinet. And it was then observed that occasions very soon presented themselves for such differences of opinion as were likely to be discovered by sects so oppositely constituted. But in the nature of our new relations with Great Britain, causes of peculiar excitement and discussion were found.

Washington and the great body of his political friends readily passed from real war to genuine peace, in conformity with the solemn assurance given to the world in the Declaration of Independence, that the citizens of the United States would thenceforth hold the British nation like the rest of mankind, "enemies in war, in peace friends." This promise they could well afford to fulfill, having signalized both their opposition to England, and love for their own country, their impatience of tyranny and devotion to freedom in the painful marches and bloody conflicts of a seven years' war. With the return of peace, to the minds of such men returned the sentiments belonging to it—justice, moderation, amity, good faith, and all those fair dispositions that lead to the mutual advantage of nations.

When, therefore, from the unavoidable delay which occurred on our part in executing that article of the treaty of peace which stipulated for the payment by our citizens of a description of debts due to the subjects of Great Britain, that government refused to surrender, in conformity with conditions in the same treaty, certain military posts on the southern margin of the great lakes, they used their utmost exertions to have our side of the covenant strictly performed, in order to secure the right dependent on it. In the same temper they endeavored to preserve an exact neutrality in the war between France and England, and preferred negotiation with both belligerents, as long as it could be honorably maintained, to war against either, as the means of repairing the actual, and preventing the fnture injury, to which our commerce was exposed by their collision.

As the opposite party had not expended their animosity in the generous trade of war, much of it remained on the conclusion of peace; and as they had not been able to demonstrate their zeal in the Revolution by such bold and patriotic evidences as Gen. Washington and his followers had exhibited, they sought now to display it by an unseasonable hostility toward Great Britain. In this spirit they insinuated that the endeavors of the administration to execute faithfully the treaty of peace, and to establish a commercial intercourse with England, manifested, with other of their measures, a monarchial tendency in their counsels, if not a design to replace us under the dominion of the British crown To color these imputations they alleged that our resistance to the encroachments of France evinced a secret partiality for England—inconsistent with the gratitude due to her rival, and the sympathy which one republic ought to feel for another.

Those against whom these accusations were directed, did not fail, in repelling them, to assert that they proceeded from politicians unduly partial to France, dishonorably insensible to the rights and dignity of their own country, and willing to gratify their lust of power at the expense of her character and interest.

It thus occurred that a habit was engrafted on the public

mind of regarding the measures of government less as they affected our own prosperity, than as they seemed likely to bear upon one or other of these antagonist nations, a habit, which, by the machinations and predominance of Mr. Jefferson, among other consequences, encouraged that fond injustice and affectionate inferiority, with which, in a more or less insolent shape, we have been since regarded by the successive governments of France.

This being the dispositions of the *ins* and *outs*—the one determined to condemn any connection with Great Britain which did not secure, not only all our rights but all our pretensions, and not only all that we pretended to, but every thing that we wished for—the other compelled to choose between the calamity of a war, and the convenience of the best agreement, which, under existing circumstances they could negotiate; it is not surprising that the ratification of Jay's treaty, in which the concessions and advantages of the contracting powers were pretty equally balanced, gave occasion to much discontent and violent censure.

In inflaming this discontent and exacerbating this censure, no one took more pains than Mr. Jefferson. In a letter to Mann Page, (Vol. III. p. 314,) declining attendance at the exhibition of a village academy, he digresses to the subject of the treaty, and takes occasion from it to sneer most indecently at the President. In a letter to Mr. Madison on the next page, (21st Sept. 1795,) urging him to answer a piece which Hamilton had published in explanation of the advantages of the treaty, he states his opinion of it in the following words—"It certainly is an attempt of a party, who find they have lost their majority in one branch of the legislature, to make a law by the aid of the other branch, and of the Executive, under color of a treaty which shall bind up the hands of the adverse branch, from ever restraining the commerce of their patron nation."

This objection implies, not that any right of the United States had been sacrificed or interest neglected, but that the commerce of Great Britain was not to be restrained. As to the word *ever*, the violence of its misapplication can be conceived only by reflecting that the treaty, in its principal articles, was limited expressly to ten years.

In the same letter he tells Mr. Madison that a number of Hamilton's pieces had been sent to him, with an answer by a Mr. Beckley; and that he gave these, "the poison and the antidote, to honest, sound-hearted men of common understanding," by way of experiment. Finding that Hamilton's pieces, in spite of Beckley's answer, produced conviction on the minds of these honest, common-sense citizens, he adds with rare simplicity, "I have ceased therefore to give them"—showing that this advocate for the diffusion of knowledge, for "leaving reason free to combat error of opinion," had no scruple in suppressing arguments however clear and convincing, if at variance with his own interested views. It does not appear that Mr. Madison could be induced to enter the lists in this controversy, finding it probably more easy to join Mr. Jefferson in reprobating the treaty, than to oppose Hamilton's logic in its defense.

No. XVII.

JEFFERSON'S CELEBRATED LETTER TO MAZZEI.

THE course of Mr. Jefferson's correspondence next leads us to his famous letter to Mazzei, which, in a futile attempt to explain it, he denominates (Vol. IV. p. 401,) "a precious theme of federal crimination." It bears date less than two months anterior to that in which he assures Gen. Washington of his total abstraction from party politics, and reviles Gen. Lee so bitterly for having intimated a doubt of the sincerity of this avowal. Being connected with a strenuous effort in 1797, to mask one of its bearings, and with an *abstract attempt* in 1824, to parry another, it extends to two distinct eras, both as it regards Gen. Washington and Mr. Jefferson himself. To the former it refers both before and after his death, to his envied popularity, and his unsullied renown; to the latter, while intent upon the acquisition of power; and after that had been enjoyed and resigned, when covetous of fame. You will therefore perceive that the task of detecting its true meaning, (and of exposing the objects with which it was written,) if not likely to require ability in a writer, will demand of the reader patient attention.

As it appears in his "Writings," this letter, so far as it relates to public matters, is in the following words. (Vol. III. p. 327.)

Monticello, April 24th, 1796.

"MY DEAR FRIEND:—The aspect of our politics has wonderfully changed since you left us. In place of that noble love of liberty and republican government which carried us triumphantly through the war, an Anglican, monarchical, and aristocratical party has sprung up, whose avowed object is to draw over us the substance, as they have already done the forms of the British government. The main body of our citizens, however, remain true to their republican principles; the whole landed interest is republican, and so is a great mass of talents. Against us are the executive, the judiciary, two out of three branches of the legislature, all the officers of the government, all who want to be officers, all timid men who prefer the calm of despotism to the boisterous sea of liberty, British merchants, and Americans trading on British capitals, speculators, and holders in the banks and public funds, a contrivance invented for purposes of corruption, and for assimilating us in all things to the rotten as well as the sound parts of the British model. It would give you a fever were I to name to you the apostates who have gone over to these heresies, men who were Samsons in the field, and Solomons in the council, but who have had their heads shorn by the harlot of England. In short, we are likely to preserve the liberty we have gained only by unremitting labors and perils. But we shall preserve it; and our mass of weight and wealth on the good side is so great as to leave no danger that force will ever be attempted against us. We have only to awake and snap the Lilliputian cords with which they have been entangling us during the first sleep which succeeded our labors."

This letter, or rather this part of it, was translated into Italian, and published by Mazzei in a Gazette of Florence. In Paris, it was republished in the *Moniteur* in a French version of Mazzei's translation, with editorial remarks adapted to its sentiments, tending to show the faithless spirit of our government toward France, the strength of the Gallican party in the United States, and the justice as well as the policy of the hostile measures pursued by the Directory toward us. From the *Moniteur* it was transferred to the English papers, after undergoing a retranslation, and in this last dress found its way to the United States. Although it bore no signature, it was immediately imputed to Mr. Jefferson, a circumstance which occasioned his favoring Mr. Madison with the following eager explanation of it. (Vol. III. p. 362.)

"*Monticello*, August 3d, 1797.

"I scribbled you a line on the 24th ult., it missed of the post, and so went by a private hand. I perceive from yours by Mr. Bringhurst that you had not received it. In fact, it was only an earnest exhortation to come here with Monroe, which I still hope you will do. In the meantime I enclose you a letter from him, and wish your opinion on its principal subject. The variety of other topics the day I was with you, kept out of sight the letter to Mazzei imputed to me in the papers, the general substance of which is mine, though the diction has been considerably altered and varied in the course of its translations from English into Italian, from Italian into French, and from French into English. I first met with it at Bladensburg, and for a moment conceived I must take the field of the public papers. I could not disavow it wholly, because the greatest part was mine in substance, though not in form. I could not avow it as it stood, because the form was not mine, and in one place the substance very materially falsified. This, then, would render explanations necessary; nay, it would render proofs of the whole necessary, and draw me at length into a publication of all (even the secret) transactions of the cabinet while I was of it; and embroil me personally with every member of the executive, with the judiciary, and with others still. I soon decided in my own mind to be entirely silent. I consulted with several friends at Philadelphia, who every one of them were clearly against my avowing or disavowing, and some of them conjured me most earnestly to let nothing provoke me to it. I corrected, in conversation with them, a substantial misrepresentation of the copy published. The original has a sentiment like this, (for I have not it before me,) 'they are endeavoring to submit us to the substance, as they already have to the *forms* of the British government,' meaning by *forms* the birth-days, levees, processions to Parliament, inauguration pomposities, &c. But the copy published says: 'as they have already submitted us to the *form* of the British,' &c.; making me express hostility to the form of our government, that is, to the Constitution itself. For this is really the difference of the word *form*, used in the singular or plural, in that phrase of the English language. Now it would be impossible for me to explain this publicly without bringing on a personal difference between Gen. Washington and myself, which nothing before the publication of this letter has ever done. It would embroil me, too, with all those with whom his character is still popular, that is, with nine-tenths of the people of the United States; and what good would be obtained by avowing the letter with the necessary explanations? Very little, indeed, in my opinion, to counterbalance a good deal of harm. From my silence in this instance, it cannot be inferred that I am afraid to own the general sentiments of the letter. If I am subject to either imputation, it is to that of avowing such sentiments too frankly both in private and public, often when there is no necessity for it, merely because I disdain every thing like duplicity. Still, however, I am open to conviction. Think for me on the occasion, and advise me what to do, and confer with Col. Monroe on the subject. Let me entreat you again to come with him; there are other important things to consult upon."

The explanation here advanced is evidently designed to impose on Mr. Madison, and therefore is naturally at variance with that subsequently furnished to Mr. Van Buren—the object of which was to delude him into the belief that Gen. Washington had never taken exception to the letter to Mazzei, and that assertions to that effect were the false effusions "of federal malice."

The design upon Mr. Madison was a double one; first, to reconcile him to the unmanliness of preferring an evasive silence, to an open avowal or fair explanation of the letter; second, to conceal from him, if possible, the obvious application of its censure to himself. As this latter application had a tendency to wound the delicacy of his self-love, it is dexterously covered by the former part of his design, and by that stratagem is made to appear as if it were intended solely to answer their mutual purpose, of avoiding an open rupture with Gen. Washington. In furtherance of this scheme, Mr. Madison is assured that in consequence of mutilations which successive translations had produced in the text of the letter to Mazzei, Mr. Jefferson could not disavow it wholly with truth, nor avow it wholly without explanations; which explanations "would embroil him personally with every member of the executive, with the judiciary, and with others;" that consequently he decided very soon in his own mind to remain perfectly silent; and that certain nameless friends, whom he consulted in Philadelphia, were clear and earnest for his persisting in this equivocal silence. Mentioning then, that he had corrected, in conversation with these frank and worthy persons, a substantial error in the copy, he shuffles down with a sort of brazen confusion to the point of the slander which was pressing against Mr. Madison's reputation; and keeping that confederate's eyes upturned all the while to the indignant countenance of Gen. Washington, slips out the following card of deception :—" The original has a sentiment like this, (for I have it not before me,) 'they are endeavoring to submit us to the substance as they already have to the *forms* of the British government,' meaning by *forms* the birth-days, levees, processions to Parliament, inauguration pomposities, &c. But the copy published says: 'as they have already submitted us to the *form* of the British,' &c.,

making me express hostility to the form of our government, that is, to the Constitution itself. For this is really the difference of the word *form*, in the singular or plural, in that phrase of the English language."

As Mr. Jefferson made this exposition, confessedly on the strength of his memory, and not from a collation of the copy with the original, I shall take the liberty of suggesting that he was mistaken in point of fact; that the word used in the letter to Mazzei, was *form*. His handwriting was remarkably neat, plain, and correct, as is known to his numerous correspondents, and appears by the *fac-simile* at the end of his fourth volume; and Mazzei, from their intimacy and correspondence, was familiar with it. The probability is, that in a letter which this person thought, or was induced to consider, of sufficient importance to be published in the Florence Gazette, he would be careful to see that no error was committed in its translation or publication; and it having been accurately printed in Italian, a subsequent error of the kind insisted on, was almost impossible. For in the French language, as in the Italian, the difference between the singular and the plural in nouns is marked by a change in the termination of two words, that is the article and the noun; as for example—in Italian *la forma*, singular, is *le forme* plural; and in French, *la forme* singular is *les formes* plural. Whereas in English, the change is confined to one word, and consists solely in the absence or presence of the *s* final. Thus, if Mr. Jefferson had written *forms*, the care of Mazzei would have ensured the appearance in the Florence Gazette, of the phrase *le forme*, which the structure of the French and Italian languages would have forced the Moniteur to represent by *les formes;* a noun that the English translator would of necessity have known to be plural, and would have so rendered. From these intrinsic evidences, it is highly improbable, to say the least, that if Mr. Jefferson wrote the word in the plural, it should have been altered in the series of translations into the singular.

But considering it in another point of view, if this alteration did actually happen, as he affirms, "in the course of its translations from English into Italian, from Italian into French, and from French into English," it only proves that the person who made the alteration, considered it, as every body else will probably do, immaterial, deeming the two phrases *form of government*, and *forms of government*, equivalent; and that the use of the one or the other made no change whatever in the meaning. Thus a sort of dilemma arises at the threshhold of his explanation, and seems to shake its horns at this assertion of Mr. Jefferson, making it either erroneous or idle. If the error of version be not unlikely, the equivalent construction put upon the phrases by the peccant translator, becomes highly probable; and if this construction is considered unnatural, the error of translation is scarcely possible.

But can it be seriously supposed by the most ignorant, or by the most learned man, that Mazzei, or any one else in Europe or America, could understand by the phrase, *forms of the British government*, the King's birth-night balls, the Queen's levees, processions to Parliament or ceremonies of the coronation? Does Montesquieu, in his analysis, or De Lolme, in his description of the English Constitution, *allude* even to these *forms*? Was the mind of Pope, when he wrote the oft-repeated line,

> "For *forms of government* let fools contest,"

inspired by levees, birth-nights, and processions? After the alleged transplantation of these ceremonies in America, did they become *forms* of our government, of a government which exists solely in our written Constitution. When Mr. Jefferson, on becoming President, announced to Mr. Macon the heads of the reformation he proposed to introduce, and commenced the list with "Levees are done away," could the venerable senator from North Carolina have understood that a certain *form* of our government was to be abolished? Are the Washington birth-night balls, which still anniversarily recur in the towns and villages of the United States, *forms* of the Federal or State governments? Were the weekly levees of Mrs. Madison and Mrs. Monroe *forms* of political or petticoat government? Or was the custom adopted by Gen. Washington of opening each session of Congress with a speech instead of a message, when he was attended by a voluntary concourse of his fellow-citizens, a *form of the British government,* "drawn over" the people of the United States?

The truth is, that as a message is nothing more nor less than a written speech, and as the kings of England open the sessions of Parliament by commission, more frequently than in person, Mr. Jefferson's custom was of a more regal *form* than Gen. Washington's, was less consistent with the frank and open carriage of a republican officer, less respectful to the legislative bodies, and consequently to the people and the States whom they represented.

On the other hand, the *forms* of the British government have universally been understood to mean its division into legislative, executive, and judiciary departments; the unity of its executive; the duality of its legislature, and the independence of its judiciary. These *forms* were imitated with more or less exactness, as they appeared conducive to the *substance* of freedom, in the Constitution of the United States, as may be seen by reference to the compact itself, and to the essays of Mr. Madison expounding it; and were unquestionably the subject of Mr. Jefferson's remark, whether he used the word in the singular or plural.

Mr. Jefferson, in a letter to John Dickinson, (Vol. III. p. 487,) in reference to the objects of the Revolution, says: —"Surely we had in view to obtain a theory and practice of good government; and how any, who seemed so ardent in this pursuit, could shamelessly have apostatized, and supposed we meant only to put our government into other hands, but not other forms, is indeed wonderful." Now here this word *forms* is used in the plural and in connection with the word *government;* yet it cannot be forced by any construction into the meaning of "birth-days, levees or processions to Parliament," which Mr. Jefferson assures his friend Mr. Madison, it always bore "in that phrase in the English language."

Thus it appears that, if we examine into the effect of the various translations of this letter, we are led to believe that Mr. Jefferson used the word *form* in the singular, in opposition to *substance* in the previous member of the sentence; and that, if out of courtesy, we admit his assertion to the contrary, we discover that the alteration of the text, which he insists on, would make not the least possible difference in his meaning. The conclusion therefore is, even from these premises, that this eager explanation to Mr. Madison, was factitious and fraudulent, intended not so much to consult as to mislead his judgment, and to prevent his taking offense at finding himself classed with the members of the "Anglican, monarchical, and aristocratical party," which had "sprung up" in the United States. For the natural import of the language, whether the word *form* or *forms* be employed, is, that those persons who had drawn over us the *forms* of the British government, that is the framers of our Constitution, had combined into an Anglican, monarchical, and aristocratical party, and were trying to draw over as also its *substance,* that is, its corruption, its executive patronage, its privileged classes, its sinecures and hereditary tenure of office. Now, as Mr. Madison's popularity and public reputation were founded on his exertions and influence in devising the *forms* of our government, (not birthnight balls, levees, &c.) and in recommending their adoption to the people, the inference, that he was implicated in the slander entrusted to Mazzei, is irresistible.

You may ask if this explanation be so shallow and preposterous, how Mr. Jefferson could venture to offer, or succeed in imposing it on a person of Mr. Madison's scholastic and practical acquaintance with our language. The answer is that Mr. Madison had been accustomed to be deceived by him, and in this case would be willing to be imposed on. Mithridates took poison so often, that at last, the most deadly and active substances would produce no disturbance in his stomach; and it is easy to comprehend how reluctant Mr. Madison would be on the occasion in question to doubt the personal friendship or to lose the political alliance of Mr. Jefferson. The latter had therefore in his favor the power of habit and the influence of self-love; agents of force enough to bias the strongest understanding. Besides, the offensive meaning of the sentence, was rendered less obvious than it might have been, by Mr. Jefferson's declining to enclose the genuine letter, though he was then at Monticello, that great mint of *press copies,* where, as you may remember, one was readily coined to appease the apprehended resentment of Col. Burr, and where, as we shall presently see, another was *struck* twenty-seven years subsequently, to bewilder the credulity of Mr. Van Buren. Instead of sending him a faithful copy of his letter, he refers him to one from Mr. Monroe, and persuades him to a conference with that gentleman, who as he had borne no part in the formation of the Constitution and but an immaterial one in its adoption, (Vol. II. p. 367,) might be the more easily employed to decoy Mr. Madison into security as to himself, and into apprehension as to the effect which an avowal or explanation of the letter would have on Mr. Jefferson, and through him on the interests of the whole party.

To mislead Mr. Madison still further, he avers that the sentence, by its alleged alteration, would make him "express hostility to the form of our government, that is to the Constitution itself"—whereas, if Mr. Madison had seen the letter itself, he would have perceived that it could produce no such effect—for certainly to say that the form of the Federal government resembles that of Great Britain—which was admitted on all hands to be the best in existence before ours was created, and to which it is related by such strong and numerous analogies,—cannot be interpreted into an expression of hostility to the Constitution of the United States, without going to the absurdity of imputing that sentiment to the fathers of our charter. This superfluous defense shows that it was the language he concealed from Mr. Madison, not that which he repeated to him,—his conscience and not his communication,—which on this occasion was his accuser. For his letter to Mazzei, as now published, does most certainly "express hostility to the Constitution itself," as well as to its framers.

But this chicanery, contemptible as it is, is not the worst part of the letter to Mr. Madison. For after admitting the letter to Mazzei to be in substance his, Mr. Jefferson expresses his determination, neither to avow, nor disavow, nor explain it, for fear of its bringing on a personal difference between himself and Gen. Washington, and embroiling him with other distinguished men. He said to Mr. Madison as he had said to Mr. Monroe: "I have written a letter to Mazzei, of a character to wound the feelings of Gen. Washington and several other gentlemen. Contrary to my expectation, it is published in the American newspapers, fortunately without my signature, but in substance as I wrote it, though with the alteration of one word, which I think changes its meaning in one respect, but which neither increases nor lessens the personal offense it is likely to give. I cannot avow it wholly because of this alteration, nor disavow it altogether because of its substantial accuracy, nor explain its alterations without bringing on a personal difference with Gen. Washington, and embroiling me with these other eminent persons. I am therefore decided in my own mind, neither to avow, nor to disavow, nor to explain it; and by this silence to avoid the personal responsibility to which it would subject me, as well as the serious harm it would occasion to my own popularity and our mutual political plans. I am anxious to get your advice on the subject, and I hope that, after consulting with Monroe, you will approve, like my honest friends in Philadelphia, this prudent and evasive silence."

Here, if we trust the indications of Mr. Jefferson's correspondence, are three citizens, who were destined to rise in succession to the highest place in the popular affection and political power of a great republic—in a government, the essential principle of which is virtue,—consulting together on a point of conduct upon which no man of honesty can possibly doubt, and, as far as appears, finally adopting a proceeding which no man of honor can approve. Is it possible to believe that Gen. Washington ever could have shrunk into such ignominious evasion? Or can the utmost stretch of the imagination conceive him consulting urgently and secretly with Gen. Hamilton and Gen. Lee, upon a step, of which the vast departure from manliness and honor, no language can describe? If there exists a being who can suppose so great an improbability, let him refer to the undisputed fact that arose out of the resignation of Edmund Randolph as Secretary of State. That gentleman—"for the purpose as he alleged of vindicating his conduct, demanded the sight of a confidential letter which had been addressed to him by the President, and which was left in the office. His avowed design was to give this, as well as some others of the same description, to the public, in order to support the allegation, that in consequence of his attachment to France and liberty, he had fallen a victim to the intrigues of a British and aristocratic party." To this demand Washington replied—"I have directed that you have the inspection of my letter of the 22d of July, agreeably to your request, and you are at full liberty to publish, without reserve, *any* and *every* private and confidential letter I ever wrote *you.* Nay more, every word I ever uttered to or in your presence from whence you can derive any advantage in your vindication."

No contrast can be stronger than the difference between these proceedings—that of Washington displaying a consciousness of rectitude, a sense of magnanimity, and an ardent love of truth. To the admirers of Mr. Jefferson I leave the glorious task of portraying the virtues which on the occasion he exhibited. Let them reconcile his silence with the sentiments of his letter abusing Gen. Lee, his evasion with honor, his secrecy with truth, either with the spirit of an independent man or the duty of a good citizen. Let them account for his conduct on any other hypothesis than that involving a consciousness of the injustice of his own aspersions; a fear of the exposure their avowal would "draw over" him personally and politically, in *substance* as well as in *form;* and an apprehension that besides this formidable array of enemies, it would be attended by the rupture of his alliance with Mr. Madison, and the consequent loss of this valuable auxiliary. For from the incompatibility between the tenor of his professions to Gen. Washington, and his communications to Mr. Madison, it was morally impossible that an explanation, which would disarm Gen. Washington, should not offend Mr. Madison. While to a private one, therefore, he was averse, a public one he actually dreaded.

There is one sentence which brings us to the *zero* of pusillanimity—to a point of prevarication, at which Mr. Jefferson's moral sense seems to have undergone congelation, and to have been attended by an instinctive assurance that a similar catastrophe had befallen his friends—a degree in the descending scale of dishonor at which shame and fear are actually transmuted into vanity and impudence. After this elaborate equivocation and dissembling, he exclaims: "From my silence in this instance it cannot be inferred that I am afraid to own the general sentiments of the letter. If I am subject to either imputation, it is to that of avowing such sentiments too frankly, both in private and public, often when there is no necessity for it, merely because I disdain every thing like duplicity"!! And to be convinced that his love of truth was as sincere as his "disdain of every thing like duplicity" you have only to remember that he assured Gen. Washington in his letter abusing Gen. Lee—which was written in the interval between the date of the letter to Mazzei and of this to Mr. Madison, "of his total abstraction from party politics"—that "political conversations he really disliked, and therefore avoided when he could, without affectation—or unless they were urged by others."

There yet remain to be considered in this explanation to Mr. Madison, two expressions, which will be found singularly significant. The first occurs in the following sentence —"Now it would be impossible for me to explain this publicly, without bringing on a personal difference between

Gen. Washington and myself, *which nothing before the publication of this letter has ever done.*" Does not the conclusion of this sentence contain of itself a complete justification of Gen. Lee, out of Mr. Jefferson's own mouth? What does it signify, but that although he was conscious of having, before this letter to Mazzei was published, given abundant cause to justify the personal resentment of Gen. Washington, it had as yet never been excited? What is it but telling Mr. Madison, that notwithstanding the many injurious and disparaging remarks, the numerous misrepresentations and calumnies in which he had ventured to indulge, in his correspondence and conversations with him and other "political friends and connections," he had hitherto managed to avoid a personal difference with Gen. Washington? If this be not the meaning of his words, they are destitute of meaning.

In the succeeding remark:—"It would embroil me too with all those with whom his character is still popular, that is with nine-tenths of the people of the United States"—the adverb *still*, is as expressive as any single word can be. The "tandem liber equus" of Virgil, so much celebrated by commentators, yields to it in significancy. It unclasps a volume of our national history which has as yet been very little read—it developes the spirit of the voluminous correspondence I have been examining, and casts a detecting light on the most obscure and invidious calumnies in Mr. Jefferson's innumerable letters to Messrs. Madison and Monroe. It now confesses to the world what it was then intended to hint to these two chosen confederates, that in spite of all his efforts to destroy the popularity of Gen. Washington, there was but too good reasons to fear that a great majority of the people of the United States remained *still* devoted to him.

The truth is, however, that these efforts were not altogether unsuccessful. Gen. Washington did retire from office, and descended to his grave with a name which, though unsullied, was dimmed for a season by the slanders thus hatched by Mr. Jefferson, and thus confided to his compeers, and with a heart that was not agonized, only because the ethereal temper of virtue is impassive to the shafts of malice. This disinterested and devoted patriot was publicly threatened with impeachment, and reduced to the necessity of vindicating himself against an open charge of pecuniary corruption. And after laying down his office, he was condemned to learn that a leading member of Congress from his own State, had reproached him in debate with a want of wisdom and firmness, and rejoiced at his retirement as an event of national advantage.

In the chicanery, slander, and ingratitude disclosed by the examination of this part of Mr. Jefferson's career, was laid the foundation of that ascendancy which he gained in the United States, and transmitted to his successors, Messrs. Madison and Monroe,—an ascendancy that has been ascribed to patriotism, wisdom and justice, by a fiction as gross in its nature, and as pardonable in its prevalence, as that which induced the Romans to believe that they drew their lineage from the gods.

The surviving partisans of Mr. Jefferson will not be proud of this political pedigree; but as it is traced distinctly through his own "Writings," has every link of its chain riveted by his own authority, it will require no little address to escape from its incumbrance. Mr. Madison, indeed, from the supereminence of his reputation and talents, and the strict account that history is likely to take of his conduct, may feel himself called on by the publication of Mr. Jefferson's side of their correspondence to declare whether, or in what degree, he conspired in those schemes which projected the shadow of a "dim eclipse" between the glory of Washington and the admiration of his fellow-citizens; and which, while the lustre of his name shone unclouded in other lands, caused it, for a space, to shed but pale and struggling beams upon his native country.

THE END

www.ingramcontent.com/pod-product-compliance
Lightning Source LLC
LaVergne TN
LVHW020110110826
845151LV00001B/121

* 9 7 8 1 4 2 5 5 4 3 7 3 0 *